Praise for *Reading with Patrick*

Shortlisted for the Goddard Riverside Stephan Russo
Book Prize for Social Justice

Shortlisted for the Reading Women Award for Nonfiction

"Penetrating, haunting . . . In all of the literature addressing education, race, poverty, and criminal justice, there has been nothing quite like *Reading with Patrick*."
—JAMES FORMAN, JR., and ARTHUR EVENCHIK, *The Atlantic*

"Anyone interested in questions of pedagogy, racism, and incarceration in America, not to mention literary criticism, will be enthralled by this book. . . . It is hard not to read this challenging book . . . and not think, You must change your life."
—JAMES WOOD, *The New Yorker*

"*Reading with Patrick* could be the most affecting book you'll read this year. To experience such a spectrum of responses—from anger to admiration, disbelief to inspiration, helpless frustration to stand-up-and-shout-cheering—should be enough impetus to get you urgently 'reading with Patrick' as soon as possible."　　　　　　　　—*Christian Science Monitor*

"[A] tender memoir."　　　　　　　—*O: The Oprah Magazine*

"Readers witness the transformative power of . . . moving lessons in both literature and life, lessons that endure and deepen in jail."　　　　　　　　　　　—*The New York Times*

"*Reading with Patrick*, Michelle Kuo's rich memoir of her literary friendship with a student in a small town in the Mississippi Delta, suggests that it is perhaps more than anything a book's ability to make its readers feel valuable that keeps us reading. . . . The act of reading gave her students the chance to think of themselves as able; it gave space, attention and value to their interior lives. . . . Instead of the tidy moral, Kuo offers a much more complex and more troubling story."

—*The Times Literary Supplement*

"In many ways . . . [Kuo's] lifelong job is to be a teacher: not just of Patrick and her students in Helena, but of us, as readers, because Kuo understands that teaching is a daily act of self-transformation, negotiation and witnessing."

—*America* magazine

"*Reading with Patrick* is as much about growing up Asian in America as it is about growing up black and impoverished. . . . [Kuo's] story is exceptional."   —*The Providence Journal*

"A moving and important work at a time when America remains gripped with inner turmoil."   —*The Herald* (Scotland)

"Her riveting narrative has been embraced globally for its compassionate message, its exploration of education and its insightful glimpse into societal inequality."

—*Hyphen Magazine*

"A powerful meditation on how one person can affect the life of another . . . One of the great strengths of *Reading* is its portrayal of the risk inherent to teaching."   —*Seattle Times*

"Honest, thoughtful, and humane, Kuo's book is not only a testament to a remarkable friendship, but a must-read for anyone interested in social justice and race in America. Thoughtfully provocative reading."   —*Kirkus Reviews*

"This memoir of teaching literature in one of the poorest counties in America is a reminder of how literacy changes lives. Highly recommended."   —*Library Journal* (starred review)

"Tender and gritty, with reflections on race and justice and pedagogy, *Reading with Patrick* is a paean to literature, to caring and to Forster's maxim, 'Only connect.'"   —*Shelf Awareness*

"Michelle Kuo's *Reading with Patrick* is a strikingly candid and insightful meditation on the relationship between a young teacher and a former student as they read together while the student awaits trial for murder in a Southern jail. Compulsively readable, the book manages to do two extraordinary things at once: it offers a poignant and moving account of a specific relationship, and it grapples searchingly with universal themes around families, race, poverty, teaching, and the power of literature. The book will continue to resonate long after you have put it down and returned to the everyday—this is what the best books, the best teachers, do."
—CAROL S. STEIKER, Henry J. Friendly Professor of Law
and faculty co-director of the criminal justice
policy program, Harvard Law School

"Warmhearted but never sentimental, and acutely self-aware, Michelle Kuo's memoir is the most profound, tender, and intensely moving portrait of a student-teacher relationship I've ever read. It shows how deeply a student and teacher can change each other's lives. Kuo knows the complications and the limits of helping, but she is brave and generous and stubborn enough to do it anyway."
—LARISSA MACFARQUHAR, author of *Strangers Drowning*

"I delighted in this book and read it in a single weekend. *Reading with Patrick* is a significant work that could swell the ranks of highly motivated and qualified teachers—people who understand they are not just transferring information but transforming lives."
—BILL MOYERS

"*Reading with Patrick* could not be more timely. Kuo underscores the power of tender attention and shows us that if we go to the margins, we all find rescue."
—FATHER GREGORY J. BOYLE, founder, Homeboy Industries, and author of *Tattoos on the Heart*

"Every American should read Michelle Kuo's remarkable memoir. Honest, generous, humble, and wise, *Reading with Patrick* will endure as a defining story for our times, and, abidingly, a testament to the power of language and of books."
—CLAIRE MESSUD, author of *The Woman Upstairs*

"In *Reading with Patrick*, Michelle Kuo takes on the subjects of race, privilege, and the debt that the human community owes to its most disadvantaged members with a bracing intelligence, honesty, and self-scrutiny. This is a gorgeous, urgent, and heartbreaking memoir."
—DARCY FREY, senior lecturer on English, Harvard University, and author of *The Last Shot*

"This book is special and could not be more right on time. It's an absorbing, tender, and surprisingly honest examination of race and privilege in America that helps articulate what is often lost, seemingly intentionally, in national debates over criminal justice and education: the inner life and imagination of a young person."   —WES MOORE, author of *The Other Wes Moore*

"Riveting . . . *Reading with Patrick* is an essential addition to our national conversation about institutional racism. It is also an empathic story of connection: between a dedicated teacher and her student; between history and our current times; and between literature and life. It is hard to imagine a more inspiring testament to the transformative power of reading."
—ELLIOTT HOLT, author of *You Are One of Them*

READING *with* PATRICK

READING

with

PATRICK

*A Teacher, a Student,
and a Life-Changing
Friendship*

Michelle Kuo

RANDOM HOUSE / NEW YORK

2018 Random House Trade Paperback Edition

Copyright © 2017 by Michelle Kuo

Reading group guide copyright © 2018 by Penguin Random House LLC

Published in the United States by Random House, an imprint and division of
Penguin Random House LLC, New York.

RANDOM HOUSE and the HOUSE colophon are registered trademarks of
Penguin Random House LLC.

RANDOM HOUSE READER'S CIRCLE & Design is a registered trademark of
Penguin Random House LLC.

Originally published in hardcover in the United States by Random House,
an imprint and division of Penguin Random House LLC, in 2017.

Grateful acknowledgment is made to the following for permission to reprint
previously published material:

Copper Canyon Press and The Wylie Agency, LLC: "To Paula in Late Spring"
from *The Shadow of Sirius* by W. S. Merwin, copyright © 2009 by W. S. Merwin.
Reprinted with the permission of The Permissions Company, Inc., on behalf of
Copper Canyon Press, www.coppercanyonpress.org, and The Wylie Agency, LLC.
All rights reserved.

HarperCollins Publishers and Bloodaxe Books: Five haiku of Issa's, four of
Basho's from *The Essential Haiku: Versions of Basho, Buson & Issa* edited with an
introduction by Robert Hass, introduction and translation copyright © 1994 by
Robert Hass. Unless otherwise noted, all translations copyright © 1994 by Robert
Hass. Reprinted by permission of HarperCollins Publishers and Bloodaxe Books.

W. W. Norton & Company: Nine lines from "Easter Morning" from *A Coast of
Trees* by A. R. Ammons, copyright © 1981 by A. R. Ammons. Reprinted by
permission of W. W. Norton & Company.

The Charlotte Sheedy Literary Agency Inc.: "Mysteries, Yes" from *Evidence* by
Mary Oliver (Boston, MA: Beacon Press, 2009), copyright © 2009 by Mary Oliver.
Reprinted by permission of The Charlotte Sheedy Literary Agency Inc.

LIBRARY OF CONGRESS CATALOGING-IN-PUBLICATION DATA
Names: Kuo, Michelle author.
Title: Reading with Patrick : a teacher, a student, and
a life-changing friendship / Michelle Kuo.
Description: First edition. | New York : Random House, 2017.
Identifiers: LCCN 2016036759 | ISBN 9780812987140 |
ISBN 9780812997323 (ebook)
Subjects: LCSH: Prisoners—Education—United States. | Alternative schools—
United States. | Prisoners—Books and reading—United States. | Race
discrimination—United States. | United States—Race relations.
Classification: LCC HV8833 .K86 2017 | DDC 371.826/927092 [B]—dc23
LC record available at https://lccn.loc.gov/2016036759

Printed in the United States of America on acid-free paper

randomhousebooks.com
randomhousereaderscircle.com

6 8 9 7

Book design by Susan Turner

For my mother and father,
Hwa-Mei Lin Kuo and Ming-Shang Kuo,
with love and gratitude

Stop thinking about saving your face. Think of our lives and tell us your particularized world. Make up a story. Narrative is radical, creating us at the very moment it is being created. We will not blame you if your reach exceeds your grasp; if love so ignites your words they go down in flames and nothing is left but their scald. Or if, with the reticence of a surgeon's hands, your words suture only the places where blood might flow. We know you can never do it properly—once and for all. Passion is never enough; neither is skill. But try. For our sake and yours forget your name in the street; tell us what the world has been to you in the dark places and in the light. . . . Language alone protects us from the scariness of things with no names. Language alone is meditation.

—Toni Morrison, Nobel Prize Lecture, 1993

CONTENTS

CONTENTS

INTRODUCTION

I WENT TO THE MISSISSIPPI DELTA WITH A SPECIFIC PROJECT: to teach American history through black literature. I imagined teaching literature that had moved me. I envisioned my students galvanized, as I had been in eighth grade, by Martin Luther King, Jr.'s "Letter from Birmingham Jail," and mesmerized, as I had been in high school, by Malcolm X's autobiography. I wanted my students to read James Baldwin, who wrote about the heroic stoicism of children who walked to school through a jeering mob. Books had taught me to admire a person's *will to confront the world, to evaluate his experience honestly,* as Ralph Ellison wrote. Books had changed me, charged me with responsibilities. And I believed books could change the lives of my students. It was unabashedly romantic. I was twenty-two.

My own origins, I believed, were prosaic. I had grown up in western Michigan in the 1980s, the daughter of Taiwanese immigrants. I walked to school, I played piano, I crushed on my brother's friends. On the first days of snow, my brother and I took our cheap plastic saucers out for a whirl and, during the summer, our parents both at work, we dutifully advanced through booklets of practice SATs, one English and one math, each day.

In certain ways, my parents had acclimated very well to the United States. They stacked foot-high collections of Michael Jackson and Joan Baez records in the living room, voted dutifully, never missing an election, and brought home for dinner the occasional bucket of fried chicken. But in other ways, my parents seemed preoccupied by their status as outsiders. They told me cautionary tales about Asians in America being cowed, killed, and then forgotten. There was Vincent Chin, in Detroit, who in 1982 was bludgeoned to death with a baseball bat, a week before his wedding. Chin had worked in an auto industry dominated by anti-Japanese sentiment. "It's because of you little motherfuckers that we're out of work," the killers, both white men, had said to him. (Vincent was not Japanese but Chinese American and grew up in the States.) The killers served no jail time. "These weren't the kind of men you send to jail," the judge stated later. "You don't make the punishment fit the crime; you make the punishment fit the criminal."

The other story my parents told me was about a sixteen-year-old kid in the Deep South, somewhere in Louisiana—this time, actually Japanese—whom we referred to as "the Japanese exchange student." Invited to a Halloween party in the early nineties, he showed up at the wrong house, dressed in a white suit as John Travolta in *Saturday Night Fever*. He rang the doorbell and was shot dead at point-blank range. The shooter was charged with manslaughter. He claimed at court that the kid moved in a strange way; his lawyer told the jury that the killer was protecting his property and that he was an "average Joe," "one of your neighbors," someone who liked "sugar in his grits." He was acquitted.

"Nobody will tell you these stories," my parents told me. "We tell you because we want you to be careful."

Be careful: That was the central message. Like many immigrants, my parents were fearful people, and they seemed determined to remind me that tragedy might be right around the corner. It only took one ignorant guy with a gun or a baseball bat. In actual numbers, the likelihood an Asian would be murdered in the 1980s and 1990s was minimal. And yet, in a way, they were telling me something important. They were trying to tell me that we did not figure, at all, in the national imagination. Indeed, until my second year of college, I never learned about Asian Americans, alive or dead, in any class, from any teacher. As an immigrant group, we were convenient on the one hand but also, ultimately, disposable. When we did well, people would vaguely point to us as evidence of the American dream, but when we were killed for being Asian, the media wasn't interested. Our dying did not betray any myth or ideal about America. Why? Because we weren't American. Our faces gave us away.

Like many immigrants, my parents believed education was both a barricade against harm and a ladder to safety and prosperity. Math, in particular, comforted my parents: It was familiar, the same in their little island country of Taiwan as it was in America. You didn't need to know English. You didn't need to learn a secret set of social rules to do math. You put in the time, and you learned how to do it. Every single night when my brother and I were in elementary school, our father drilled us with math problems. He yelled when we got answers wrong; we cried; our mother guiltily brought us tea.

I spoke late and was shy. My pursuits were solitary. I could, for instance, play the piano with great feeling—once, in a fit of zeal over a Chopin cadenza, I banged my head against the stand. Like my mother, I disliked indolence, and, in my moderately competitive public schools, this quality got me far. I enjoyed pleasing my parents and, for Christmas in the sixth grade, gift-wrapped my report card. I read copious numbers of books, though in retrospect it couldn't be said I was particularly good at it. I liked moral absolutes and was poor at grasping parody. I read *Don Quixote* and thought he was a hero. I read *Middlemarch* and wanted to be Dorothea, married to a man of knowledge.

But other readings rewarded my earnestness. I felt, for instance, personally summoned when Martin Luther King, Jr., wrote, *So the question is not whether we will be extremists, but what kind of extremists we will be.* I read Malcolm X, also from Michigan, whose mother had been committed to a mental hospital in my hometown of Kalamazoo. He warned black readers not to trust white liberals: *I don't care how nice one is to you; the thing you must always remember is that almost never does he really see you as he sees himself, as he sees his own kind. He may stand with you through thin, but not thick.* And I heard that same reprimand in James Baldwin, who said that liberals bought all the right books, have *all the proper attitudes—but they have no real convictions. And when the chips are down and you expect them to deliver on what you thought they felt, they somehow are not there.*

They somehow are not there. I took this allegation literally. Where should I put myself?

In suburban Michigan, in the quiet of my bedroom, these iconic readings of antiracist rhetoric cast a spell over me. They effected a clandestine evangelization of a kid primed to be a good disciple. It was not enough just to learn, just to read. Not enough to admire a black writer. Admiration was nothing. If your passions went unmatched by actions, you were just playing a role, demonstrating that you knew what to praise and what to reject. *Education*, for me, became laden with a meaning at once specific and spiritual. To be educated meant you read books and entertained ideas that made you feel uncomfortable. It meant looking in the mirror and asking, *What have I done that has cost me anything? What authority have I earned to speak? What work have I put in?* It meant collapsing your certainties and tearing down your self-fortifications. You should feel unprotected, unarmed, open to attack.

There was a problem, though: Baldwin, King, and Malcolm spoke only of black and white people, and I was neither. What had Asian Americans fought for, died for? What had we cared about? History textbooks and popular culture didn't tell me. When an Asian-looking man appeared on television (a rare occurrence), my heart beat very fast. The question was never *Will this be a joke?* but rather *What kind of joke will it be?* If it turned out I was wrong and he was simply like any other minor character—no accent, no distinguishing characteristics, unmemorable—I felt satisfied and, even, grateful.

I found my role models in books. W. E. B. Du Bois, Ralph Ellison, Richard Wright, Alice Walker, Maya Angelou—each of these people seemed as fearless to me as Asian Americans seemed afraid, as essential to American history as we were irrelevant. I went to Harvard for college and met activists for the first time; the ones I most wanted to emulate had parents who had fought for civil rights and against the Vietnam War in the sixties and seventies. They had been at the March on Washington and heard Martin Luther King, Jr.; they had taken part in the Black Power Movement. I imagined households steeped in conversation. What was it like to inherit a history of passions and resentments? I wondered. Did it make you stronger? Did it embolden you? Was this why I was weak, sweet, obedient?

I steeled myself. I would start from scratch. I would root out like weeds the effects of my parents, the tendency to choose safe options, to get ahead, to feel secure. I would embrace irrational measures. In college I worked at a homeless shelter, where I slept overnight on Fridays and signed up for extra shifts precisely when I had papers due. I dropped pre-med and majored in social studies and gender studies. I edited a small magazine about race and class and sexuality. And when I met other Asian Americans, those bound for consultant and hedge-fund jobs where they would make six figures, my judgment was harsh. Silently, through my narrowed eyes, I told them, *I know you, and there's not too much to know.*

As graduation approached, I wondered what I wanted to do. I considered activism; I admired activists the most. But I wasn't good at it. I'd tried working at a feminist nonprofit, where I had to lobby congressional staffers, and discovered I had a tendency to apologize for intruding on their time. More broadly, I thought it was too difficult to change the minds of the powerfully self-interested. What I wanted to do was straightforward, immediate work in places that needed people. Then I met a recruiter from Teach for America, an Asian American woman who told me that schools in the Mississippi Delta, among the poorest places in the country, faced a drastic teacher shortage.

This was the first time anyone had described to me the state of the present-day Delta. This land of cotton and extreme poverty had served as the stomping grounds of the early Civil Rights and Black Power Movements. Bobby Kennedy had toured the Delta as part of a war against poverty. Stokely Carmichael had coined the term *Black Power* there. The Delta was a place where heroic people had been maimed, shot, arrested, and killed for their belief in change. King himself was killed in Memphis, the Delta's northernmost tip, while rallying for sanitation workers;

James Meredith commenced a legendary solo walk across Mississippi but was shot by a sniper on his second day; and Fannie Lou Hamer, a sharecropper, had been arrested and beaten for organizing people to vote.

Why hadn't I heard about how people in the Delta lived now? I wondered. Was it because few progressives and members of the educated middle class—the disappointing liberals of Baldwin's day—wanted to visit, much less live there? I couldn't help but wonder if this place had vanished from the national consciousness when the Civil Rights and Black Power Movements ended. Was rural black poverty, unattached to white violence, too unglamorous to attract celebrated leaders willing to speak for its cause?

The fiftieth anniversary of *Brown v. Board of Education* was approaching, yet on a recent national reading test for fourth graders, 45 percent of white students had passed, as opposed to 13 percent of black students. Considering the Teach for America job, I began to think I could pick up where the Civil Rights Movement had left off. "This is our hope, and this is the faith that I go back to the South with," Martin Luther King had said. "Go back to Mississippi, go back to Alabama, go back to South Carolina, go back to Georgia, go back to Louisiana, go back to the slums and ghettos of our Northern cities, knowing that somehow this situation can and will be changed."

I wanted to touch that heroism or at least work in its shadows. I believed in James Baldwin's injunction: *If we . . . like lovers, insist on, or create, the consciousness of the others, . . . we may be able . . . to end the racial nightmare, and achieve our country, and change the history of the world.* And I felt I knew what Baldwin asked from me: reparation that required my whole body, my whole being. *It is the innocence which constitutes the crime,* Baldwin wrote of whites in 1963. *For these innocent people have no other hope. They are, in effect, still trapped in a history which they do not understand; and until they understand it, they cannot be released from it.* Yes, I told myself, I would prove that I was no innocent— Baldwin's softer, and more damning, term for ignorance. Teaching in Helena, Arkansas, a rural town located in the heart of the Delta, might help acquit me of Baldwin's charge.

Nearly a thousand miles from my parents, I easily made the decision to go to the Delta. When I told them, over the phone, they were befuddled, then angry. "You're going to get killed down there," my mother said.

At this I chortled loudly. This made my father stern.

"It's not funny, *mei mei*," he said, using the Chinese word for *little sister.* "It's dangerous down there."

Growing up, I'd attributed to my mother and father a particular hysteria, a sad misapprehension of America, where I— unlike them—was born, and belonged. This feeling had persisted through college.

I started to tell them the literacy statistics and, detecting my pious tone, my parents cut me off.

"Are you even going to get paid?"

I replied that the local district gave a salary.

"It won't be much," my dad said. "You want to throw away your Harvard degree?"

I was hurt. But within a day I was joking about their disapproval with my friends.

TEACH FOR AMERICA ASSIGNED ME to an alternative school incongruously named "Stars," which the local administration used as a dumping ground for the so-called bad kids. These were the truants and the druggies, the troublemakers and the fighters who had been expelled from the mainstream schools. Stars was a kid's last shot at staying in the system before being banished, entirely, from public education.

This is where I met Patrick, who was fifteen and in the eighth grade.

Mild-mannered, he walked with more hunch than swagger. In class, he preferred listening to speaking. Patrick never bullied anybody. He never cussed anybody out. He appeared to abide by a self-imposed code: Keep to yourself, don't mess around, don't get involved with other people's trouble. But he was willing to break his own code for a cause: Once, he leapt between two girls to stop a fight, and, in the process, got slammed to the ground.

Other students rushed and jostled to get to the front of the lunch line. Patrick hung back. His mind always seemed to be somewhere else: Frequently, while he was working, he would hum to himself, often not realizing it until someone poked him. He left papers strewn about his desk or unfolded them from his pockets. His grin was a half grin, as if he'd once trained himself to smile fully but had since abandoned the project.

More than anything else, Patrick seemed lost, as if he'd gotten on the school bus by accident. And indeed, just a month after he arrived at school, he stopped attending.

It wasn't hard to imagine why Patrick had stopped coming to school. Maybe it was just depressing. It could be violent, and when students got into fights, the school sometimes called the police. Shoved into a police car with the rest of the school watching, some pair of kids, freshly scratched and bruised, would spend the weekend in county jail—where, as one teacher put it, they could "think about where they're going in life." And we, the teachers, were also violent: For more minor incursions, like cussing out a classmate or teacher, students were paddled. Corporal punishment was legal in Arkansas and widely practiced in these parts. Stamped with ARKANSAS BOARD OF EDUCATION, an updated paddle had been engineered with holes to make it swing faster. I did not personally paddle, but like most teachers who have sent kids to the principal's office, I was complicit. Still, by far our most common method of disciplining a student was simply to send him home. Since all the students qualified for a free lunch, they liked to joke that if you wanted to mess around, you should do it in the afternoon.

In spite of everything, many of my students, including Patrick, remained optimistic about their futures. Patrick said he wanted to graduate and become a mechanic. He said he'd like to visit New York. Other students wanted good jobs so that they could take care of their grandparents. And when I looked for the source of this hope, most kids told me it came from God. This belief in God, this idea that because human beings were made in God's image their value was inherent, was foreign to me, but the longer I lived in the Delta, the more sense it made.

I often thought of the words Baldwin had written to his nephew: *This innocent country set you down in a ghetto in which, in fact, it intended that you should perish.* Except in the Delta, the ghetto was not a corner of a city but an entire region of the country. This ghetto is all my students knew, and it occurred to me that if you live in a place that you cannot leave, where you can't travel or work if you can't afford a car, where land is endless space that's been denied you, where people burn down their houses because the insurance money is worth more than the sale price, where the yards of shuttered homes are dumping grounds for pedestrian litter, where water is possibly polluted by a fertilizer company that skipped town, you want to believe that you do not at all resemble what you see. You want to believe that your town's decay is not a mirror of your own prospects, that its dirtiness cannot dirty your inner life, that its emptiness does not contradict your own ambitions—that in fact you were born linked to beauty, to the joyous power of resurrection.

Yet for all the hours I spent thinking about my students' fundamental beliefs, I fretted mainly about the tasks in front of me. How to get them to read and write and talk. How to get students like Patrick to show up at school. I generally tried not to think too hard about the perils that lay ahead of them, after they finished school. I didn't entirely acknowledge everything they were up against. In other words, had an oracle knocked on my door and told me what the future held for Patrick, I wouldn't have believed it. I would have shut the door. And maybe that would not have been wrong of me: There are just certain kids for whom you bring all your hope.

PART
I

A Raisin in the Sun

Where Helena sits on the banks of the Mississippi, the river is quiet, peaceable. Summer songbirds talk with frogs, with a *tsee tsee tew tew cheer cheer*. Wild dewberries bloom on the bluffs, where they dangle, ripe but unplucked. In the water below, catfish form shadows, ready to gorge on what the wind shakes in. For thousands of years the river routinely flooded these banks, building the most fertile soil in the world. In the mid-nineteenth century, plantation owners yielded from this soil a single crop—cotton—and cotton made it slave country.

Slave owners in the Delta were the richest moguls in the nation, and the wealthiest 10 percent of Arkansas's population owned 70 percent of its land. Steamboats competed with railroads to transport cotton from Helena. After the Civil War, the lumber industry took off, and the swampy hardwoods in the Delta offered yet another source of wealth. People flocked here for wages at the twenty-four sawmills and the docks, the fish fries and the juke joints, the opera house and the saloons. Toss dice, haul wood, make moonshine, repeat. Helena was, as Twain wrote in 1883, the *prettiest situation on the river* and the *commercial center of a broad and prosperous region.*

In 2004, the year I arrived in Helena, Twain's city was hard to imagine. On Cherry Street, the town's main drag, wooden planks covered windows. There was a No LOITERING sign on an abandoned storefront even though the actual loiterers were across the street, hovering around the town's only liquor store. The marquee of a long-shuttered store had become the canvas of a prankster: STARBUCKS COMING SOON. Sincerity was more likely to be found on the marquees of churches, which abounded. No SUCH THING AS REHAB WITHOUT JESUS, said one. There was no coffee shop, no bookstore, no movie theater, and no more than a handful of restaurants. When I asked where to get good coffee, people recommended McDonald's. (It wasn't bad.)

Helena had begun an effort to market an enchanting part of its history, the blues, at the old train depot, which was converted to a museum. The museum shares stories and photos of black musicians who sang in Helena, lived in Helena, visited Helena, used Helena as a stepping-stone to Chicago, or retired in Helena when Chicago didn't work out. Their names are evocative, often involving infirmity or animals: Blind Lemon Jefferson, Howlin' Wolf, Super Chikan. Exhibits here have hopeful titles—*A Heritage of Determination*, reads one, or *Struggle in a Bountiful Land*—but few visitors.

People say Helena's decline truly began with the closing of Mohawk Rubber and Tire Company. When it shut down in 1979, the middle class, both black and white, fled. Then Arkla

Chemical, a fertilizer company, was shuttered. The bowling alley, the movie theaters, the shops, and the nicer restaurants followed suit. Those who grew up here left, trying to find jobs in Little Rock, Memphis, Fayetteville, or Texas; families stopped coming here to live. When I first arrived in Helena, I worried what locals would think of teachers who left the community after Teach for America's standard two years. But soon I realized my question presumed that leaving was novel to the experience of living in Helena. What was novel was that young teachers would travel here at all. "The saddest day is high school graduation," one grandparent would later tell me, referring to the kids who had found opportunities elsewhere, "because those kids won't come back."

People here got what jobs they could. Old men knocked on doors, asking to pick up sticks in the yard for money. The guard at the county jail also worked part-time at McDonald's. A big employer was the casino, technically in Mississippi, just across the river. Funerals provided a steady stream of business. If you drove down Plaza Avenue, on a block no longer than half a mile, there were three funeral homes, a tombstone store, and a flower shop. On a lawn in front of a store, large blank headstones lay flat, reflecting the light. Walmart also did well. On any given school day, teenage girls could be found browsing the many aisles of its baby section. (Outside—on weekends—the high school church group peddled abstinence pamphlets.) Phillips County, of which Helena is the seat, was one of the poorest counties in the country, and ranked last in the state of Arkansas in public health. Its teenage birthrate was higher than that of ninety-four developing countries. There were regular shoot-outs in town. Drugs were a problem, and police officers were busted by the feds for trafficking.

White people did live, eat, and work here, but their children were hard to spot in daylight. They attended DeSoto School, one of many private schools in the Delta established to circumvent integration. When DeSoto was opened in 1970, a dedicated cohort of white families deliberately sent their children to the newly integrated public schools, which flourished in their early years: Helena's basketball team, a pretty picture of black and white players, became one of the best in the state. But as the economy tanked, property values plummeted, and everybody fled Helena, DeSoto—at first a minority bastion of racists—transformed into an evacuation site for the remaining white families. Helena's public schools, Central High School and Eliza Miller, are 99 percent black. As of this writing, DeSoto has yet to matriculate a single black student. Thus, in a city so small that the combined graduating class of its high schools is fewer than two hundred students and so remote that one must drive a hundred miles to see a movie, two groups of kids grow up, one white and one black, rarely interacting.

MY FIRST MONTHS IN THE Stars classroom had a surreal aspect. Most students had never encountered an Asian person before, and they stared. "What you is?" they'd say, and then, with a serious expression, ask if I was related to Jackie Chan. (Others, less polite, said, "Fuck you, Chinese bitch.") Once, a sixteen-year-old student took a piss in a classroom, on a dare. Another kid came to school with his legs covered with welts from a switch. "Should I call child services?" I asked other teachers. No, no; that was just how you kept discipline around here. When kids got in trouble at school, it was universally known, they preferred paddling to suspension. "They're used to that," the secretary explained to me. "And they don't want to go home."

I was shocked by all of this, but I was shocked, primarily, by myself. I yelled. I got mean. At first I tried to appear strict, in a bid to be taken seriously, but this contortion took on a life of its own. To the twelfth grader who called me a Chinese bitch, I said he'd be lucky if he got a job at McDonald's. To a boy who told a girl she was fat, I snapped, "So are you." I tore up a student's drawing, which I'd thought of as a doodle, in order to jolt him into paying attention; he never forgave me, and I will regret it forever. I bribed a mother to sign a permission slip for a field trip. The mother, an absentee drug addict, was angry at her daughter, my student, for calling child services on behalf of her younger siblings. I went to the house. The mother said she'd sign the form if I got her a color TV. We compromised: I'd go to Walmart and get her a kiddie pool. ("Your children are gonna love this," said the cashier at Walmart, shoving my purchase into a huge plastic bag. "Days get hot here.") Another time a kid grabbed my butt, and I sent him to the principal; she asked me, "Paddling or suspension?" I told her, "Let him decide." He chose paddling.

I began to speculate that the modern Delta did not exist in the American consciousness because it disturbed the mind. It crushed part of our American mythology. What had the Civil Rights Movement been for—the violence, the martyrs, the passionate actions—if its birthplace was still poor, still segregated, still in need of dramatic social change? A world of meaning had been built and had now collapsed. Here, one began to worry that the movement was a fabrication of the nation's imagination. And indeed, much later, a sixteen-year-old boy, whose older brother had been killed by a white man while robbing a flower shop, would approach my poster of Martin Luther King's March on Washington with genuine suspicion. He put his face right up to the photograph so that his nose touched an image of white protesters in the crowd.

"You made that up," he told me.

"What?" I asked, confused.

"White people ain't gonna help no black people." He believed I'd photographically doctored the photo.

THAT FIRST SEMESTER OF TEACHING was so relentlessly challenging that I barely recognized the cliché I was enacting: middle-class outsider visits, shudders.

I was constantly making classroom rules that I then constantly modified. Raise your hand. Don't curse. Don't put down your classmates. Don't use the word *faggot*. Don't slap—don't poke—just don't touch anybody. Never put your head down. If you put down your head for the whole class, you get a zero. For most infractions, students would get a "warning." If they got two warnings, they'd have to go to the corner, where they wrote a "reflection" or, if applicable, an apology. If they refused, I sent them to the principal. This had worked in my summer training in Houston. But the students here were older and, having been subjected to much worse punishment, didn't care. They had perfect behavior in one circumstance: when our school police officer occasionally stepped into our room. (We had no guidance counselor, no music or art teacher, no functioning library, no gymnasium, no sports teams—or any teams, for that matter—but we did have him.) His presence transformed the class: Whenever he stood there in his blue uniform, his baton hanging from his belt, the kids suddenly became deeply absorbed in whatever I was trying to say. From across the room, the officer winked at me.

I began to distrust my own system. I distrusted punishment. Should a person who forgot to raise his hand suffer the same consequence—a warning—as a person who called another dumb? Shouldn't the word *faggot* trigger a collective, "Kumbaya"-type discussion rather than a targeted reprimand? Distracted by issues of discipline—the police, the paddling, my own inner Mr. Hyde—I'd suddenly remember to ask myself what I actually hoped to teach. What did I want students to learn? I was an English teacher, but it seemed I could go days without thinking about a book.

A book—even the word seemed outmoded in Helena. Before school began, the Stars principal had warned me that the eighth graders were reading at a fourth- or fifth-grade level and that I, accordingly, should find appropriate "content." I either did not understand or did not want to know what this meant. So I gave my class a James Baldwin short story, and they got frustrated because the language was too hard. I gave them a speech by Malcolm X, hoping to rile them up, but it bored them. And I showed them a video of a young state senator named Barack Obama, who had just made a splash at the 2004 Democratic National Convention. "My father was a foreign student, born and raised in a small village in Kenya." Everything about Obama's speech, its historical references and its exhortations, seemed too distant for them to grasp.

What was I doing wrong? I wondered. Was it purely a matter of reading comprehension? Historical blind spots? My lack of control over the classroom? My inability to connect with them? I became afraid to share any piece of writing in the black tradition that I considered precious. If it meant nothing to them, maybe it should mean less to me. Deciding to try one last time, I introduced Lorraine Hansberry's *A Raisin in the Sun*. Characters spoke to each other directly, the reading level was easier, the format—a play—was new to them, and the story centered on a black family.

It was a hit. The angry banter between Walter and Ruth,

husband and wife, got laughs. Their complaints about living in a crowded house got nods. Ruth's despair over discovering she's pregnant made the room go silent. And the students universally loved the grandma: All seemed to know her. Born in Mississippi and religious, she scolded her son for wanting to start a liquor store, slapped her daughter for saying there is no God, and yelled at her daughter-in-law for wanting an abortion. As I assigned parts, the students clamored to be cast in her role. "She don't play," they said admiringly.

Why, I asked the students, did they think the grandma had left Mississippi to move to Chicago?

"Because there isn't much for us down here," one student said easily, and I felt vertigo at the word *us*. Others nodded in easy agreement.

For the first time, our conversation about American history was not a strain. Usually the students were so handicapped by a lack of basic knowledge that we made no progress. They hadn't known, for instance, when slavery ended or recognized the vocabulary word *emancipation*. They hadn't known that promises to give former slaves land had been broken. They'd vaguely heard about violence against black people in the Delta, but most didn't know about the massacres of black sharecroppers who had tried to organize in our county, nor did they recognize the word *lynching*. But this one question, why a black family would leave the Delta, was not difficult for them to answer.

I talked about Helena's history of violence, which was a taboo topic—for people black and white—in town. This violence, I said, helped drive the mass migration to cities like Chicago. I talked about governments that stood by or even participated in the intimidation of black people. And I passed around a picture of a lynching, a dangling body burned and charred, its edges eerily blotted out. If my students could see how brutal the conditions were, I thought, they might find a channel for their anger and a reason for pride in the history of black resilience.

"This isn't right," said one student, looking disgusted. He passed it on. Another studied it and shook his head wordlessly. Then he, too, passed it on.

Their twin emotions, outrage and sobriety, formed for me a coherent whole. When I learned about lynching in middle school, indignation had made me feel powerful.

Then the photograph stopped at David, a spindly kid who lived with his grandmother and liked to sketch animals. He gazed at the picture and did not move. He looked as if he had stopped breathing. Then he turned over the picture and put his head down.

My neck burned; a knot grew hard in my stomach. It was against my rules to put your head down. The students watched and saw my weakness.

"If you don't lift your head," I said, trying to sound firm, "you're going to get a zero."

Finally David muttered, "Nobody want to see that."

The moment he said it, I knew, instantly, that I had failed to understand something essential. In the tone of his voice, in the sudden change of his demeanor, he was telling me that I had crossed a line. I retrieved the photo from his desk, and even a quick glance at it made my heart skip a beat. It looked different now, something I didn't at all recognize; some other teacher must have found it, printed it, and passed it out.

I walked to the front of the class and resumed my place at the board. I wrote some words idly, so that my back could be turned and the kids could not see my face. My chest was exploding. How could I be so casual or, worse, smug about a lynching? I had confronted them with their history, treating it like a secret whose exposure would transport them to a painful but necessary enlightenment. I'd meant to be daring and transgressive in bringing up the history of violence against black people. But maybe David and the others wanted school to be a refuge from that memory.

I had expected to be guilty of other things—of sentimental-izing their conditions, of patronizing them with my sympathy. But I didn't expect to be smug. *Here, look, learn*, says the smiling teacher with mysterious motives; *learn about your history or get a zero.*

After class, I put the photograph facedown in my drawer and never looked at it again.

2

The Free Write

IBEGAN MY SECOND YEAR OF TEACHING IN THE SAME FOG OF discouragement that I'd ended my first. Except now I was even more sick for a bagel, a bookstore, a movie theater, a coffee shop. Increasingly, I spent Saturdays driving the seventy-two miles to Memphis, Tennessee. Despite its storied history, what mattered most to me was that Memphis was a city. With traffic, and traffic lights! Coffee shops, happy hours, Thai food, parking lots, tower cranes, families out for walks, young people dressed up with somewhere to go, Asians! Cars honked, drivers lurched, the city sang; you knew, deep in your heart, that somewhere not too far away a store was selling tofu. In blighted areas, graffiti shouted joyfully from the walls; for all the poverty in Helena, you never saw it. Even a mediocre tag, I grasped with a jolt, suggested a loftier youth malcontent than the one in Helena: a spirit of public rebellion, a confidence about who your enemy was (property, society, state, the man), a thrill in using color to demand that people see you, even the where-withal to get spray paint.

Meanwhile, the nicer pockets of the city offered a different kind of wasteland, where you could feel passionate about consumption and empowered by anonymity. At the café in a Barnes & Noble, a man cut me in line—in the rare cases where there was a line in Helena, nobody cut—and, recovering from my shock, I leapt to action. "Apologize!" I yelled at him, in a teacherly way. What did I care? I'd never see him again, which was probably what he'd been thinking. "Apologize!" I repeated, louder, unhinged. The man looked chagrined—it was unclear whether on my behalf or his own. "I apologize," he said meekly. At the counter I greedily ordered a muffin. And a coffee. And a fizzy drink, just for the hell of it.

In this café, marveling at how spacious and airy and clean everything was, I pecked out law school applications on my laptop, occasionally stopping to eavesdrop. I'd decided that law school would give me a semi-respectable excuse to leave the Delta behind. My self-interest was not unmixed with idealism. Ever since I'd studied the Civil Rights Movement, I'd admired the NAACP Legal Defense Fund and wanted to work there; the stories of lawyers and their battle to desegregate the South in the 1950s and 1960s had drawn me to the Delta in the first place. But, also, I was just desperate to get out of there.

Then something happened. I started to like the Delta. One Sunday I went to a student's church, a clapboard shack crammed with people in dresses and suits and big hats, and clapped and danced and sweated. Another time I spent all afternoon just taking pictures of the kudzu wilding up the telephone poles—strange, gorgeous, improbable triangles of thick green. I stopped going to Memphis every weekend. I added ice to my tea and drank from my mug on my porch, in arm's reach of a blooming fig tree, from which I could pluck dessert.

In the classroom I had finally learned how to banter with students and assert authority with ease. In late September, a student interrupted a lesson to ask me if I was related to Yao Ming. I looked at him coolly, letting the silence hang. Finally I said:

"You related to Kobe Bryant?"

The other students started guffawing—at him, not at me.

"Ms. Kuo, that be racist," he tried, affronted.

"Think about it," I said. And I continued with the lesson.

When I called my parents to tell them I'd applied to law school, they were intrigued. They didn't know any lawyers themselves, but they liked the sound of it. Nobody messed with lawyers. Getting sued was one of their chief associations of America before they arrived, and living here reinforced it. But it had never occurred to them that their daughter could be the one suing.

Now they asked, with enthusiasm, "If you get in, you'll leave Arkansas, right?"

For me their excitement was a clue: If they liked an idea, maybe I should be suspicious of it.

"I guess I'd leave," I said.

"Good. You won't have kids making those Chinese sounds at you," my dad said.

"They were bad kids," my mother said, laughing, as if I had already left and the kids were just memories from my past.

I felt immediately that I had erred in portraying my students. I must have complained too much. I considered admitting to my parents that I hadn't applied to law school for the right reasons, that I was starting to make a life in the Delta with my students, and that I'd begun to find ways to reach them. But it seemed like a lot of trouble to explain these little triumphs to my parents. I wanted them to like and respect me. Law school and the prospect of my departure seemed to have cheered them up, and I decided not to ruin it.

PATRICK HAD BEEN IN MY class since the beginning of the year, but he was quiet, and it was easy to miss quiet students. He always chose a seat in the back and kept his head low. His voice was low, too. "Patrick, could you speak up?" I often heard myself saying—at which he smiled slightly, as if I had said something funny. He seemed at once distracted and alert. His eyes searched the walls of the room, seeking a place to settle. A couple of times, from his seat, he reached his arm out to touch a nearby bookshelf, knocking on it softly to see what it sounded like. And he was empathetic. Once, a student slapped another, lightly, on the back of the head. Patrick winced and looked away, as if he'd been slapped himself.

There were students who no longer interested me, in whom I'd found a hard, mean edge. My fifteen-year-old student Ray was one of these. One teacher said, "He's always got an ugly face on, don't he?" Another told me, "Don't even try—the devil's already got him." Even though what he needed was a counselor, I did try for a while. I felt hope when Ray stole a poster of mine, a Picasso Blue Period in which a blind man is eating; I thought it must have moved him. Once, I got him to write a poem. But those acts were anomalies; generally he was impenetrable. He never laughed, even if the whole class was keeling over about something funny. He put his head down a lot, and if you tried to talk to him, he called you a bitch and told you to get the fuck away. Rumor had it that his mother was an addict and, unlike a lot of the kids, he appeared to have no grandparents in his life. And still I got tired of trying to show him I was on his side.

By my second year teaching, I had started to regard students in a utilitarian way: Who would respond with enormous success to just a little adult interest? Few students answered that question better than Patrick. He wanted to try; he was thirsty for encouragement, yet he had failing grades. Patrick could excel if somebody was there to push him every minute. But he kept missing classes. Now I knew why he'd been sent to Stars; he simply did not come to school.

In December, he'd missed so many classes that I was worried, concerned he would fail his upcoming exams. I called Patrick's house. I wanted to know why he was absent. A male voice said, "Pat's sick," and hung up. Worried that Patrick had dropped out, I decided to go find him.

Patrick lived in the "ghetto in a ghetto," as my students called it, where the shootings were so frequent that the city council had threatened to impose a curfew. Most of the neighborhood's house numbers had faded, and many of the houses were vacant. A group of teenage boys walked down the middle of the street, challenging cars to swerve around them. I drove back and forth, lost, until finally I gave up and pulled over. A boy rode by on his bike, and I asked him if he knew where Patrick Browning lived. "Pat stay right there." He pointed to a small square house with a porch, just a few feet away.

I knocked on the screen door. It was dark inside. A man in an undershirt got up slowly from the couch and limped to the door.

"I'm Patrick's teacher, Ms. Kuo," I said, through the screen. "I think we've spoken on the phone before?"

He looked at me. "Yeah, yeah," he said. Then he dropped back into the darkness.

Another figure approached. It was Patrick. His face emerged into the sunlight and, seeing it was me, he smiled—a huge, boyish glow at being noticed, at being favored. He suddenly seemed years younger. Then, with a twitch, he remembered he hadn't come to school.

He said very fast, "The bus didn't come." Then he looked away. He knew he wasn't a good liar.

"I missed the bus."

Then, "I'm sorry, Ms. Kuo."

We sat on the porch.

"Doesn't . . . doesn't anybody"—I turned to make sure the front door was closed—"make you come to school?"

"It ain't on them, it's on me. They tell me to, you know, but sometimes I just don't really feel like . . ." He trailed off. "My mother, she real busy; she's always at work. And my daddy, you know . . ."

He stopped, not wanting to say anything bad about his father.

"How did you end up at Stars, anyway?" I asked.

"I got in an accident when I was eleven," he began. "Gas was cheap, a dollar for a gallon, and I had a whole gallon of gas. I was just playing in the backyard, pouring gas onto some sticks on the ground. Just pouring gas for fun, really. I wasn't thinking about gas being flammable. It was real stupid. I ignited a whole jug; it flew into a fire. I looked down and my pants were burning. Pretty quick the whole yard was on fire. Lucky my sisters, they was there, and they got a towel."

I had been in the Delta long enough not to be surprised that he was in the backyard casually starting a fire. There wasn't much to do in Helena besides going to Walmart, and boredom kept you from thinking straight. It wasn't malicious. It was the opposite. He was trying to find something to do that wouldn't bother anybody.

It reminded me of Richard Wright, who, at the opening of *Black Boy*, starts a similar project. The son of a sharecropper, Wright had grown up in the Delta and spent several years in Helena in the 1910s. Four-year-old Wright had *ached with boredom* as he watched the coals burn in the fireplace. *An idea of a new kind of game grew and took root in my mind*, he wrote. *Why not throw something into the fire and watch it burn? . . . Who would bother about a few straws*, he thought, tearing a batch from an old broom. The fire rewarded his attention; it crackled and blazed. *My idea was growing, blooming.* How would the fluffy white curtains look, he wondered, if he held lit straws against them? Soon, to his fright, the house was in flames.

Patrick looked down at his leg, stained by burn marks in large, irregular splotches. "I was in the hospital for maybe weeks, out of school for months. Teachers was supposed to bring work to my house but never did." His voice was flat, not angry, as if such failure was ordinary. "The hospital got a TV, and I saw the towers go down."

The towers: It was jarring to connect him to 9/11, or to any national experience, and for a moment I realized that, in my mind, the Delta existed as a place disconnected from the rest of the country.

"I had to learn how to walk again. Bed rest for two or three months. I got behind. I had to do seventh again. And then eighth. Then I got sent to Stars."

I tried to imagine his life at home. His mother would have been at work during the day. Something was going on with his father. Maybe he had gotten used to a dull kind of freedom, looking out the window, flipping through channels, watching other dropouts on the street, getting cheap weed. The structure of school must have seemed alien.

"I saw you break up a fight," I said. "Why did you do that?"

An immense line creased his forehead and he looked down. "May is my cousin. Liana was my neighbor. I don't want to see my cousin get in a fight with my neighbor. I don't like to see people fight. Why? And we're all in alternative school, so it don't make sense. Maybe they just ready to give up on life; that's the only reason I can think of."

I nodded, and then handed him a postcard of Rodin's *Thinker*. I'd written him a note on the back, saying the statue reminded me of him.

He looked at the picture carefully, holding the corners with his fingertips. "Thank you, Ms. Kuo."

I'd chosen him to go on a field trip that weekend. Would he like to join?

"Yes, ma'am," he said. I handed him a permission slip.

"Thank you, Ms. Kuo," he said. "Thank you."

I told him to stop thanking me.

I told him I knew he could make it through the eighth grade.

"Yes, ma'am," he said, in a soft, low voice.

I told him I would work hard for him, but that he would need to work hard, too, through a lot of small steps.

"Yes, ma'am," he repeated, this time turning his head slightly so that his eyes met mine. It was getting dark and there were no streetlights. Yet his eyes offered a small, certain source of light. I wondered if mine did, too.

I told him I'd like to see him in school tomorrow; did he plan to come?

From the way he nodded, in that serious way of his, I knew that he would.

I told him I would be at the ceremony when he graduated

from high school. At that, he grinned. He had a gap between his front teeth that I hadn't noticed before.

Hearing myself make this promise out loud stirred me, made me want to stay in the Delta. This was who I would be: a person who stayed.

When I stood up and started walking toward the street, he seemed surprised, as if he felt I was being careless.

"It ain't safe here, Ms. Kuo." He followed me past the porch, and I realized he was escorting me to my car.

Ms. RILEY WAS MY ONE good friend at Stars. She sang gospel, quoted the Bible and Tyler Perry, and made chicken dumplings that she shared with me over lunch, occasionally feeding a spoonful straight into my mouth. Gentle with me, she was tough on the students. Once, a pair of girls had torn up a roll of toilet paper and scattered it across the bathroom; she confiscated the rest of the rolls. "The good will go with the bad," she'd said, like a prophet, the streamer of loose tissue dangling behind her like a banner. Officially Ms. Riley was a "teacher's assistant," but as often happened in the Delta, where teacher shortages were severe, assistants taught classes. Ms. Riley taught reading.

Over lunch one afternoon, Ms. Riley read the audit report released by our new superintendent. "Fools been running the town, Ms. Kuo," she said as I leaned over her shoulder to read.

In Helena it is the rare person, black or white, who attempts to defend the public schools. Each year brought a new disgrace. In my first year teaching, our test scores were among the lowest in Arkansas. In my second year, 2005, the Arkansas Department of Education seized power over the Helena school district, deposed our superintendent, and dispatched its own replacement from Little Rock to investigate financial corruption. Among other scandals revealed by the audit was the allegation that an administrator received a raise, unauthorized by the school board, from $90,000 to $124,997 in one year. First-year teachers made around $27,000. Assistants made less than half of that.

"Have you seen Ms. Madden around?" I asked.

"Ain't seen her all week," Ms. Riley said.

The attendance record of Ms. Madden, our principal, rivaled that of our worst students. Her major contribution to the school thus far had been to change its name from Stars to Hope. Months later she would change the name back to Stars, for reasons I never figured out, and a decade later she would be indicted for embezzling over a million dollars from a federal food program that gave money to hungry children. But at the time she was just a twenty-seven-year-old woman who, in addition to her job at Stars, ran a daycare program.

Our fourth principal in a year, Ms. Madden would last the longest. Our first, and best, Dr. Rankin, had gotten her Ph.D. in counseling children and forged real relationships with students who landed in her office. Within months of my arrival, she had been "transferred" to the Transportation Services—overseeing the buses. She had been replaced by a Mr. Horton, an assistant superintendent whose assignment to Stars was intended as a punishment for cooperating with the state's investigation of financial corruption. He sued or threatened suit, and then he, too, left Stars, only to be replaced by Mrs. Eckleson, who lasted a few months. Students referred to days when a principal was absent as "free days"—days when rules were lax and they could test boundaries. They hid in the bathroom during class, let out screams in the cafeteria, and tried to provoke fights; the clever ones stopped short of anything that would get them in serious trouble. And any kid could see that teachers, having nobody to hold us accountable, became lazier. We left campus earlier and didn't try as hard.

My friend, Ms. Riley, had grown up in Helena, and she talked a lot about what life had been like during segregation. Buses carrying white children would splatter mud all over the black children as they walked to school, but they didn't care: They walked together; they had one another. No neighbor ever stole, no door had to be locked; if you went out and forgot you left your clothes drying on the line, a neighbor would see them flying and bring them into your house and not a thing of yours would be gone. Children respected parents; parents respected education. According to Ms. Riley, integration had ruined a lot of it. Black teachers, generally not welcome to teach at newly integrated white schools, lost jobs, while white teachers kept theirs. When Central integrated, administrators began to offer alternatives to paddling, because they didn't want the few black teachers who'd found jobs to whip a white child. And, anyway, white families had started DeSoto, so what had been the point of it all? Helena had been better off segregated.

Trying to make sense of Ms. Riley's words, I recognized that they were more than mere nostalgia. In a neighboring Delta school that had undergone integration in 1968, I'd read, the school board had closed the all-black school and refused to re-hire its black teachers. The teachers sued, but the judge dismissed the suit, writing, *This is another instance where a school system has accomplished integration as required by Law, which unfortunately resulted in adjustment that caused certain of the teachers to become victims of the "constitutionally required process."* It was not hard to detect his disdain for integration and his apathy at the prospect of punishing black teachers for it.

* * *

AROUND THE SAME TIME PATRICK went missing, I had discovered one fail-safe. It was the "I Am" poem.

> *I am*
> *I feel*
> *I wonder*
> *I hear*
> *I see*
> *I understand*
> *I say*
> *I dream*
> *I try*
> *I hope*
> *I want*
> *I pretend*
> *I cry*

The poem has a deceptively simple structure. It looks like easy credit: Fill in the blanks. But it was a trick. It forced you into self-reflection. What do you know about yourself? What do you want, what have you lost? It required tough students to cop to an internal life. If you asked them these things out loud, they'd laugh at you.

Once they started working on the poem, nearly every student wanted to write about somebody they'd lost or feared losing. And I could tell, by their eagerness to talk, that it wasn't often that they met an outsider who found their trauma novel or their stories freshly sad. Though their vocabularies were limited, everyone seemed to know the words *heart disease* and *diabetes*. A grandparent's death was devastating, because he or she was often the main caretaker. The stories could be dramatic. A pastor impregnated a student's cousin, who was fifteen or sixteen. A stepdad, high on heroin, threw battery acid on his stepdaughter, and she lost a leg. An alcoholic playing with a gun accidentally shot and killed his niece.

Aaron, a bright, wiry kid, one of my best students, took to the assignment immediately. "Can I write about my nephew?" he asked. "He's two and already going bad."

"You're so great," I said, confused about why he was even at Stars. "Why were you sent here?"

I assumed it was marijuana.

"Fighting."

"Really? I can't tell."

At this he brightened. "Miller was messing me up," he said. "It's easy to get into it out there."

For all of Stars's problems, its small classroom size was perhaps what Aaron needed. At Stars, he said, "You see everything." What did he mean, everything? I had asked. "How much help people really need," he replied.

Aaron spoke in a clinical manner, as if he did not belong to the body of students who needed help but rather was assessing them distantly. And I realized that small class sizes were not just beneficial for the obvious reason—that larger classrooms ignored, worsened, and evicted the problem student. For a student like Aaron, who lived on the borderline of success and failure, the small classroom provided a magnifying glass with which to evaluate his peers: What did they want, what ticked them off, how did they lose their tempers, what help did they take or choose not to take? Seeing these possible mirrors of himself allowed him to realize he wanted to be different.

At Stars I never saw him fight; he remained, in all ways, an ideal student. He was bright, he was curious, and he had perfect attendance. In his house, attendance was "not optional," he'd said, and he showed up even when he had a cold. His mother and grandma had both graduated from high school, and they expected the same from him. This—regular attendance—would turn out to be one of the most basic predictors of success for my students at Stars.

For his "I Am" poem, Aaron wrote: *I hear everyone cursing around me, so I curse, as well / I see my aunts and uncles fighting all the time, so do as I see / I cry when I get a whooping for cursing all the time / I try to be good, but I always find some trouble to get in / I hope one day I will break out of my hard shell and be somebody new.*

Sitting next to Aaron was Tamir, who looked afraid. He peered at Aaron's paper, as though this was the kind of assignment one could copy. I went to him. His paper was blank except for his name. His handwriting was tiny, nearly imperceptible—a common technique, I'd begun to realize, to protect oneself from correction.

In a low voice, not wanting other students to hear, he said, "I don't know what to put."

"Sure you do." I kneeled down to the desk. This had become my favorite part about teaching: the prodding, the slow prying apart of words, the transfer of mind to page.

"How about this one?" I pointed to *I see.*

"Ms. Kuo," he said, "things I see ain't nothing worth talking about."

I fell silent. We looked at each other, his eyes serious and bright. He wanted to write. He had gone through a lot, things that I could never really know about. I wished there was a way to tell him, *I know I don't know you. But I want so much for you, and that is real.*

"I'll bet there's somebody in your life who really means something to you," I said.

Tamir blinked. There was someone. He hedged, deciding whether he should say it out loud. "My auntie," he said finally. "But she passed." Now he looked at me questioningly, unsure whether her death disqualified her from being seen.

"But I'll bet you still see her."

Tamir lit up at that thought.

He asked, "How you spell *aunt*?" and I spelled it.

He wrote: *I see aunt happy in haven with here father.*

"How about this, Ms. Kuo?" He pointed to *I wonder.*

I said, "There's no right answer. It just has to be something you really feel, the kind of thing you fall asleep thinking about, you know." Then I stood up and said loudly, so that others could hear, "You've got this." He nodded.

He wrote: *I am red like the sun as it rises / I hear a dog barking as I try to fall asleep / I pretend I don't feel anything / I wonder if I am going to live to be eighteen.*

After Tamir finished his last line, he read the whole poem to himself. Then he asked if he could use my computer to type it.

Miles, an eighth grader freshly dumped from Miller, was also reluctant. He'd arrived to Stars with a reputation: My friend Vivian, who taught at Miller, had said a couple teachers were ready to throw a party when he left. But he seemed fine at first. He dressed neatly. His shirt was always tucked in; his pants never sagged.

"Get out of my face, China woman," he said when I neared him. Then he made a mocking sound, *ching chong*, and stared at me to see what reaction he'd produced.

I simply gave Miles a rueful look, affecting a distant sadness, as if he had hurt himself. Then I said, "At the end of this class period"—here I pointed to the clock deliberately, slowly— "you're going to apologize to me for insulting my heritage. And it's going to feel great."

In the background, students snickered. "Ms. Kuo got him good."

I was used to the Asian-mimicking sounds by now. The first time a student had made them, my stomach cramped. I thought of my grandfather, who had walked me to school every morning of the second grade, even in the stinging winter cold. He was twice an immigrant: born in China and rendered a refugee in Taiwan after 1949, he had recently arrived in the United States. One day, classmates made similar sounds at him, singsong and grotesque. I begged him to stop walking to school with me. Eventually we compromised; he agreed to walk behind me.

Now I had enough experience to hide the memory. My lack of anger appeared to calm Miles.

"Did you know my brother?" he asked. "He went to Stars."

"Who's your brother?"

"Brandon Clark."

My heart fell. Brandon had been one of my first students. He was the one who had been killed robbing the flower shop. On New Year's Day, he'd gone into the shop with two other kids, including a quiet student of mine named William. The third, supposedly the ringleader, had pointed a BB gun at the elderly couple who owned the shop. But the husband had a real gun and emptied a clip of five rounds. The kids scrambled. One bullet hit the back of Brandon's head just as he reached the door. He'd been holding the bag of money and it went flying: The total amount stolen was one hundred and three dollars.

Days after Brandon died, I had asked students to write about him and how his death made them feel. Somehow Ms. Jasper, a teacher's assistant who had recently paddled a sixteen-year-old with severe learning disabilities, caught wind of what I was doing. She burst into my room.

"Chickens coming home to roost, Ms. Kuo," she yelled.

"You telling the students that it be *okay* what Brandon doing. A boy got hisself shot and you're writing little poems about it."

I was dazed. The students stopped writing. Was she right? Was writing silly? Did it do little more than endorse Brandon's crime? I hesitated. Ms. Jasper came from the same generation as Ms. Riley. She believed in the vital black community that seemed, in the past three decades, to have lost its moral high ground. In her eyes, to write about Brandon was to grieve Brandon, and to grieve Brandon was to claim his innocence. By having students write, by authorizing emotions other than shame, I had authorized Brandon's robbery. For her, shame was a source of dignity.

The flower-shop owner who killed Brandon had not been arrested. He claimed self-defense. It was Miles who would later doubt the veracity of my poster of black and white protesters together in the March on Washington.

"Brandon was a good person," I said to Miles, right as the bell rang.

He examined my face to see if I was lying.

TRUE TO HIS WORD, PATRICK came to school soon after I visited him at home. And then he began to come every day. He'd get off the bus holding his books in that lost way of his, as if his arrival was a mistake, but now that he was present, he did well. You never had to worry that he'd erupt over somebody picking on him and get sent to the office to be whacked by the wooden paddle.

I had asked the students to tape their "I Am" poems on the walls, to make them proud of their own writing. Then I noticed something surprising: They wanted to read one another's work. Certain students—who, during my attempts at collective reading, put their heads down or slapped the head of a studious classmate, trying to keep him from "being good," as they called it—would now stand attentively in front of a classmate's poem, tracing the line methodically with an index finger, not saying a word.

"This is good," one of them would finally say. And then, often, they gave the same reason: "This is real." Patrick, like many of the others, read every piece of student work.

After I'd watched them do this for a few days, I suddenly realized what I had been doing wrong. I had not tried to sell reading. I had not spelled out how a book could be personal and urgent—that it was like an "I Am" poem. Besides *A Raisin in the Sun*, students still had not connected with any book I had assigned. So I tried a new tack.

"You all talk about fronting," I said to them. "What do you mean when you say that word?"

"It's when someone pretends to be all that."
"It's like being fake."
"It's when somebody tells you one thing but doesn't
    do what they say."
"It's when somebody clowns, trying to get attention."

I wrote on the board, *People think I'm _____ but I'm really _____.* I asked them to fill in the blanks. They wrote:

*People think I don't care, but I really love my mom and
    want to make her proud.*
*People think I don't want to learn, but I want to get my
    education.*
People think I'm dumb, but I'm really smart.
People think I'm evil, but I'm not.

Patrick wrote, *People think I don't care, but I do.*

"We all front," I said. "You know why I love to read? It's because books don't front."

They were listening—it was working.

"You can hear what people are thinking in books," I continued. "They do crazy things, but you can figure out how they feel. You get to figure out what's happening to them on the inside."

We talked about what it meant to see only the outside of people. I asked, "Why do people keep their insides hidden?" The responses were painfully insightful, and the most common was a variation on this one: "People are afraid that if they're honest about what they want, they won't get it."

I realized that I needed also to give them a sense of ownership over the people and stories in these books. I researched black writers for teenagers: Walter Dean Myers, Sharon Flake, Sharon Draper, Sister Souljah, Nikki Grimes, Jacqueline Woodson. I ordered these books and then I read them. I felt these writers knew better than I did what stories the kids needed. The heroes were people who looked like them, talked like them, and faced the problems they faced. In *Tears of a Tiger*, by Sharon Draper, Andy, a teenager, blames himself for his best friend's death. In *Jazmin's Notebook*, by Nikki Grimes, Jazmin, fourteen, is her mother's primary caretaker. In *Begging for Change*, by Sharon Flake, Raspberry has to decide whether or not to welcome her estranged father back into her life. A state fund for new teachers had given me eight hundred dollars for the classroom, and I spent it all on these books.

"Ms. Kuo, why are you bothering? You know they ain't going to read them," Coach Dodd yelled from his window, watching me lug a box to my classroom. Coach Dodd was the recently hired "guidance counselor." An assistant football coach at the high school, he was sent to Stars because he needed a faculty position. If you asked him how he was doing, he always said, "Same crap, different toilet."

I tried, like a matchmaker, to help students find books they might like. Demand grew, word passed quickly about which books were good, and my shelves were plundered. Pretty soon I saw these books clutched to chests and carried from class to class. The students guarded them like amulets. New readers pored over the books, whose inside covers gradually acquired territorial graffiti—*This a good book, JG.* "Who's JG?" they'd ask, pondering. When they figured it out, they were often shocked.

"Jasmine loved it," I'd respond briskly.

Worn and read, the books were gathering dignity.

Did the students know, I wondered, how they looked when they read? Concentrated, absorbed, serious. I took their pictures. This was before camera phones, so real suspense built as they waited for me to get my film developed. And when I brought the photographs in to class, they studied these unexpected portraits of themselves.

I decorated the walls with their pictures, which, like watchful spirits, seemed to encourage us. We finished one book after another, charting the number of pages read by coloring in rectangles on a grid hung on the wall. Silent reading became an institution in my class. Among the best qualities of silent reading, I was learning, was that it was impossible to guess who would be good at it. You could never know the quiet a person craved. Kayla, recently sent to jail for fighting, enforced silent reading most strictly. When a student disturbed the peace with whispering, Kayla stiffened and threw a piercing glare. Liana and May, the same girls whose fight Patrick had recently tried to end, curled up in adjacent beanbags, as if silent reading was a kind of cease-fire.

* * *

EVERY MORNING I AWOKE AT five. I prepared lessons, I graded quizzes, I drove to school at six-thirty and waited in the parking lot for the janitor to open the gate. I developed weird habits around food. At school I didn't eat, and at home I was always eating. I gained a lot of weight; I lost a lot of weight. I talked to myself, in my head, all the time. How I'd screwed up or what I'd done well. Sometimes I found that I was talking to my students. I talked to them, by myself, out loud. "I know you know better," I'd catch myself saying into space, or "This writing is beautiful."

My notebooks were strange, filled with often-contradictory self-exhortations and resolutions. *Be kind. Don't be afraid to be mean.* Sometimes the notes read as if I had joined a cult: *Change is happening every day. No spiritual work is ever wasted.* And there were notes from Dostoevsky that felt directly relevant: *Work tirelessly. If, as you are going to sleep at night, you remember: "I did not do what I ought to have done," arise at once and do it.* On my less-frequent jaunts to Memphis bookstores, I found myself browsing the self-help aisle for books like *Staying Positive* or *How to Unclutter Your Life*, the latter of which I bought and subsequently lost under piles of papers, books, and clothes in my filthy house. I had neither the time nor the inclination to clean. When flies bred in the kitchen, I simply put up sticky squares of flypaper, which collected so many victims that they tumbled off the tape and onto the counter.

"MR. THOMPSON," I SAID.

Mr. Thompson, the permanent substitute history teacher, didn't turn around. He was playing Minesweeper. It had been nearly a year since the history teacher quit, and the school still hadn't found a replacement.

During my free period, I sometimes tried to track down students who had been absent. Out of the corner of my eye, I saw Patrick and Miles on the computers, watching music videos, their large headphones like earmuffs.

"Do you mind if I steal Miles and Patrick to make up work they've missed?"

Frowning at the screen, eyes fixed on the numbered squares, Mr. Thompson was immobile, his index finger on the mouse the only sign of life. "Ms. Kuo," he said, not moving, "you know you don't need to ask me for permission. Take 'em all, if you want."

Miles and Patrick followed me back to my room and sat at desks next to each other. I slid into a third desk and rotated it so that I faced them both.

I gave them their writing folders. Miles was angry that I had taken him away from his free time. He knocked the folder off the desk. Then he sneered.

"Don't tell me I got an attitude," he said. "I don't got no attitude. What I got is nobody."

Patrick, bent over at his desk, glanced up. "That ain't no reason to disrespect everybody."

Miles stiffened. He looked up to Patrick. Patrick never teased people, never bothered them—not about their appearance, not about who their family was, not if they struggled with reading.

Others looked up to Patrick, too. "Patrick don't pick," someone said. And it was true. He kept to himself. He seemed a lot older than Miles, even though both were now sixteen.

"We all got our problems," Patrick said. "My uncle, he killed my great-auntie over some crack. Over some stupid high. How do you think that feels? But see, here, people around you just trying to help you. Ms. Kuo, people like her don't come 'round every day." They both looked at me, diminutive at my desk. "She ain't trying to hurt nobody, she trying to help. You gotta take that help now, before they give up on you."

Miles blinked.

Patrick continued, "Because they gonna give up on you in a few years. Trust me, I know."

Miles looked down. Nobody spoke.

Patrick stared at the wall of windows, where the sun shone through our mounted pages of vocabulary words, each word distinct in marker—*jubilant, diligent, grave*. He had used that phrase again: *give up*. How had he put it before, when we were sitting on his porch, about the kids fighting? "Maybe they just ready to give up on life." How did he know that feeling so well at sixteen?

But he seemed fine at the moment, and I needed time alone with Miles. I nodded at Patrick, gesturing toward the beanbags. That meant silent reading. He nodded back and went to our shelf to choose a book. I saw him touching spine after spine, trying to decide.

"Hey," I said to Miles. His arms were crossed. "When you're ready to write, just say, *I'm ready, Ms. Kuo*. And I'll be right here." Miles tilted his head down at the paper, at the blank spaces next to the simple prompts: *I am, I feel*. Perhaps, like Tamir, he honestly didn't know how to finish these sentences. I took a risk and brought up his brother.

"You miss Brandon?"

He nodded, then turned away. "I can't look at my mama in the eye, 'cause I know she thinking about her son. Thinking about all the shit he done, wondering if I end up the same way."

"Do you think you'll . . . you'll end up the same way?"

"I don't know the future," he said tersely. "Only God know." Miles swallowed; he'd said too much. Now he was determined to say nothing. We each waited in silence for the other to speak. I broke.

"I've got an idea. Why don't you write an 'I Am' poem for your brother?" I said.

"How?" he asked, in spite of himself.

"Where do you think Brandon is now?"

"Heaven." He didn't hesitate.

"What's he doing there?"

"Having fun."

"There. You just got your first line."

This made him smile, but the smile disappeared as soon as he glanced at the first blank. His face twisted—he didn't know what to do.

I said, "How about, *I am Brandon Clark in heaven and having fun.* Hurry and write it, before you lose it."

He wrote.

"What I do now?" he asked simply. The next line read, *I feel.*

"Well, how do you think he's feeling right now, up there?" And we talked through the lines like this for the rest of the hour.

Occupied by Miles, I had forgotten to talk to Patrick. This was like Patrick—he didn't demand your attention. I wondered what book he'd chosen. Knowing this would make me feel as if I hadn't lost track of him.

On the way to lunch, I spotted him carrying *The Wonderful Wizard of Oz* under his arm.

MY PARENTS CALLED LATER THAT day. "Have you heard from law schools?" they asked by way of greeting. I had almost forgotten that I'd applied and now resented being reminded.

"Thanks for asking about my day," I said.

"How was your day?" they asked.

* * *

FOR THE NEXT FEW DAYS, Miles returned to my room—during lunch, during breakfast, or during "free periods" where teachers let them sleep or play on the computer. He had never worked so hard in my class before. He kept revising and revising again. "This be spelled right, Ms. Kuo?" he asked. "This sound good?"

In objective terms, the poem was sentimental. It was written in simple language. It should not have taken so long to write. He should have known how to spell *heaven, everyone, misses;* he should have known what a comma was. But in terms of where he had begun—his distrust of writing, his grief about his brother, his aggressive outbursts—the poem was a triumph.

I hear my mom pray every night about how she misses me / I want nothing to happen to my little brother the way it happened to me / I tell my mom, Keep your head up and stay strong, because I am getting good care in heaven / I worry about nothing because Jesus has my back / I cry and Jesus comes and wipes my tears from my face / I try to make it in the NBA in heaven / I hope everyone is not worried about me / I am Brandon in heaven, having fun.

I drove to Kinko's in Memphis to have the poem enlarged to a gigantic 36-by-44-inch size—as large as the classroom's posters of Malcolm X and James Baldwin—and hung it in the front of my classroom. Next to it was an eight-by-ten photograph of Miles smiling. And every morning for the next few weeks, before classes even started, he would drop in to look at my wall, making sure his photograph and poem were still there. "You love that poem I wrote, don't you, Ms. Kuo?"

I did. "Of course I do."

His mother later told me that she had laid the poem on Brandon's headstone.

* * *

"WE ARE GOING TO KEEP writing poems," I told them.

"This isn't real work, Ms. Kuo," said Gina, a quick-minded, spirited girl who'd gotten into fights at Miller because people made fun of her weight.

Gina wasn't the first to say this about our creative work. Like others, she thought grammar worksheets were "real work," likely because they were tedious. I ignored her and smiled. Then I asked the kids to think of metaphors for hope. We brain-stormed. A candle, a window; a patch of light, a playground; a tree because it looks up, a hole a dog digs.

Patrick began to write. He tilted his face close to the paper, nearly crouching. He wrote with his left hand; it moved across the page, smudging ink on the side of his palm. I peered over his shoulder, but he was concentrating so deeply he didn't notice that I was there. His paper was full of words crossed out. He crossed out *mind* and wrote *blank mind*. Each word presented difficulty: It didn't express what he felt; it didn't look good; it wasn't spelled right. Every word that failed him, he viewed as a personal failure—he wrote like a writer.

"Ms. Kuo, how you spell *drought*?" he said. "Never mind." He got up to get the dictionary.

Finally, he brought me the result.

> Pat is a dog
> an animal in the streets
> with a blank mind.
> In a collar in the yard,
> cooped up behind a fence,
> no master to train him or feed him
> Always finds his own way.

Judged as some low-life creature,
Not trusted nowhere but
Around other dogs.
Valued only by a price.
Half-dead from
the drought,
Thirsty for water.

I was dumbstruck. This, his first effort, was, in some fundamental way, a real poem.

Patrick wrote his title last: *The Neighborhood Beast.* He stretched his neck, making a loud crack, and I realized how hard writing could really be. Physically, it changed you. You forgot to breathe. Your hand hurt. Your shoulders were sore. But it carried emotional challenges, as well. You risked a lot when you decided to write. You took off a mask. You said, *I feel these things; now tell me I'm silly.* You said, *I tried to make sense of some stuff; now tell me I'm wasting my time.* Only you would ever know how hard you concentrated, how you broke open a new space inside. The point of it was never connection with others, but if connection did fail, then that space shrank a little. A classroom made everything riskier. What if you spelled something wrong? If you couldn't even spell it, did you have a right to use it? What if somebody saw your teacher help you and claimed you didn't write it yourself? What if people thought you were a kiss-up or soft? Or pretending to be someone you're not? What if it was too late, everyone knew you'd never been good at school? Freedom to take these risks, concentration, intrinsic desire—these, I realized, were the conditions for writing, or any meaningful work.

I started to assign free writes in the classroom. The free write was not graded. It was not corrected. They could write anything they wanted, any way they wanted. I would not look for errors; I would not circle their desks looking over their shoulders; in fact, if they wished, they could keep their work. If they wanted someone to read what they wrote, I would feel privileged to do so, but I would mark nothing on the actual writing.

How to describe the incredulous looks on their faces when I explained this to them? Demarcus said, "Then I just ain't gonna write nothing." Cassandra said, "You're supposed to teach us." Yet every student wrote. And during this strange time of silence—the heavy, deep sounds of breathing, the arrhythmic scratching of pencil, the surprising absence of talking—there was a palpable sense of desire.

Some students never doubted the exercise. Patrick immediately bent his head over the page and began to work, his left hand moving across the paper, gathering ink. Periodically he'd crumple up a draft and put it in his pocket.

Kayla, tough, with big eyes, and who threw a notorious punch, had been sent to Stars for fighting. She told me she didn't understand why she fought. Maybe, she speculated, it was because she liked to do things she was good at. Lately she'd hung on to every word I said. In the span of three weeks she'd torn through all four books Sharon Flake had written. For her "I Am" poem she had chosen to imagine her mother, who had five kids and worked two jobs—a preschool during the day and the casino at night. In another assignment, she'd written, *I want to make something happen in life but it seems that there's this one thing that's holding me back and I just can't seem to find out what it is.*

For her free write, she wrote a letter to herself:

Dear Kayla,

How have you been doing these last few months. Fine I hope. Have you been in any more fights. I hope that when trouble come your way, you would just hold your head held high and walk away with a smile on your face. I know how you get sometimes, but hey! What's fighting gonna do, nothing but make things worse than what they are already is.

In my future I want to be a young lady teaching poetry to young teen girls. And when I leave out of that school door I want these students to change their mind and start all over again. I want them to always forgive their self for every mistakes they make in life, Because mistakes happens its okay.

All of my students, even the skeptics, bent their heads in silent concentration, a ribbon of feeling unfurling on the page in front of them.

Because mistakes happens its okay.

That mixture of innocence and experience.

I know how you get sometimes, but hey!

When the seven minutes were up, they always asked for more time.

3

The Fire Next Time

In March, I got a voice message from the admissions office at Harvard Law. I'd gotten in.

I called my parents. *"Gong xi,"* my mom said, breaking into involuntary laughter, a happy cry, disproportionate to how I felt. *Congratulations.* My father grabbed the phone and said now he had an excuse to go out to dinner. It seemed that it'd been a long time since I'd made them happy. Perhaps when I graduated from college. So I did not tell them that I wasn't going to law school, that I had decided to stay.

"See you soon," I said. They were visiting in May. They barely heard me.

Then I called a friend already enrolled in an elite law school, hoping for his alternative viewpoint.

"Isn't there something radical about staying in the Delta and

teaching here?" I asked. It was a relief to speak in this way—
I didn't even know the word *radical* in Mandarin.

But he, too, spoke a different language now.

"Radical?" he said, as if he hadn't used the word in ages.
"You can make real structural change by getting a law degree.
You can't do that staying in the Delta." He started to talk about
everything he was learning. He sounded different. Actually, a lot
of my progressive friends who had gone to law school had
changed. There was a difference in how they carried themselves.
They seemed more sure, more worldly. Their indignation was
more concise. They talked about trials and suits. They talked
about precedents and distinctions. They knew the names of
banks and corporations and firms, and the names mattered.

"Don't be a martyr."

I felt wounded.

He asked if I'd been reading all the stuff about state surveil-
lance in the *Times*.

"The *Times*?" I repeated idiotically. Apparently my vocabulary had changed, too.

"Yes," he said drily. "*The New York Times*. Maybe you've
heard of it."

There were hardly any items in the *Times* about the Delta, I
thought, but kept it to myself.

"What are you teaching these days, anyhow?" he asked.

I swallowed and cleared my throat. The "I Am" poem now
seemed stupid. I worried he would think I was babying the students, when, in fact, I had been pushing them very hard. And he
would definitely not know the names of the young-adult writers
I'd discovered.

I said, "Amadou Diallo and police violence and democracy."

In reality, this lesson hadn't gone well and I had truncated it
after a day. But my friend and I had both come of age when Di-

allo was killed. The New York City police shot forty-one bullets; nineteen hit him. Diallo, a twenty-three-year-old immigrant from Guinea, was unarmed. To my disappointment, the students were not exercised over it. They thought he had a funny name and joked that the police in Helena didn't know how to shoot a gun. It hadn't occurred to me that they wouldn't relate. The violence of white police officers wasn't a major issue in the Delta: The police force, like most across the Delta, was 100 percent black, all the way up to the chief, and black people were not a minority here. What really angered the kids about the police here was that they dealt drugs and didn't investigate the deaths of their friends who got killed. Our lesson quickly digressed into the quotidian. What was it like in *New*, *York*, *City*, the students asked, pronouncing the three words as if each were a distinct place. Did it have bowling alleys?

"Diallo? Wow, that's great," my friend said, impressed. "But it's time to move on, Michelle. With a law degree, you can multiply your impact."

PATRICK FLOURISHED AT SILENT READING. Books kept his focus. His taste in books was eclectic: Langston Hughes, a Dylan Thomas anthology, a rhyming dictionary. At a school ceremony in the spring, he won the award for "Most Improved" student. I hadn't nominated him; even our absentee principal had noticed that he'd started coming to school. When his name was announced, he looked surprised; he'd never won anything before. Students cheered. He walked up to the stage, his gait slow and hunched, not sure how to act. External affirmation made him sheepish. He turned to the students, who were still clapping. Then, suddenly, he raised both arms up in the air: a victory pose. Everybody laughed.

Soon after Patrick won his award, a scruffy New York film-maker, Richard Wormser, with wrinkled slacks and graying hair, descended on Helena. He had been told by several people that if he wanted to talk to the "at-risk" kids in Helena, he should come to Stars. Richard had recently done a film about Elaine, Arkansas. Just fifteen miles inland, near the center of Phillips County, Elaine was "the country" to Helena residents. It was in Elaine that Richard Wright's uncle had been killed by whites for owning a thriving liquor business that they coveted. The night he was shot, his family fled to Helena, loading their clothes and dishes into a farmer's wagon and rolling away in the dark. There was no funeral, no farewell, no burial. *This was as close as white terror had ever come to me and my mind reeled*, Wright wrote. *Why had we not fought back, I asked my mother, and the fear that was in her made her slap me into silence.*

Wormser's film, I gathered, told the story of the "Elaine riots," as they were called around here. That was a misnomer. The "riots" had been a straight massacre of black people.

It began at a church: Black sharecroppers had gathered to discuss their plans to sue planters for failing to pay them. Whites stormed into the church, firing inside. When one white person got shot, the town erupted. Within days, hundreds of whites poured in from neighboring counties, hunting down any black man, woman, or child—in the open streets, in the cotton fields, anybody in plain sight. Federal troops came, too, armed with machine guns. According to some historians, they helped shoot down black people. Five whites died; hundreds of black people died. The police arrested only black people, depositing them in Helena's county jail. Because no whites were charged, no murders of black people were recognized.

In speaking, Richard and I quickly realized what we had in common: We both wanted to know what, after all that brutal history, people in the Delta went through today. Standing out-side my classroom, we talked as a sea of students let out of fourth period moved from the classrooms to the cafeteria.

"Who's that?" he asked, pointing at a slowly ambling figure with stooped shoulders.

"That's Patrick," I said. I watched Richard watch Patrick. It wasn't just me, I realized: There was something distinct about Patrick that made you want to help him.

"What'd he do to get dumped here?" Richard asked, in-stantly understanding the gist of our school.

"Bad attendance," I said. "A lot of students are sent here for that. But then we don't help them. So then they start missing school again."

Richard wanted to film Patrick, and within days he and two others in his film crew showed up to get some footage of him at his house. Patrick seemed flattered by the attention. Did they want to see his go-cart? We followed him to the backyard. He'd fixed the sprocket himself, he said, the chain and everything, and the only thing left was the brakes. He bent down, tightening a bolt. Then he showed them how the wheels moved: They spun flawlessly.

He looked up and beamed. It had taken Patrick just a few seconds to captivate the film crew.

"You think you want to be a mechanic?" asked the camera-woman.

"Yes, ma'am," Patrick said.

Richard got the camera going and asked Patrick what he thought of Stars.

Patrick said a lot of nice things about me. He said I'd motivated him to come to school. He said I called or went to his house when he was absent. "None of that happened at Miller. That's why I flunked," he said. "That's why I don't think I'd never flunk here at Stars, because Ms. Kuo, she care so much."

It made me happy to hear about myself in this way. One of the crew members turned to look at me, and I detected her admiration. Back at the school, Richard pivoted the camera toward me. I heard myself say, with the guileless passion of a zealot, "The most fundamental thing is just to make sure these kids feel cared for. And it's that simple."

ONE WEEKEND AFTERNOON IN MAY, I took a walk through my neighborhood, trying to find the Maple Hill Cemetery, better known as the "Confederate Cemetery." I walked past what had once been a mansion: pillars, square windows, steps leading up to the porch like a wide white ladder. A woman with Down syndrome was sitting at the top of the steps, petting a cat. She was one of the few white people left in the neighborhood.

I kept walking. A stray dog poked his head into a discarded bag of chips, and I watched the dog as two kids watched me. I waited for them to yell, *Ching chong.* Nothing—I was relieved. Soon the procession of poplars and oaks ceased, so that there was no shade from the hot sun. I began to sweat in the terrible heat. I took off a thin hoodie, revealing a tank top. My neck was dripping. The Victorian homes had disappeared and been replaced by one-story shacks so uncomfortably close to the street they revealed their interiors to passersby. Instead of glass in the windows, plastic wrap was duct-taped to the frames. Several of these buildings were churches. One marquee said: JESUS IS YOUR TICKET TO HAVEN. Another advertised: MIRACLES HERE.

More stray dogs appeared. I recognized a street name where one of my students lived and became worried that he would see me in a tank top. I put my hoodie back on. People sat outside their houses, watching me, fanning themselves. A toddler played with a dirty plastic cup.

I stopped. There, in the distance, was the cemetery, its green, sunlit hills of unseemly majesty. Large strong stones were shaded by thick trees. The entrance had an arched metal gate. It was, by far, the nicest public space I'd seen anywhere in Helena.

I ascended one hill, then another, until finally I reached a plateau of paved stone under a dense shelter of cedars. At the center stood a tall monument. I strained my neck to see the top: a sculpture of a soldier, mustached and holding a rifle. At the top was engraved, SHILOH. And then, CHICKAMAUGA. Above thirteen stars, it said, OUR CONFEDERATE DEAD.

Then, in etched capitals: THIS MONUMENT REPRESENTS AND EMBODIES HERO-WORSHIP AT THE SHRINE OF PATRIOTISM AND SAC-RIFICE, DEVOTION TO THE MEMORY OF THE LOST CAUSE, AND HONOR TO THE SOLDIERS KNOWN AND UNKNOWN, WHO REST IN ITS SHADOW.

"Hero-worship," "the lost cause"—where the hell was I? Or when? In 2006, in a majority black area, where cotton production and slaveholding had once skyrocketed in tandem, one of the city's rare public spaces still memorialized the Confederate cause.

The Union army marched through Arkansas in 1862 and took Helena, choking off supplies to Vicksburg, the site of a bloody battle in 1863. Union soldiers, twenty thousand of them, manned the defense of Helena; they evicted people, took control of farms, and freed slaves. Not just in the Delta but across the South, slaves pinned their freedom on making it to Helena. The volume of emigrants was staggering. Thousands of people poured into Helena, "wandering around the camp thick as blackberries," as one Wisconsin soldier observed.

The Confederate Congress passed a proclamation that any black soldier who fought for the Union would be executed. They fought anyway. The first black regiments in Arkansas were formed in Helena. By the end of the war, more than five thousand black volunteers in Arkansas would serve—85 percent of these were from the Delta.

Where were the memorials to the black soldiers and refugees? How much had gone wrong in this long century that so few traces of them could be found? The black cemetery in town, called the Magnolia Cemetery, was a sorry sight, unkempt, its tombstones hidden in knee-high weeds. The neglect and erasure of these stories belong to the long, unfulfilled history of black emancipation in the Delta.

The end of slavery brought new injustices. Reconstruction helped lift black people to power, but the quick demise of that power brought more despair.

Within a decade of emancipation, a vicious system of sharecropping had already developed. It worked like this: At the end of the year, around Christmas, the sharecropper would be called to the plantation office to get paid for his year's work. It was often a moment of *bitterly dashed hope*, as Nicholas Lemann writes. The sharecropper would be handed a piece of paper with a single number. Sometimes it represented the amount he owed the planter; other times, after a year's worth of work, he'd earned just a few dollars. It could be fatal to ask for a detailed accounting. *The false-promise aspect of sharecropping, the constant assertion by planters that your poverty was your own fault—you and he were simply business partners, your loss was right there in cold type on the statement—made it especially painful*, Lemann writes. *As a sharecropper, you found your life was organized in a way that bore some theoretical relation to that of a free American—and yet the reality was completely different. There were only two ways to explain it, and neither one led to contentment: either there was a conspiracy dedicated to keeping you down, or—the whites' explanation—you were inferior, incapable.*

The fever of a black emigration movement to Liberia testified to the desperation of rural black Southerners. Helena became the birthplace and hotbed of activists for this early Back-to-Africa Movement. The first convention of the Liberian Exodus Arkansas Colony took place in Helena, at the Third Baptist Church, in 1877. Still, very few would make it to Liberia—no more than one hundred people from Phillips County; they were too poor and too far inland, and white planters would not release them from their fabricated debts.

At around the same time that black people in Helena were organizing to get out, Frederick Douglass vigorously denounced any kind of movement in favor of migration, whether west, north, or to Africa. Great work, he exhorted, needed to be done in the South. For Douglass, the South was a home and homeland, a *ground of his political powers and possibilities*. In 1879, he declared, *The colored people of the South, just beginning to accumulate a little property, and to lay the foundations of family, should not be in haste to sell that little and be off to the banks of the Mississippi. A man should never leave his home for a new one till he has earnestly endeavored to make his immediate surroundings accord with his wishes. The habit of roaming from place to place in pursuit of better conditions of existence is never a good one. . . . It is a more cheerful thing to be able to say, I was born here and know all the people, than to say, I am a stranger here and know none of the people.*

Douglass's optimism fueled his insensitivity. If black people could fight and win the Civil War, they could fight and win their freedom now. For as much as black emigration reflected the assertion of power of individual black people, it also admitted the triumph of mean and lawless Southern states. Above all, Douglass was a dreamer: He believed in the promises of

Reconstruction, refusing to accept that it was a dead project. He had not anticipated that black people would express freedom by abandoning the South he'd hoped to reconstruct. The world's most famous fugitive wanted black people to stay in the South.

Douglass was in the minority. Other black leaders understood, more profoundly than he did, that the oppressive institutions of the South would continue unfettered and uncorrected.

This was true in Helena. Like other states across the South, Arkansas jailed ex-slaves as a way of extorting their labor. Before emancipation, jail populations were mostly white, as masters needed their slaves' labor and bailed out any who were arrested. But after emancipation, these jails' inhabitants were disproportionately black. Local courts acted as *a conveyor belt for labor-starved employers throughout the state*, as the historian David Oshinsky writes. Charges were minor, and sentences harsh. In Phillips County, two ex-slaves were convicted for forging orders for one quart of whiskey; one got eighteen years in prison, the other thirty-six.

One former slave described the new system as *worse than slavery*, because the freedom was fake and the game rigged. Ex-slaves and their children continued to do the same work that they'd always done: building levees, clearing swampland, and harvesting cotton. Industrialization soon made the work even more perilous. Coal mines, sawmills, and railroad camps had a high number of fatalities.

Still, other sources of dignity persisted and bloomed. Black parents started their own schools. In Phillips County, a shady grove served as a classroom. Another classroom was a floorless mule stable. Quakers from Indiana came to help; locals called them "nigger teachers and nigger spoilers." Black soldiers stationed in Helena raised two thousand dollars to help the Quakers build Southland College, soon to become the first black institution of higher learning west of the Mississippi River. And there was always the blues. Saloons and juke joints were packed with people who danced, flirted, fell in love, and shared the bootlegged liquor that, in Arkansas, flowed more freely than in Prohibition-strict Mississippi.

But the blues and the free schools could not stop the violence propelled by white supremacy. From the end of Reconstruction to the Second World War, more lynchings occurred in Phillips County than in any other county in America. During the Elaine massacre, as the historian Nan Woodruff writes, one teacher in Phillips County witnessed *twenty-eight black people killed, their bodies then thrown into a pit and burned;* he saw sixteen more hanging from a bridge near Helena. Grif Stockley cites a Memphis newspaper's account, *Enraged citizens also fired at the bodies of the dead negroes, as they rode out of Helena toward Elaine.* And a local resident testified, "When we saw them shooting and burning them we turned running and went to the railroad east from there, and the white people tried to cut us off. They were shooting at us all the time. . . . By 5 o'clock that evening, there was near 300 more white people coming on with guns, shooting and killing men, women and children."

In 1923, four years after the massacre, the desire for violence still raged: Over ten thousand people attended a Klan rally in Helena, arriving from Tennessee and Mississippi. Meanwhile, an NAACP field secretary visiting the Arkansas Delta had recently concluded that *rural districts of Arkansas are more unsafe for colored people today than they were thirty-odd years ago; perhaps more than they have ever been.*

Masses of people left Arkansas. Instead of Liberia, they aimed for the North. In the 1920s and 1930s, Arkansas saw a higher proportion of its people leave than any other state in the country. One-third of its black population left. Then came a transformative machine, the mechanical cotton picker: It could pick a thousand pounds of cotton an hour; a human could pick just twenty. Suddenly, black labor—indispensable to the Delta for nearly a century, for which a bloody civil war had been fought, vagrancy laws invented, jail sentences falsely imposed, penitentiaries built, rebellions crushed, and schools closed during planting or picking season—was an anachronism, and blacks were cast off like old shoes. Those who could go north continued to do so. The exodus grew.

In Arkansas, as across the South, the people who left tended to have higher education and some connections. Those who remained, often living in the most remote and interior parts of the Delta, lacked means to leave. They could not read or write. And they were afraid: of violating their "contracts" with their employers; of violent reprisals against family and loved ones who could not leave; of places that were unknown and unfamiliar. Bad conditions could impel one to leave, but they could also sap one's strength to go. Much has been said about the difficult and courageous journeys of those who migrated to cities like Chicago, New York, and Los Angeles. But few have considered those who stayed. Perhaps, then, Douglass, who was so unfeeling toward the black migrants of 1879, can be forgiven: He was expressing sympathy for those who stayed behind.

Living in the Delta today meant living under the shadow of this age-old question: Do you have the means to leave and live elsewhere? I was beginning to grasp that the Great Migration of the early twentieth century—like the Civil Rights Movement, like the emancipation of slaves—offered its own parable of salvation. In this story, black people made a choice to gain freedom by breaking out and merging into the teeming melting pot of the North. In this story, escape was heroic: You got *out*, you fled north, you did it for your children, you did it for your dignity, you did it to survive. In this story, what matters is not so much where you left but that you did. In this story, where you left— the Delta, the Black Belt, the whole Deep South—hardly ex- isted. Eventually, like a bad memory, like the past itself, it would disintegrate.

So the story of the Great Migration shrouded from view those who could not leave or those who chose to stay. They were, likely, among the most destitute. The ones with the least contact with the outside world. The ones most accustomed to defeat. And yet they—perhaps by virtue of these very characteristics— endured. They grew old, they had children, and the world their children entered was bleak. There were few jobs. The schools were bad. The stories of mob violence seemed far away. The main thing, some told their children, was that you had to lift yourself up on your own.

Patrick, Miles, Tamir, and the rest of my students were de- scended from the people who had been left behind.

IN A WEEK, MY PARENTS were due to arrive for their visit, and I still hadn't told them that I planned to stay in Helena. My friends gathered to help me strategize.

"Wait until the end of the weekend before you tell them," one said. Another disagreed. "Tell them from the beginning. Get it over with." "No, no," said another, "wait until after they've seen everything."

Until after they've seen everything. This made me hopeful. A plan was made. We would eat cornbread and ribs. I would show them my classroom. Wall by wall, picture by picture, poem by poem. I would take them to an event called "Delta Idol," a big fundraising event for a Boys & Girls Club that my friends were starting. Kids from across Phillips County, from Elaine to Marvell to Helena, would dance, sing, read poetry, and perform. DeSoto kids would take part, too, making this event the first one in a decade at which white and black students shared a stage. I'd show them the press release my friend Danny and I had written, which the newspaper had published verbatim.

And last, everyone agreed, I needed to clean my house.

FOR THE WEEK BEFORE MY parents' arrival, I'd planned a field trip to Cleveland, Mississippi, for a workshop on rap and spoken word. I'd begun doing this more regularly, picking up a few students in the morning and taking them on day trips—to the Memphis Library, to Beale Street, to bookstores.

I was a bad driver, which pleased my students. They caught every mistake I made: a missed turn; a bump over a curb; a red light skipped. Once, having pulled into the wrong driveway, I backed the car into a mailbox trying to get out. "Shit," I said.

Patrick, usually brooding, was delighted.

"Aw, Ms. Kuo cussing!"

"Ms. Kuo, you get your license from a Cracker Jack box?"

"You're supposed to teach us, not kill us."

"Man, this how people in China drive? I'm never going there."

"Don't call her Chinese! Ms. Kuo was born in America," Patrick offered.

"But she's still Chinese."

They liked that in my car there were fewer rules than in my classroom. What this meant, practically speaking, was that they could bicker without fear of reprisal.

They liked, too, the opportunity for music. They fiddled

with radio stations and rummaged through my CDs. They never took to my repertoire of Nick Drake, Sufjan Stevens, Iron & Wine. They squabbled over who got to choose what music.

Patrick was the one who found my 2Pac CD. He put on "Changes" and tapped his fingers along the dashboard. "Man, it's getting crunk in here," Tamir said from the backseat. "Tupac, he's hard."

Up front, Patrick was listening to the words.

"But you made it in a sleazy way, sellin' crack to the kid," he repeated to himself as he peered out the window.

I followed his line of sight: a boy, no more than eight years old, riding a scooter. Patrick nodded at the kid, who saw Patrick and, staring at him distrustfully, rode on. "Do you know him?"

"Naw," he said. "Just trying to be friendly." He began to hum.

The driving was always more fun than the destination. I never had to tell the kids to look out their windows. Patrick always had his rolled down, as if the wind blowing in was proof that we were going somewhere. A car felt powerful. A car could zoom across vast empty spaces, unceasing flat land, quickly. No place seemed impassable. And no one spoke as we crossed the Helena Bridge over the Mississippi—for most, it was the first or second time.

The quiet in the car as we went over the bridge was the quiet of silent reading.

MY PARENTS ARRIVED FOR A three-night visit. We ate ribs and cornbread. They attended the silent auction my friends had organized for the Boys & Girls Club and bought an expensive drawing of a duck that we knew would end up in the basement. After each performance they clapped genuinely, and my father swayed during the gospel singing. My mother and I shared a look of surprise.

On the last full day of their trip, they came with me to school. I steered them toward the students' poems on the walls. My dad read one halfway through, then walked away. My mother made herself popular by handing out mechanical pencils that she'd brought from Indiana, where my parents had recently moved. But it was the after-school math class that lit my parents up. Patrick, Miles, Aaron, and others were at the front board, working on their own problems, and my father was unable to stand still. "No, no, this way is faster," he said, charging to the front. He took my dry-erase marker. My mother laughed to herself, recognizing him.

The students giggled; his style was the opposite of mine— blunt, direct, easy. Now he handed the marker back to Miles. Miles solved it my dad's way and then turned back to see if I was watching.

"See?" my dad said triumphantly. "Faster." Maybe I didn't know my parents at all.

The students towered over my father, so that he looked like a bespectacled Asian elf. He started to do another problem, a tricky one involving subtracting fractions. Explaining it, he got so animated that his glasses nearly fell off.

Later that evening, we drank iced tea on the porch. I was feeling hopeful and my heart was beating very fast. Just tell them, I thought.

"So I've been thinking," I began. "I've been thinking I might stay for a couple more years. There's this thing you can do, it's called deferring; a lot of—"

"Here?" they said in unison.

My father's face contorted. My mother put her hands over her face.

"Here?" my dad repeated, shocked.

They had already started telling people that I was headed to law school, they said. What was I trying to do? Make liars out of them? If I wasn't really planning to go, why did I bother applying?

"You're so much smarter than this—" my dad continued, waving his hands, gesturing to the street. When he said *smarter*, his voice hit a strange pitch. I could see the pulse in his neck.

"Are you happy?" my mother interrupted. "Look at you," she said in Mandarin. "Look at your body." She was referring to my weight gain. "Do you know how you sound? You don't know. You sound old. You sound so serious. When I talk to you, I think, my daughter's forgotten she's young. You don't care about how you look; you don't care that you don't have a boyfriend. It's like you don't want to be happy. It's just school, kids, school, kids. They're not your own kids. Do you even want to have kids? All your friends here are couples. They don't care that you're lonely. It's not their fault; it's just how couples are. I care, only your mom and daddy care." She took a breath. "You're not normal. Your cousins, they're normal. They get married, study science, become happy. It's so easy for them. They're so easy. They listen to their parents. Why can't you be normal? What happened to you? You know, nobody wants to marry Mother Teresa."

I was stunned. I hadn't realized how much they hated that I was here.

She kept going. "You've changed since you went to college. We shouldn't have sent you to Harvard; everybody there thinks they can change the world. You think you can? Look at the newspaper; nothing changes. You think you're so special? You think you're better than your mom and dad? Because you read all those books, because you like to *help* people?" She laughed derisively. "You think your mom and dad don't help people? We help *you*. We help you go to school. We help you go to college. We give you a house to sleep in and we work every day."

My father gripped his chest as if it hurt. "You look down on your parents," he concluded.

Then he stood up and walked away, not waiting for my mom.

She followed him, worried.

Early the next morning I drove them to the airport in Memphis. We stopped for breakfast along the way, but we spoke little.

"We're a happy family, aren't we?" asked my father finally. Then he answered himself decisively. "We're happy."

After I'd left them at the airport, I found that I did not want to go home. Instead, I drove up and down Highway 61 between Memphis and Helena, my neck in knots, thinking about my parents.

Once, at a car wash in Kalamazoo, when I was around ten years old, my dad pulled up behind another car and we heard a high-pitched scream: "Hey!" A woman leaned out and shouted at us from behind. "You chink and your chink daughter cut in line." Had we in fact cut in line? This is the question that preoccupied me, as I didn't know what a chink was. My dad bolted out of our car and yelled right back at her: "You motherfucking bitch." I shrank back; everybody in the lot would hear him say bad words. But, to my shock, the woman shrank back, too; she hadn't expected that he would talk back. His cursing was fluent. His temper was wild. I was scared he might punch her right there. But he didn't. He returned. Now he was yelling at me, as if I, too, had done something wrong. "Remember you're American. You're an American citizen. You were born here. Do you understand? Do you?"

When my parents introduced me to neighbors, I sometimes detected surprise on their faces when I spoke, as if they had momentarily forgotten I lacked an accent and the presence of out-siders had reminded them. My person, and specifically my English, was at once a peace offering, a riposte, a battle cry. *Listen to her*, my parents seemed to say; *she has no accent, she is one of you*. To my parents my brother and I were American—not Asian American, not Chinese American, just American. Maybe it was the times. But it was also a sign of what they were willing to give up.

Few of my friends in the Delta understood the power my parents had over me. "You're like a little girl around them," one roommate had admonished. "How can they tell you what to do? You're an adult." But one can never overestimate the extent to which many Asian parents make their disappointment unbearable. The caricatures in popular culture are untruthful mainly because they never go far enough. For my family, at least, there was the usual stuff, the yelling and tears, the shaming and guilt trips.

But all of that is a red herring. Maybe the secret of their effectiveness was what they declined to say. They thought nothing of emptying their savings for my lessons and my books. They did not hope for too much success in their own lives; ours were more important. They did not think to ask my brother and me to do chores—they believed studying was a full-time job. They didn't read to me, because they were afraid I would adopt their accents. They cared so little for their own histories that they didn't make me learn their native tongue. For them the price of immigration had always been that their children would discount them in these ways.

"You look down on us," they'd said to me, with a stricken expression. This wasn't the first time my parents had said it, but it was the first time I heard it. And so I could not suppress a reluctant, painful tenderness. So they didn't know how to talk to me; so they didn't know how to help me reason out loud what I wanted. So what? Big deal. Grow up. And maybe they knew something about me that I wouldn't admit.

Once, Ms. Riley heard the kids make their derogatory Chinese noises at me and yelled at them: "Ms. Kuo is a minority just like us. Why you trying to hurt her? You hurt yourself." The students got very quiet, ashamed. They'd turned their heads to examine my face and my features afresh. I could see them pondering our relationship. Not foreign, not Yao Ming's relative: I might be somebody like them. How I loved Ms. Riley for saying this. How I loved that she was saying, *We are like each other, you and me.*

The *yellow race*, the *Mongoloid race* (Supreme Court), the *obnoxious Chinese* (Supreme Court again)—each term separated Asians from whites, amalgamating distinct cultures into a single deportable entity. Until *Brown v. Board of Education* in 1954, Chinese kids in Mississippi were prohibited from attending all-white schools on the grounds that they were "colored." In Arkansas, introducing a formal ban in 1943, a state senator said, "I know none of you gentlemen think Negroes are as good as your children, and I don't think any member of the yellow race is as good as my children or yours, either."

During the war, nearly seventeen thousand Japanese Americans came to the Arkansas Delta a hundred miles south of Helena as prisoners. Rounded up mostly in California and put on a seven-day train ride across the country, they encountered abandoned and snake-infested land on which dirty, half-finished barracks had been built. In some areas, there was a watchtower but no running water. It did not matter that the majority of the newly incarcerated were born in the United States. *The Japanese race is an enemy race*, wrote the general who headed the Western Defense Command, and *while many second- and third-generation*

Japanese born on United States soil, possessed of United States citizenship, have become "Americanized," the racial strains are undiluted.

In the Delta, the Japanese Americans cut down trees, cleared the land, and planted crops. Some had farmed in California; others had been office workers who had to learn for the first time how to use an ax. Their work would increase the value of the land—previously worthless—seven- to fifteen-fold. Fearing that the Japanese would buy this land and stay after the war, the state legislature passed an act declaring *no Japanese or a descendant of a Japanese shall ever purchase or hold title to any lands in the State of Arkansas.*

Ms. Riley was telling the students we belonged in the same picture—the Delta's history of white supremacy. Her words expressed the very reason I had come to the Delta: to show my solidarity. Yet now they seemed far-fetched. The struggles of those Asians in the Delta were no more mine than were the struggles of my students and of Ms. Riley. My ancestors were not from here. My grandparents hadn't been interned during the war or prohibited from attending these schools. I had a very short and simple history in America: My parents had come from a country nobody had heard of and that I didn't know much about. And so I had turned—it was becoming obvious now—to the black tradition as a surrogate, as a way to fill in the absence of my own history and claim an American past.

I kept driving. I pulled into the Lucky Strike casino and then pulled out. I went north and south and then north again. Along the highway there was a stand of pecan trees, mysterious crosses, fields that had gone fallow, and an old tree that stood in water.

"Here?" my father had said, swinging his arms to gesture at the place. This was not the America he and my mother had come for. They did not know it. In Helena, one immigrant group after another had disappeared: the Delta Jews, the Delta

Lebanese, the Delta Chinese, all once significant parts of Helena, all gone. They were immigrants: This is what made them who they were. They moved. It was an oddly clear moment. How my parents saw the Delta was closer to how my students saw it, as a dead end, a place to escape.

In proclaiming our bond, Ms. Riley had prompted me to wonder where my loyalties did lie. My parents had been too modest. They hadn't told me much about their histories because they thought there was nothing special about them, about their journey. And I thought, my heart breaking a little, that my error had been to take them at their word. They should be the first with whom I claimed solidarity, these fleshly, plodding, scolding beings who treated me as if I belonged to them. And perhaps I did. Perhaps I did have a duty to them.

As was often the case, the things my mother said made me recoil in part because they were true. My closest friends were almost all coupled. Almost daily I was down the street at Danny and Lucy's house; they had two cats, and I was like their third, coming in and out when I pleased, dozing off on their couch. Often when I came to, there was chili on the stove and a blanket on me, and the two would be tiptoeing about, whispering softly so as to not wake me. After dinner Danny tried to teach me guitar as Lucy sang to the tunes we played. My roommates this year were also a couple, a Catholic and a Jew, who argued about whether, when they eventually had children, they should have a Christmas tree. Even the repetition of the argument was a glimpse of a domestic life that I wasn't close to having.

But the real smoking gun for my mother's charges lay in my conversations with my only single friend, Vivian. We talked about the Delta as being like a remote island: If you were single, you'd stay that way. There wasn't anyone our age. We whined about how much weight we gained from stress and all the fried food we ate. We noted pointedly that nearly all of our friends who had decided to stay for the long haul were coupled.

I had to admit that I was lonely. The unattractive truth was that I was nearly twenty-five years old and had never had a boyfriend. The year before I came to the Delta, I had gone to England on a scholarship. It was there that I really drank for the first time, had my ears pierced, and suffered the humiliation of a relationship that went unrecognized. I left England a bit sorry for myself, but by the time I got to the Delta that summer, I pretended none of it had happened, reverting to my high ideals from college, where I had decided dating was what other women did and behaved as if this showcased the intensity of my commitments and my disinterest in triviality. I had been proud, very proud, of contradicting the stereotype of Asian women as feminine and exotic. I had joked to people that I was a feminist celibate; I wore overalls and mismatched colors; I spoke passionately about the superiority of female friendships over bourgeois heterosexual romance. But now I felt embarrassed. My proclamations seemed too loud. A significant way to interact with the world eluded me.

And Vivian was leaving. She had gotten into graduate school for public policy at the University of Michigan and had stopped by for dinner earlier that week. "Today Mr. Cooper"— her principal at Miller—"chased a kid down the hallway with his paddle. I think the kid started a fight or something." She raised her arm to demonstrate the gesture: fist gripped, ready to strike. "Anyways, the kid got away." Vivian laughed ruefully, and for a moment I didn't recognize her. Her laughter at the school's dysfunction felt like permission to leave.

In a functional school, like the ones I'd gone to growing up, the staff acts as a basic unit, and a troublesome student is handed off between adults like team members handing off a baton. The principal sets up a parent-teacher conference, the counselor organizes regular sessions, adults convene and design a plan for the child. But central to the experience of a dysfunctional school is the feeling of giving up. To give up is to send a disruptive student out of one's classroom, excluding him from the lesson you hoped would change him. To give up is to banish her to the whims from which the school ought to be a protection. When our principal was absent, students who were sent out of a room as punishment had nowhere to go. They wandered around Stars, banging on doors, trying to get into any classroom. "Lock your door," Ms. Riley had advised. "They'll bang and bang but they'll go away."

Were my parents so wrong? Most parents, immigrant or not, don't want their kids to move to the Delta. My parents wanted me to get married, have kids, a good job, money. Their idea of happiness was very American. It seemed to me that just about all the people in my life had already given me permission to leave. Why would I stay? It was an outrageous idea. I was an Asian American woman from Michigan—what ties could I have to this place? Now I saw only the absurdity of my whole attempt to live here. Who did I think I was?

By the time I pulled into my house, in the near dark, I had decided to leave. I took a long, hot shower. When I got out, I happened to catch myself in the mirror. For the first time since I got to the Delta, I saw that I looked pretty, and I felt startled.

TWO WEEKS AFTER I'D MADE my decision, the district announced that there was not enough money to keep Stars going. All of its students and teachers would be sent back to Central, the main high school. So the district's experiment, if it could be called that, with alternative learning had lasted seven years. Stars would disappear from Helena with scarcely a conversation. The only murmur of reflection came from white families who lived in the wealthy neighborhood hundreds of feet from Central; they voiced concerns about the "danger" of bad kids being so close to their homes. You couldn't blame them, really; were they any more objectionable than the majority of middle- and upper-class families, of all races, who chose to live in suburbs because of safety—because of their distance from "danger"? In other neighborhoods in this tiny city, bricks were lobbed randomly at the front windows of homes, the elderly were beaten and burglarized, and people were held up at gunpoint in their driveways.

Students turned to me and asked, "You gonna be at Central, too?"

I shook my head.

Patrick put down his pen. The class got very quiet. The computer made a dull buzzing sound.

"I'm going to law school," I said. "I won't be here next year."

There was a long silence. Finally Monica, one of my most sweet-tempered students, broke it.

"Ms. Kuo, you're not gonna be a good lawyer."

"Why?" I threw my hands on my hips, mock-offended.

"Because you're too nice."

I looked at everyone.

I said, "I am going to miss you." I said, "You are the strongest people I know." Patrick looked at me, not blinking. He seemed to drink my words in. Aaron did, too. Gina. Monica. Kayla. They all believed me. That they believed me—that they didn't think I was just being nice, or trying to get paid, or trying to get them to do something—struck me. In the grand scheme of things, a year isn't long. But we'd spent every day together, and had come to trust each other.

On the last day of school we had a "field day," of eating burgers and playing outside.

"Stay, Ms. Kuo," Monica said. I didn't think I detected any judgment in her expression.

I DID STAY UNTIL THE very last day of summer. I played Ping-Pong at the temporary space for the new Boys & Girls Club. I sat on my porch reading Marilynne Robinson's *Gilead*. To be useful, she wrote, was the best thing people hoped for themselves; to be aimless was their worst fear. It took a long time to pack up my classroom; I didn't want to throw anything away. I kept my stickers, which, it turned out, had been a hit with the fifteen-year-old boys. I kept their free writes. I kept their pictures. I kept a drawing from Patrick that said, *Caring Teachers*, which included a picture of me.

ON THE NIGHT BEFORE I left, I went to see Danny and Lucy. We talked all night. I told them about the homeless shelter where I had worked. You get the man toothpaste; he tells you the police are harassing him at the airport, where he usually sleeps. You talk for hours. You give him a subway token in case you have no beds the next night. After your shift, you move on with your life; you spend money on things you don't need; you worry about things that don't matter. Did this make any sense? When you see somebody who has been absolutely abandoned—in tatters, freezing, foul-smelling, with alcohol on his breath and speech slurred—and you look him in the eye, shouldn't you be transformed permanently, shouldn't your life change permanently? It was obvious to them what I was really asking.

"How long are you going to stay, do you think?" I said finally. They said gently, without judgment, that they weren't in a rush to leave. Danny and Lucy said they wanted me to be happy. They gave me a guitar.

I set off on a hot, bright morning, and it was only then, as I drove out of the Delta, that I realized Baldwin's assertion of our common humanity—that whether black or white, *we are part of each other*—was grounded not in effortless human feeling but in work.

One can only face in others what one can face in oneself, he had written. The belief in an ideal of common humanity, in love, wasn't the right starting point—belief was something you earned. You gutted yourself, were gutted. You put in work; you confronted pain. You wrested your despair, as he did, into a belief in our inseparable destiny.

I had demanded my students put in hard work. I had made David put in work when he looked at that picture of a lynching. He put his head down. Did he do that because he saw an ancestor humiliated? Or was it about the classroom itself? Had he detected, and then resisted, a role desired from him—of bearing witness to a grotesque spectacle, of finding comfort in the fact that the spectacle was terminated?

And I had made students put in work by writing. Liana, fifteen, Patrick's neighbor, taken care of by her grandma: *Dear lord, the mane thing I don't understand is why my grandma can't find a good boyfriend and a good job so she can take care of me and my sister why can't she just hit the lotto or something or get some money what about the 40 acres and a mule.*

"Forty acres and a mule?" I asked her, surprised. No other student knew the phrase. "Where'd you learn this?" I pressed.

She said, "My grandma." It hurt her to think about somebody breaking a promise to her grandma.

Miles had kept writing. But his next poem was a demented twin to the first: *I wonder will that man suffer for killing my brother / I see the shop and I think of my brother / I want the man kill / I feel like a king when I get done.* I held the paper and sat half paralyzed. My ears burned as it sank in that writing hadn't given him "closure," an end to bitterness, the proverbial new beginning. To the contrary, writing had swung open a door to anguish and more anguish.

And Patrick had put in work. Patrick had continued to show up at school on his own steam. Every morning he got up. Every morning he got on the bus. I had been bewildered by his absence in the beginning. But now it made sense. Why should he attend? Would his world really get better if he graduated? What would he do afterward? Nobody in his family had ever graduated from high school. Still he came to school. He wrote a poem about an animal in the streets. He read about a wizard in Kansas. He appropriated Dylan Thomas. *Dark is a way and light is a place*, he wrote in his notebook. "It had good sound," he said.

In *The Fire Next Time*, Baldwin wrote: *We . . . must, like lovers, insist on, or create, the consciousness of others.* And my students had. They had insisted, and I had become more conscious. But there remained an unspoken truth, understood by everyone in the room: I could leave. I could walk out of the classroom, if I really felt like it, and never come back. That I could leave, and they could not, was my trump card.

The cliché, that I'd gotten out of it more than I'd given, was true. What I had now was a metric for judging what a meaningful day might look like. The metric was this: Could you form a live, difficult connection with a person from entirely different circumstances? A connection so genuine that you forgot that you were even attempting to make one? So urgent that you wanted to show up the next day and that person believed you would? If you could do this, then you had a shot at not being full of crap, at making your liberal ideals substantial, a part of your bone and flesh.

I had asked students to put in the work, but what work had I put in? I thought I'd put in a lot, but as I drove away, two years seemed like nothing. Maybe I hadn't changed at all. I recalled now the bad days of teaching, days that brought to the surface the ideas I had of myself, ideas of my benevolence or patience or strong convictions, and utterly collapsed them. A kid would taunt another—retaliation, eruption, chaos. I would stand there, my arteries bulging in my neck, as they watched me, waiting to see what I would say.

Some must have thought I was fed up. That I wanted to give up, get in my car, and go. Probably true. But most of the time I also felt the opposite. I felt the day could be salvaged. The kids who lost it would feel that they messed up again: Today's explosion had erased yesterday's success, cleared the scoreboard, and flung them back to zero. But I would go to them and talk to them. I'd say, *Nothing can take away what you've done. See that picture of yourself? See that book you're reading?* I'd say, *It's human to self-destruct, to fail, to fall down, to feel bad, to get up again. You're strong, you're good; trust me.*

The words did matter. They built someone up. But there were some students to whom I seldom had to give the pep talk. Students like Patrick showed up and offered wisdom of their own.

One afternoon in April, after a week where it had rained every day, a leak in the roof destroyed a lot of our classroom books. The students despaired. Monica scratched at a water-logged book. I panicked.

"Stop crying, y'all," Patrick said. He stood up and walked out. A few minutes later, he returned with a bucket and mop.

PART
II

Goes out,
Comes back—
The loves of a cat.
                    —Issa

4

The Death of Ivan Ilyich

L AW SCHOOL QUICKLY RENDERED ME UNRECOGNIZABLE TO MY- self. For the first time in my life I did not feel like a good student. In class I was timid and afraid to speak. My grades were mediocre. I worried about whether I sounded smart. The people who seemed the smartest applied rules swiftly and without hesitation. They were able to do what had been asked of them: to think about a problem abstractly, without being distracted by the likelihood that real people had inspired it.

On the first day of our contracts class, the professor told us a story of a woman whose husband had died. Because of a technicality in the man's life insurance contract, the insurance company denied his wife money. When the professor explained the technicality, we were appalled. Should she get her insurance? Nearly the entire class of eighty raised our hands, yes. When, three-quarters of the way through the semester the professor read us the same case, only a handful of us voted the same way.

I was reading Leo Tolstoy's *The Death of Ivan Ilyich* during that first semester. Ivan is a judge, formerly a lawyer, formerly a law student. He works hard; he ascends; he awaits promotions; he despairs when he does not get them; he gets them; he resumes ascendance; he is appointed a judge. In every way, he tells himself, his life has been correct, decent, and good.

But everything changes when he becomes ill. The physical pain startles him. He moans, he thrashes. And he begins to hear a voice inside of him.

What do you want? asks the voice.

Ivan replies that he wants to not suffer, that he wants to live.

The voice replies, *To live? To live how?*

Ivan finds that when he listens to the voice the pain goes away.

Ivan wonders to himself if he has not lived as he should have. But how could that be, if he has done everything one ought to?

And when it occurred to him, as it often did, that it was all happening because he had not lived right, he at once recalled all the correctness of his life and drove this strange thought away.

LAW SCHOOL MARKED THE FIRST time in my life I had access to moneyed events: recruiting parties, thrown by corporate law firms. By the beginning of my second year, I spent lots of time in a black dress and my mother's pearls, assuring recruiters that I was *very* interested in mergers and acquisitions. Each event in this boozy season of restaurant-hopping—whether it was wine and salmon cakes at Chez Henri or a giant chocolate fountain at the Charles Hotel—was designed to seduce you. You were meant to apply to the firm, then to work there over the summer, and finally—assuming you weren't too obvious about your hangovers—to receive the Offer. The seduction worked in conjunction with other forces: necessity (law school debt was enormous), social pressure (everybody else was doing it), and rationalization (much of the world is run by corporations, and you should know how they work). You tried your best to blot out the advice of a law professor who called the corporate route "the path of least resistance" and suggested that "when you die, you don't want your gravestone to say, *He kept his options open.*"

Between my second and third year in school, I spent a month at a law firm in Manhattan, becoming a "summer." The work was asphyxiating, although my paycheck astonished me. Besides the free five-course lunches, every few evenings the summers were treated to an event involving open bars and fancy food. The firm held, for instance, a "diversity" event to celebrate Asian Americans; its keynote speaker was advertised as "the Asian guy on *Survivor.*" Another evening, we attended a gourmet cheese–making tutorial. One firm sent its summers to a night at trapeze school.

Each summer was assigned a lawyer-mentor. Mine dutifully treated me to lunch at an excellent Japanese restaurant in Manhattan. I liked him because, unlike the other mentors I heard about, he didn't appear to care much about recruiting me. My mentor was actually a year younger than I was, but he had the manner of an old man. He was haggard and spoke of body aches. He talked about alcohol a lot. He was Korean American, I gathered, and had gone straight from college to law school to the firm. With cryptic nostalgia, he recalled his test-taking days. I wondered if the tests reminded him of a time when he knew exactly what hoops to jump through, no questions asked.

For these four weeks, my New York was much like Tolstoy's Moscow: We had dull work that we interrupted by eating and drinking, and the next day we returned to our work that was dull, which we again interrupted with eating and drinking. I loved my eating and drinking; I hated it, too.

When my mother and father visited me that summer, we met for lunch outside the law firm's building in Times Square. How very *immigrant* they suddenly looked, peering up at the skyscrapers. How very long their journey to the United States now appeared. More than thirty years ago they'd come to Michigan from their obscure island nation of Taiwan, learned English, gotten jobs, raised two children in a Midwestern suburb, and now, towering over them, was proof that they had *made* it: Here, in this tall building, their daughter worked. My father—the sort of person who ponders, at lunch, what he wants for dinner—asked me to describe the five-course meals I was treated to, and I obliged. It was hard for my parents to understand my observation that none of the associates seemed happy, so I didn't belabor the point.

My job at the firm ended after four weeks. As part of its recruitment strategy, the firm had agreed to pay for my internship at any nonprofit for the remaining summer. After cleaning out my office at the law firm quickly—there was nothing I wanted to save—I stayed in New York to work at an organization for kids, called The Door. It was a boisterous Hull House for young people: dance and rap classes, onsite counselors. I helped get a visa for a Chinese kid who'd been trafficked. I felt happy. During these four weeks, I lost the BlackBerry my firm had loaned me, which I was expected to return at the end of the summer—it was somewhere on my desk at The Door or, possibly, not on my desk. On a Friday morning, buoyed by a workers' rights training that I'd organized, I received a phone call on my private cellphone. "Where are you?" It was the law-firm coordinator for summers.

"What do you mean?" I replied. Apparently I'd missed the ceremony for summers who got offers, the details of which had been conveyed via the missing BlackBerry.

"Well, you got an offer," she said. "Thanks," I responded, nervously wondering if she could now revoke it.

Other summers called their parents when they got offers; I didn't.

I tried to date, or to learn how to date. Inevitably during these dates I would talk about teaching in Helena. As with any intense experience, it was hard to put into words, and it was still recent enough that I did not yet think of it, or want to think of it, as my past—as, merely, a "good experience." Perhaps this explains why I would revert to talking about the Delta in the future. "If I had a partner who was willing," I would say on a first date, "I might go back and live there."

And I wondered why these dates went no further.

Mostly I entered my last year of school preoccupied, like everybody else, by the hunt for a job after graduation. I had the offer from the firm but was on the fence about taking it. I considered working for the government or for nonprofits. Students at Harvard were lucky in this way; jobs at nonprofits were scarce and when they did hire, they tended to choose unfairly from the top-ranked schools. My friends at other law schools who desperately wanted to work in the public sector were bound for the private sector instead. I had the luxury of options. But where should I work?

I'd come to law school with the idea of fighting for education as a civil right. Since college, I'd admired the civil rights lawyers from the 1950s and 1960s, who had risked their lives to desegregate schools in the South. I'd had my sights set on the NAACP Legal Defense Fund (LDF) and interned there the summer after my first year of law school. But I discovered that schools were no longer the battleground for civil rights lawyers. Judge Robert Carter, formerly a leading attorney for the LDF in the *Brown* litigation, reflected on the iconic victory in an essay published in 1980.

A primary mistake lawyers had made, he wrote, was that they assumed an integrated education meant an equal education. They could not be blamed for thinking so: Until *Brown*, school districts in the South publicly, openly, and shamelessly short-changed black schools, and a bulk of the evidence compiled by *Brown* lawyers showcased the glaring disparity in per-pupil allocation of funds, dismal salaries for black teachers and principals, and decrepit facilities. But it was only after *Brown* that they understood *the fundamental vice was not legally enforced racial segregation itself; that this was a mere by-product, a symptom of the greater and more pernicious disease—white supremacy. Needless to say, white supremacy is no mere regional contamination.*

In the North, affluent whites fled to the suburbs to avoid being in the same schools as black people. Residential segregation was and remains the most common cause of racial isolation among children: It is why white children go to schools with white children, black children with black children, and why schools are more segregated today than in 1954, the year *Brown* was decided. Meanwhile, in the South, the governor of Arkansas blocked the schoolhouse door with state militia. In rural areas like the Delta, a slew of small private schools opened. By 1980, Judge Carter had already seen the writing on the wall: Integration would not happen in his generation. *For the present, however, to focus on integration alone is a luxury only the middle class can afford. They have the means to desert the public schools if dissatisfied.* For the sake of children's education today—for the sake of *real life*, as he put it—people should *concentrate on having quality education delivered to the schools these blacks are attending.* W. E. B. Du Bois's

words in 1935 seemed prescient: *There is no magic* to either segregated or mixed schools, he warned. *The Negro needs neither
segregated schools nor mixed schools. What he needs is Education.*

Others held to the dream of school integration. The point
was not that black children *needed* the presence of white children
to learn. Rather, as sociologist Orlando Patterson wrote, integration *brings Afro-Americans and Euro-Americans together at a
time when their life-long attitudes are being formed.* Studies showed
that whites who went to school with black people *tend to be more
tolerant and more in favor of greater educational and economic opportunities for Afro-Americans.* Black children, in turn, acquired access to social capital and valuable networks to broader groups.
As Justice Thurgood Marshall wrote, *Unless our children begin to
learn together, there is little hope that our people will ever learn to live
together.*

I stood somewhere between these two views, but I was rapidly learning that my view, and anyone's views on the matter, had
been made irrelevant by the Supreme Court. On a hot day at the
end of June 2007, I climbed the steps of the Supreme Court with
the entire staff of the LDF to hear its decision on a landmark
case. In a hushed, packed room, Justice Roberts read an opinion
that prohibited the school districts in Seattle and Louisville from
taking race into account when assigning students to schools. Justice Roberts called the systems *racial balancing,* and wrote that
Brown stood for the proposition that schools could not assign
students by race. *The way to stop discrimination on the basis of race
is to stop discriminating on the basis of race,* he opined. Dissenting,
Justice Breyer remarked from the bench, "It is not often in the
law that so few have so quickly changed so much." Dissenting as
well, Justice Stevens said that the majority, in rewriting the history of *Brown,* was a *cruel irony.*

I, too, felt deflated. I'd come to law school thinking I was somehow closer to the levers of power. But the Supreme Court ruling essentially signaled to civil rights lawyers that the issue of school integration was a dead end. Here were two local school districts that had confronted their histories of segregation and voluntarily attempted to integrate. But the Supreme Court had called their systems unconstitutional. As education-law professor James Ryan wrote, *many who believe in the goal of integration, including myself, cannot help but feel a sense of loss and betrayal.*

The next summer I worked at the law firm and at The Door, two places that could not be more different. I was shooting darts, trying to figure out where I belonged. By the beginning of my third year, I had decided that if I could get one thing out of law school, it would be the acquisition of basic skills that could be useful to poor people in crisis: What do you do if your landlord tries to evict you? If your boss doesn't pay you for your work? If the government deports your father or mother? I applied for a fellowship to work at Centro Legal de la Raza, a nonprofit in Oakland, California, in a neighborhood called Fruitvale, which would later be made famous as the place where Oscar Grant was killed by police. My clients would be mostly undocumented Spanish-speaking immigrants. "It's not glamorous work," a lawyer there said, winning me instantly. "But it's one of the few places where people feel safe to come and ask for help."

I got the fellowship. Money would still be tight—less than what I had made as a teacher in Arkansas, cost of living adjusted, and less than some California public school teachers. But the tiny salary seemed like proof that my conscience was intact.

THEN DANNY CALLED ME FROM Helena with some bad news. "You had Patrick Browning as a student, didn't you?" he began. I thought he was going to tell me that Patrick had died.

But it wasn't that. Patrick had killed someone. He was in jail. He had gotten into a fight and then stabbed the person three times.

I was stupefied. It had to be a mistake. Patrick could not have killed someone.

I talked to Danny some more. Did he know, I asked, the visiting hours for the jail? Was it open on Saturday? I wrote professors to say I would be absent.

SATURDAY MORNING, THREE DAYS AFTER Patrick was arrested, I made it to the Phillips County Jail before visiting hours ended. It looked like a benign structure from the outside: brick, stout and short, two stories.

The lobby had a low ceiling, stained with water marks. Its lone decoration was a framed black-and-white photograph of a sheriff sitting on a horse. A sign instructed visitors to give all valuables to the guard at the desk. The only other person waiting with me was a boy who looked like he was in middle school. He handed over his bag of Doritos.

The guard walked me through a narrow hallway. He looked sideways at me, puzzled. "You know what he did, right?"

"Patrick was a wonderful student," I said simply.

Not replying, he pointed toward a glass window. Patrick was waiting on the other side.

When I walked toward the window, I almost expected the Patrick I remembered: gap-toothed, half-grinning, a sheepish mixture of the wry and pensive. That look that greeted me when he didn't do his homework, when I visited him at his house, when I said something nice to him.

Patrick's face had thinned. His striped prison garb was two sizes too big. His mouth was turned downward. He looked older—he was older. It had been two years since I'd seen him.

He looked very surprised to see me.

I picked up the black phone hung on the wall.

"Ms. Kuo, I didn't mean to," he blurted out, in a tone of supplication.

Those were his first words to me. They sounded common, the words of a child who had done something wrong. In reality, he was no longer a child; he must have been eighteen or nineteen now. But I suppose in my mind he still was one.

I asked him what happened. He told me that he'd come home that night, looking for Pam, his youngest sister, who was in special ed. She was sixteen. He knocked on a neighbor's door. Nobody answered. He went home again. This time Pam was walking up to the porch with a man called Marcus. They looked high; he was definitely drunk. Marcus started to talk crazy to him. Patrick told him to get off the porch. Marcus wouldn't get off. Patrick thought Marcus might have a weapon in his pocket. He got scared and picked up a knife, which, he said, was on the porch because he'd used it to fix his nephew's stroller that day. He'd just meant to scare the guy. But they fought. Marcus limped away, and Patrick was about to go inside when he saw that Marcus had fallen near the sidewalk. The police came. They handcuffed Patrick. He told me that he'd been in jail for three days, that there were bad people there, and that the jail was like hell.

I asked him what kind of relationship Marcus and Pam had. "They were having sex," he said. He stopped. "I didn't mean to kill him," he said again.

He was silent. We looked at each other through the glass. He shook his head. "Ms. Kuo, I don't even know."

The way he said it—"Ms. Kuo, I don't even know"—made him seem more familiar.

We talked more. How were his dad and mom? Fine. Making it. How was the food? Bad, real bad. How was school? He couldn't keep up. Just stopped going. He tried, he really did. But he didn't want to talk about it.

The officer came to get me. Time was up.

I rose and thought about the last time I'd seen him. Toward the end of our year together, some form of self-knowledge had begun to flicker inside Patrick, a self-knowledge too tremulous to be called *pride*. But I would have called it a kind of warmth toward oneself. "I can hear myself in here," Patrick had told me about our classroom. Now that warmth had either disappeared or gone dormant. Whatever gains we'd made had receded. Did those gains still matter?

I told Patrick I'd write. It was a promise, I reminded myself, that I must keep.

I HAD BEEN TAKING A writing class when Patrick was arrested. After I returned from visiting him, I started to write about my time teaching. Frenzied, concentrated, I wished to remember everything. Two years had passed since I'd left the Delta, yet the names of certain students returned to me like reflex. Miles, Tamir, Kayla. Writing was like stepping back into an old dream.

At first, writing felt urgent and necessary. Writing joined me to Patrick, allowing me to remember who he was and my time in the Delta. In the privacy of my room, I could confront the Delta and consider what I had and hadn't done for it. I tried to evaluate myself honestly. I asked, with dread, whether there was any connection between my leaving and Patrick's dropping out of school. Like a vaccine that injects you with a strain of illness, writing infused a kind of negative life. I was admitting danger, admitting fallibility, and in so doing I was becoming stronger.

But that strength also felt odd. For, by the time I was done writing, it felt very nearly as if I was done with *Patrick*. No detail from my memory of him had gone unravaged; his gestures started to repeat themselves.

In trying to remember him, I had treated him like someone who was lost. In my writing, Patrick had become a thing on the page, somebody who existed to serve *me* and my need to not forget the Delta.

FIVE WEEKS PASSED. IN NOVEMBER of 2008, Obama won the presidency. On a windy Boston evening, I searched three newsstands before I found one that hadn't sold out of *The Boston Globe*. I wanted Patrick to see Obama's triumphant picture, to feel a part of this historic event. I put together a package, also enclosing James Baldwin's *The Fire Next Time*, marking an *X* in the margins of passages I liked. I had never shared the book with the students, afraid that they would be bored.

And I wrote him a letter. It began in a too-civil manner. *How are you? I am well.*

* * *

There was a black male in a red shirt lying face down [sic] *just to the left of the hedge bush with blood under him. Myself and Ofc Rose was on scene as I rolled over the victim, he was gasping for air. I then try try* [sic] *to find a pulse but could not find one there was 2 large what appeared to be stab wounds to the upper chest area on the victim and his eyes were fixed and dilated.*

In the spring of my last semester of law school, I showed Patrick's police report to my professor, a former public defender whose ruthlessness I hoped Patrick might benefit from. I had enrolled in her criminal defense clinic and been assigned several cases. My main client was a heroin addict charged for assault and battery—of his mother. She was a sixty-seven-year-old diabetic from Mexico, whose five strokes had put her in a wheelchair. The whole family was fed up with him. He'd stolen her disability checks, left her place ravaged with needles, and nearly gotten them evicted.

My professor had told me to find out where the mother lived, knock on her door, and convince her to drop the charges.

"You want me to talk to . . . to talk with his mother?" I said, swallowing nervously.

"Who else?"

I'd done what she asked and gone to the apartment. But— perhaps to my own relief—the mother refused to budge.

Surely this professor, of all people, could uncover some aspect of the case that might help Patrick.

Patrick's warrant stated *capital murder,* meaning lethal injection in Arkansas, and had since been reduced to first-degree murder—still an overcharge. Jury trials are expensive and time-consuming, and the overcharge is a standard prosecutor's tactic, intended to scare the defendant into taking a plea. The state also overcharges for a simpler reason—because it can. To overcharge sends a message: *We have the power to really hurt you, so obey us.* The sentence for a first-degree murder conviction is life; the sentence for manslaughter, three to ten years. Few defendants— including those who are innocent—want to take a gamble on a jury trial that might send them to prison for life.

Only in certain cases—where, for instance, the defendant has the public's sympathy—does the prosecutor undercharge, or charge with the law in mind. The white guy in Louisiana who'd shot the Japanese kid at point-blank range on his doorstep was charged with manslaughter, for instance, in consideration of two legally relevant factors: the "castle doctrine"—that one's home is one's castle, and a man has a right to defend his castle—and genuine fear. These two factors could certainly have been weighed in determining the appropriate charge for Patrick. But Patrick was not a white man living in the suburbs, so he was charged with first-degree murder.

My professor didn't seem surprised by the overcharge. "He'll need to try to get that charge down," she said, leafing through the pages. Then she asked, "Did he talk to the police?"

"He signed a waiver," I said.

Her face fell.

"There wasn't a lawyer with him?"

"No." I hurried on. "It says that he was read his Miranda rights, but, to be honest, I doubt he knows what *Miranda* is or what those rights entail."

She was uninterested in this argument: This is true of most criminal defendants who are poor and uneducated. The law on *Miranda v. Arizona* barely makes exceptions for defendants who are mentally handicapped.

"He confessed?"

"Yeah. And his dad signed a statement, too."

She closed the file. He'd confessed; no question existed as to legal innocence. Patrick was the one who did it. The case was just ordinary, a fight that had ended badly but not unpredictably. He had won the fight and then he told the police everything. He had protected himself too much and then he hadn't protected himself at all.

She handed the file back to me. "I hate to say that it's too late," she said. "But there's not much you can do."

This was not a "close" case. She, an experienced defense lawyer, was telling me to not have hope.

* * *

I TOOK THE BAR EXAM over the summer and moved to California. It was September and my life was set to begin. The fellowship in Oakland was to start in a month and a half.

My mother flew to San Francisco to help me unpack. With her characteristic meticulousness, she ironed each piece of clothing—blouses, blazers, dresses, slacks—shaking her head tragically at the wrinkles wrought by the long journey west. When she thought a blouse and a blazer made a particularly good match, she placed them together on the same hanger. I took my mother for a walk in the neighborhood. "You'll be happy here," she said, pleased.

I was to live in the Mission District in San Francisco. My friend Adina had found the two of us an apartment; we signed a yearlong lease and paid the security deposit. We were excited to live together. Down my street was Tartine, Mark Bittman's favorite American bakery. On a single block were three excellent bookstores, arrayed in puzzling and wonderful proximity to one another. On one side of my neighborhood, Diego Rivera–inspired murals greeted me in fantastic swirling colors. If I walked in the other direction, the names of businesses amused me, playful or ironic or obscure—like the restaurant Foreign Cinema.

At every corner, a bar advertised happy hour. Big, gorgeous sheepdogs shared the streets with preposterously small Chihuahuas. Accenting the streets, always, were people and more people, dressed chaotically in argyle, boots, leggings, and rebellious-looking hats. Gentrification had begun, but the rent was still affordable.

The day after my mother left, my friend and her husband visited. We took the bus to Ocean Beach and looked out at the Pacific. The salty air, the pale drama of the fog—the California that had existed in my fantasy was now reality. Sharing a loaf of sourdough, the three of us sat on the sand and followed the sound of barking yelps to a herd of seals on a nearby island. A golden retriever chased a ball into the ocean and emerged triumphant and sopping, treasure in jaw.

PEOPLE IN MY WORKSHOP TOLD me that my writing about Patrick was good enough to get published. I felt guilty considering this. Then I tried to comfort myself: The writing was not triumphalist, it did not downplay my moral failure; I had tried to depict Patrick and my students warmly, humanely. Did that effort mitigate the exertion of power, the betrayal of intimacy, that was intrinsic to telling someone else's story?

A teacher had put me in touch with *The New York Times Magazine*, and an editor offered to publish it as a "Lives" column. I made a pact with myself: If Patrick didn't like it, I would not publish it. I mailed Patrick the essay I'd written about him.

But he didn't write back. Had he even received it?

I told the editor to go ahead and publish.

Then—after the deed was done—I worried. I worried what Patrick would think. Would he find my portrait wrong? What if he thought I only cared about writing his story and didn't really care about him? It was a strange, sudden, unexpected opposition between *writing* and *caring*. I had never doubted the latter; indeed, I had built my whole identity out of it. Anybody who knew me knew I was a clichéd bleeding-heart liberal, sure, but my heart truly bled! Now my act of publishing seemed to have undermined my sincerity.

I made another little pact with myself. *When you go back in October to see Patrick*—I had planned one more visit before my job started in Oakland—*you'll show him the piece, face-to-face.*

* * *

ON A SATURDAY MORNING IN early October, almost exactly a year since I'd last seen Patrick, I drove to Helena's county jail. There was no traffic. The streets were empty. Having lived in San Francisco for a month, where the sheer effort required to park your car can steal your soul, I was incredulous at the parking spot I found squarely at the entrance.

I sat down in the waiting area. At the front desk was a sign in orange block letters—OPEN—but there was no guard.

This time, the only other person there was a woman, who wore a shirt that said, DON'T ASK ME SHIT.

After ten minutes a guard appeared, holding a jumbo-sized bag of hot chips.

I told him I was there to see Patrick Browning.

"You can't see him," he said.

"But aren't visiting hours now?" I asked, confused.

"Maybe I ain't feel like getting him," he said. Then he winked.

Now I understood. He was "just playing" with me and wanted me to play back. I was no longer puzzled—indeed, had he been professional, I probably would have been more surprised.

Mock-affronted, I furrowed my brow. At this, he cocked his head.

"You got a boyfriend?" he asked. Suddenly I felt his hand on mine. "You don't got no ring." He puckered his lips at me, then grinned.

In the Delta, banter was sexual harassment. It didn't really matter what you looked like, as long as you were under fifty.

He introduced himself—his name was Shawn; he was *very* pleased to meet me.

Shawn said he'd give me the lawyer's room, which was better than speaking through a Plexiglas shield. I wasn't sure why. Was it because he knew I wasn't a family member? Or because he thought I had traveled on a long journey from the Orient? Or because I had let him flirt with me?

He walked me to a private room labeled INTERROGATION in faded stenciled letters. The room was dank and musky. A bucket sat near the corner, collecting water. Above, a purplish-black splotch spread on the ceiling. I tried to hold my breath, not wanting to inhale the vaguely toxic smell. Patrick emerged. He was shocked, and then he smiled.

"How are you?" I asked.

"I'm all right, ma'am. I'm doing all right."

As if suddenly remembering something, he said, "How are you, Ms. Kuo?"

"Good."

"Where you be living now?"

"California."

He repeated carefully, "*California.*" He seemed to be trying to recall the word, or a map, in his mind.

I asked him how his family was.

"They be all right." He paused and we both were silent. He realized that I expected him to say more.

"Yeah, sometime while back they visited. My sisters, my daddy, they all crowd inside the window," he said.

"You've got three sisters?"

"Yes, ma'am."

"No brothers?"

"Naw."

When I was a teacher, I had known very little about Patrick's background. Certainly I hadn't known that he had three sisters and no brothers. Now I realized that this was an essential fact.

His mother must have asked him to look for his sister because he was the only son, the man of the house.

"Your mom didn't come?"

He shook his head. "She got work and, really, it be . . . it be hard on her to see me. It's been months since I seen them."

His family did not live far from the county jail, no more than five miles away. I must have looked surprised, because he looked down. "To be honest, ma'am, I don't like seeing them this way." He stopped, searching for the right words. "I *smile*, but you know . . . but I don't like to put on *no front*. So I just ask them not to come."

Patrick fell silent again.

"We don't have to talk about it," I offered.

School had been where we connected, and I wanted to know: Why had he dropped out? How had it happened? I cared as much about these questions as I did about the question of what had gone wrong one night a year ago. I suppose I believed, on some deep level, that none of this would have happened—that we would not be here in jail—had he stayed in school. Secretly I imagined there had been a noble reason for him to quit; perhaps somebody, his mother or one of his sisters, had gotten sick, and he needed to get a job to support her.

"So when did you"—I was about to say *drop out*—"stop going to school?"

My tone was unnaturally casual.

Patrick looked away. He didn't want to talk about this, either. "I tried . . ." he began. "I wasn't getting all that treatment you was giving me at Stars. I really didn't learn too much *trigonometry*." He enunciated the word slowly, not wanting to get a syllable wrong.

"Is that what got you down, math?"

"Yes, ma'am."

"What grades were you getting?"

"Low grades."

"Like we're talking . . . Fs?"

He hung his head.

"I ain't know nothing about trigonometry, to tell you the truth."

"You were good at math," I said, remembering his fractions.

"Not *this* math."

"You didn't ask your teacher for help?"

Patrick kept his head down.

"Did you think about asking him?"

I tried to keep my tone neutral. Then it occurred to me that it didn't matter what tone I used or even what I said. It was an unsalvageable conversation: I had been his teacher, and he had dropped out.

"Just didn't have a lot of . . ." His voice trailed off. "It be a lot of pressure to ask."

There was no way—absolutely none—that our math classes at Stars had prepared him for trigonometry. Certainly my after-school math class hadn't. And the official math teacher at Stars coached the baseball and football teams at Miller, which meant that he frequently left the school hours early, for games and practice, leaving the police officer to chaperone.

Just a few minutes ago I'd been mystified by the question of why Patrick had dropped out; now I could picture it perfectly. I could picture him in his math classroom, in a sea of thirty faces, slipping by unnoticed in a seat in the back, observing the others. I imagined him starting to miss classes. Math, in particular, is cumulative: If you miss one day, the next day you're lost. I imagined him returning after having disappeared, hoping for a fresh start. Then he'd be given a worksheet that danced with triangles and shapes, with words like *sin*, *cos*, *tan*. He must have felt baffled. I had never known Patrick to ask for help. He took help if you offered it, but he didn't ask for it.

Then I thought, coldly, that he did have a tendency to give up easily.

I leaned back in my chair. So the topic of school was like the topic of family: a dead end.

"So have you talked to your public defender?"

"My what?"

"Your lawyer."

"Naw. I don't know him."

"Do you have a trial date?"

He shook his head. "Man, I don't know *nothing* about that."

"Do you know what you're being charged for?"

For the first time Patrick leaned forward, realizing that I might know something that he didn't about his case. He was flustered. "Ms. Kuo, what I be charged for? Nobody told me *nothing*."

His charge—of course. This was what he wanted to talk about, what he thought I could do to help him now. I knew some basics but hadn't expected that I would be the one to communicate them.

I chose my words carefully. Where once I had tried to think of creative ways to explain *theme* and *symbolism*, I tried now to avoid using abstruse legal terms: *mens rea, malice aforethought*.

"It all has to do with state of mind," I began. "There's first-degree and second-degree . . ." I paused, not wanting to say *murder*.

"*First*-degree is when a person intends to—"

Patrick broke into my words, the first time he'd interrupted me. His body tensed, his voice reached a desperate pitch. "I didn't *intend* to hurt him; I was just looking for my *sister*. He got to talking crazy with me, about the bloods, the gang he be in. He be talking really crazy. I tried to walk off and he *grabbed* me."

"Do you remember what he was saying?"

He drew back in his seat, embarrassed by his outburst. "I don't remember much," he said in a low voice. "It's confusing, it all happen so fast."

I cleared my throat. "How did you feel during that moment?"

"Ms. Kuo, I wasn't really trying to hurt him, or to"—he stopped, gathering strength—"kill him." At the word *kill*, he fell silent. "I just . . . I just started crying when they say what I'd done. I really didn't intend to; I was really just looking out for my little sister."

"Do you remember why you were crying?"

"They say I killed a man! I ain't . . . I don't know."

His voice broke, its pitch strange and high. Patrick covered the sides of his head with his hands, his fingers gripping his scalp.

Until now I'd resisted wondering about who the dead man was. What had he been like? He must have had a family, a mother and a father and brothers and sisters. They were a strain to think about, these grieving others. Abstractly, I understood that their grief eclipsed that of Patrick's family, but I could not summon them.

It seemed impossible to hold both Patrick and Marcus simultaneously in my mind. To have sympathy for one was to doubt the other. It was like some constraint of astronomy, where two stars could not be gazed at together, the light of one affecting the other.

"Manslaughter," I continued. "Manslaughter is different from murder when"—I hesitated again, not wanting to use the word *killing*—"when what happened is not intentional."

But Patrick had shut down, fatigued from his own memory. Shawn poked his head in, pointed at his watch, and disappeared.

I knew I had to leave soon, but I still hadn't let Patrick read what I'd written about him. It was only fair, I thought, that he knew the writing existed.

I pulled the slim *New York Times Magazine* out of my bag.

"I wrote this about you," I said. "It's about you and my teaching at Stars." Would he like to read it?

"Yes, ma'am," he said, in a manner so automatically compliant that I knew he hadn't really heard my question.

"Why don't you start?" I said. I pointed to the first sentence on the page.

Patrick leaned forward, tense from concentration. Suddenly I realized he was nervous. When was the last time he'd read anything out loud—a book, a magazine? And with a teacher, no less? His left hand was shaking, and he clenched his fingers into a fist as if to tame it. His right fingers held the paper gingerly, as if it might tear.

I calculated how long it had been since I had him as a student. Three years and four months. He had dropped out of school the year after I left the Delta. Technically speaking, the last grade he had completed was the eighth grade.

I had an urge to stop the exercise, but Patrick had plunged forward. He started reading very fast, affecting confidence. But immediately he stumbled on the sentence referring to himself: *There was something capacious inside him.*

"Sorry, Ms. Kuo," he said.

I saw his face burning, and then I realized mine was also.

We hobbled along. He read: *a mixture of wry and pensive.* Then he gave me a sideways glance, waiting for my correction.

"Sorry," he said again. "I'm forgetting things."

I saw his eyes darting downward to the last line, near the bottom edge of the page, which promised an end to the assault of consonants and vowels.

The ethics of writing about Patrick had occupied me so much that I hadn't even imagined we would encounter this basic problem: He was so out of practice that he could barely read. This was the real Patrick, the one who I didn't know because I was too busy remembering who he used to be.

Later that day I would ponder the self-absorbed foolishness of my exercise: What had been the point? I should not have put him in such a position; it was cruel, he was embarrassed. At least I could have explained to him, honestly and simply, why I had written it, the original reasons, before I had gotten caught up with my self-doubt: *I wrote this because writing is how I understand things. I wrote this to get closer to knowing you, and myself, too.* Or I could have helped him read, explained the meaning of words. But it had been so long since I'd taught that I'd lost my teacher's instinct and let him stumble on alone, ashamed, uncomprehending.

Finally, Patrick reached the last lines in the piece: *I haven't been able to resist guilty feelings over Patrick.* He hesitated at the word *resist*, the too-sibilant word faltering in his mouth. *"Resist,"* I corrected him, and he repeated the word.

When Patrick reached the end at last, he let out a breath. I sensed his shoulders loosening, heaving downward. I relaxed, too.

He traced the page with the tip of his index finger, as if enjoying its glossy surface, its feeling novel to his skin.

"What did you think?" I asked, my tone false and bright.

"It's"—he searched—"good."

We looked at each other. He sensed he ought to say more. He said, "You got good memory." Then: "To be honest, Ms. Kuo, I don't remember all that."

I asked, "Do you remember when you brought in the bucket and mop?"

He shook his head.

I asked, "Do you remember when you escorted me to the car?"

He shook his head again.

I might as well have been writing about somebody else.

"I remember it raining," he offered. "I remember all that rain." Then he said, "You know, it wasn't the best school, but you was there and you cared. It made going to school—you know, made it really mean something, somebody that care for you."

He looked away. Then he flipped to the other pages, stopping only on the ones that had colorful pictures.

"You made all this?" he asked, after he had flipped through it.

I frowned, confused. Made what? "Oh, no," I said, understanding. "It's a magazine." I flipped to the cover and said, "See what it says?"

He read aloud the cover, *The New York Times Magazine,* pronouncing every word.

Then: "People in New York read this?"

"Well," I said, "a lot of people outside New York read it. Maybe millions."

This number didn't appear to mean much to him.

"You been to New York?" he asked.

I said I had.

"How do you get there?"

"I took a plane," I said. He nodded, as if he understood. To make conversation, I asked him if he'd ever been on a plane.

"No, ma'am."

"Have you been outside of Arkansas?"

"I been to Memphis one time." He paused. "And I been to Mississippi, too, because you got to go through there to get to Memphis."

I looked down, quiet.

Patrick said, "Yeah, these be broken and don't fit."

He thought I was looking at his sandals. They were orange and too big—like a clown's shoes. The flap hung out.

"Oh," I said. "That can't be comfortable."

"No, ma'am. It ain't."

We sat there silently. We stared at the shoes. He dangled his arm, fingering the lone seam that held together flap and sole.

Patrick shook his head and he opened his mouth to speak. Then he stopped himself. He seemed hesitant to tell me something.

I nodded at him expectantly.

"I got to think about my"—he trembled—"*daughter*."

The word was like a foreign term in his mouth.

Startled, I asked how old she was.

"She be more than a year old now." He stopped. Then he said, "I guess I ain't no . . . no *role model*."

To no one, he said, "It is what it is."

Again silence.

Again I broke it.

"What's her name?"

"Cherish." Patrick's face brightened slightly. "But I call her Cherry."

"Who thought of the name?"

"Her mother. Because she got a niece named Treasure."

I nodded. I didn't know what else to say. Was my visit over? It didn't seem right to leave yet.

"When was she born?"

"June," he said.

"So you got to be with her for around three months."

"Yeah."

"What does she look like?"

"They say she look like me." His mouth twitched, nearing a grin. "Big jaw, bright skin." Then his mouth went slack again, the smile unfinished. "That what they say, anyway."

"That is really sweet," I said.

His head fell downward, his mind somewhere else. He lowered his voice.

"Ms. Kuo," he whispered finally. "Somebody—" He stopped. "Somebody in here told me I stabbed a man thirteen times, fourteen times."

He looked into my face searchingly. Suddenly I realized that he didn't know whether it was true.

"Who told you that?"

"Just this guy who said he live across the street from me. He said he was there. He here in the sixteen-person cell now. He told a whole lot of people here that."

"Patrick," I said. "Look at me."

He looked.

I didn't remove my gaze. "I read the police reports when I came here before," I said slowly. "They said you stabbed him twice in the chest, once in the arm. So—it's not thirteen times." My voice became very low. "Okay? Don't believe what those people say."

He let out a breath. Then his head drooped toward the floor. I watched the lines in the back of his neck.

"Hey," I said. "Lift up your head."

With reluctance, he bent his head upward. His eyes searched for mine but, finding them, darted away.

"People in your family love you very much," I began. It had been so long since I had given a pep talk to a young person; I pressed forward with my clichés. "We all do."

In the air my words sounded empty—who was I to speak,

who was I to console him?—but Patrick had already leaned forward, alert for the first time, as if my words fed him in some primal way. I suddenly remembered my student Kayla; while driving her home, I'd given her a word of encouragement—a throwaway line, perhaps that she was an intelligent young woman, which seemed utterly obvious. She radiated gratitude: "Ms. Kuo, that's the first positive thing I heard all week."

"I remember you so well," I said to Patrick. "You were really wonderful in my class, and I know you—" I stopped. "I know you still are."

He nodded seriously, trying to smile. In this painful gesture of civility, he was trying to show me that my words meant something to him, or perhaps that my effort to say encouraging words meant something.

I stood up to leave. He stood up, too.

"I'll write you," I said.

"All right," he said.

He didn't say, *I'll write you back*.

He didn't say, *See you soon*.

I reached for the door, but he got to it first. He opened it for me.

"Thanks for coming to visit me, Ms. Kuo."

Ms. Kuo. Who else still called me that, with that tone? To him, I had no other name.

I looked for the guard, searching both ways down the dusty hall. Then I saw him, still holding the massive bag of chips. I nodded, signaling that we were done.

We walked side by side, passing by a door labeled LIBRARY. I halted suddenly.

"What's that?" I pointed, excited.

He kept walking. "There ain't nothing there but plastic silverware."

* * *

I STEPPED OUTSIDE INTO THE motionless heat. The warmth startled me—it had been cold inside.

It was a Saturday morning and the downtown was silent. Businesses were shuttered. Stores were vacant. Next door a jumble of planks and litter lay on the ground. This was the Delta. How to describe this—the stifling absence of people, the stillness that was also beautiful?

I was twenty-two when I first came here. Antarctica attracts misfits who find beauty in the world's end. I saw a similar beauty everywhere in the Delta: in the kudzu wilding up telephone poles, the cypress trees standing in high water. I had been told teaching here was hard, that it would break the weak. But what was a battle without a wound? Wounding was what I had signed up for.

Now I had left, moved on, survived, progressed. Now I was back as a visitor, and Patrick was alone. Inequality between us had widened. We'd both grown up, and the years divided us. He thanked me without expecting me to come back. He expected little from me or from anyone. Maybe he'd suspected things would go wrong. Maybe the shock that he was feeling was that *it* had now happened, in this way of all ways, he who stayed out of trouble, he who kept a distance from others, observed others hurt each other, hurt themselves. He hadn't expected to escape from it all, but he never thought he'd end up here, at the bottom.

In my time in the Delta I had often thought about free will and how the question of its existence was central to rural black life. The looming question—the invisible shadow—that worried and confused the kids in Helena was this: Would you rise higher than those around you? So much of anyone's identity is determined long before birth. But among my classmates at law school, I'd begun to wonder how it had happened that we, the entitled, could not comprehend, could not embrace, how free we really were—or at least how much freer than most.

Most of my classmates at Harvard had accepted their offers to work for law firms. For a few, law school debt—and the need to pay it off—was very real; for others, working at a law firm really was their dream; but most weren't sure why they'd accepted. A friend told me he'd just gotten an offer from Arnold & Porter. I had never heard of it, but from his tone I understood that this was an important firm.

I asked, "Are you going to take it?"

His lips twitched. "I'm not sure." He looked trapped by his good fortune.

I tended to treat people like mirrors, as if they carried secrets about myself, and now, searching his face, I wondered: Was this who I was, too? Did I just go about my life half-making decisions to justify my preferences and comforts?

Standing by my car outside the jail, I thought again of Ivan Ilyich. He behaves exactly as he should. From his bench he commands petitioners. He talks to them in a certain way, aware of his power but softening the fact of it. In every way, he tells himself, his life has been correct, decent, and good. *But in general Ivan Ilyich's life went on as he believed life ought to go: easily, pleasantly, and decently. . . . In all this one had to know how to exclude all that was raw, vital—which always disrupts the regular flow of official business.*

I thought I'd been brave to move from the East to the West Coast; I'd rejected the law-firm offer, chosen to work at a nonprofit, and was starting afresh. Correct, decent, good, Ivan had thought about his life—had I started thinking this way, too? Ivan, it seemed, had not done anything explicitly wrong. But in his educated social circles, he'd developed an attitude, an orientation toward others. This attitude was one of expectation that his life would be comfortable rather than uncomfortable, that he could be spared an exercised conscience.

Had I turned my back on all that was *vital* in life? As I thought about Patrick in jail, my conscience started to agitate.

It occurred to [Ivan] that those barely noticeable impulses he had felt to fight against what highly placed people considered good . . . that they might have been the real thing, and all the rest might have been not right. His work, and his living conditions, and his family, and these social and professional interests—all might have been not right. He tried to defend it all to himself. And he suddenly felt all the weakness of what he was defending. And there was nothing to defend.

Alone on the street, I tried to figure out what had just happened between Patrick and me, no longer teacher and student. What had we talked about, really? Somehow I had thought we would have more to say to each other. There was a cliché about teaching: Once a teacher, always a teacher. But there was truth to it. Your sense of responsibility to your students never leaves you. You wonder about the different paths they might have taken. You wonder if you failed them.

A voice inside said, *If you hadn't left, Patrick might not have ended up in prison. You owe him something.* And the voice continued, *Stay here. Drop everything and stay a little while.*

Don't be crazy, I argued back. Your job starts in *three weeks.* What, you're going to call your future boss and say, *Sorry, I can't come after all*? And the funders who interviewed you and gave you money to work there, what will you say? *Hey, I need to go to Arkansas to . . .* do what? It's irresponsible; it's flaky. You're an adult now; act like one. And Mom and Dad actually approve of you; they think you've gotten your act together; you took your bar exam and probably passed; you have a job and they like California. Mom just helped you move in all your crap, all those dresses and dishes—where are you going to store it all? And a subletter—you'd need to find a subletter for your room. Adina is going to hate you. She had to look at so many apartments before she found this one.

You're not thinking straight, I told the voice, because you feel bad that you've moved on and Patrick's here in jail. You feel bad that he has a baby daughter and he's afraid to think about her. You feel bad that writing about Patrick meant so much to you and then turned out to mean nothing to Patrick. You feel bad that you made him read when he didn't know how to read anymore. You feel bad because the essay was really not about him, it was more about you, about who you used to be. How naïve of you to think that when you let him read on a beanbag in your classroom, when you sat on his porch, that you changed his life. Now you see Patrick in jail, alone, not expecting anything of you or anybody—Patrick blaming himself, Patrick not knowing what he was charged for, Patrick not even knowing how many times he stabbed a person, just knowing he took away a life. Now you know who you aren't, who you weren't.

No, said the voice. *That's cynical. Why should optimism be a crime? You were a believer. When you woke up each day, you decided that showing up to work mattered. And it did. Remember the kids' silence as they read? You didn't have to enforce it. Because everyone understood: For twenty minutes or so they had gone somewhere new, someplace private and safe. It's in moments like these that we realize how capable we are of quiet and care: The consciousness is filled to the brim. From the outside of the Delta classroom, it can look hokey or insignificant. From the outside, it's smarter to talk about the Delta with a certain educated tone of fatalism mixed with ambition: "Until there's a massive redistribution of wealth and a national effort to revitalize this historically neglected region," you might intone, adjusting your glasses, "there's very little hope." But on the inside nothing seemed so sure. On the inside so much could happen in one day, in one hour.*

And then you left. You justified your leaving by saying you wanted to learn the law, because it was a powerful language to know. And perhaps you can make some broader change. But maybe you've forgotten the language you started to learn in the Delta: the one that allowed you to connect with people from different circumstances. This is a powerful language, too, and maybe you've forgotten it. Maybe this is the only language that matters. Sure, yes, you're going to work for a nonprofit. But in a place like New York or the Bay Area, a nonprofit has plenty of educated do-gooders to choose from. You're simply more disposable. It's not wrong to want to come back to the Delta. It's not shameful to be motivated by the feeling of being needed. Don't block out your desire to feel a part of what is raw and vital. To embrace what is not part of official business. Just—don't—think.

My defenses began to soften. I thought about what I could do here, if I decided to come back. Help him with his murder case? But the case was straightforward; my teacher had said so. I could teach again. But where? Stars had shut down. Maybe the Boys & Girls Club: I never got to see the new facility I helped build. I could write more, about the Delta. But writing was pointless if all I had to say was *It's too late.*

Don't write: Writing is part of the problem. Writing requires that you close the door. It's what sad people do. You were a person who did stuff, stayed close to people: You answered the cellphone when a student called, you were that person people would talk about and say, She was there for me.

Accept this picture of what happened: You left prematurely. You stumbled upon law school, showing up basically by accident. You gave in to your parents. You were weak. You thought that teaching was not prestigious. You thought the Delta was not a place to make a life.

But what can staying do? I wondered. Was staying just a way

to make myself feel better, and make up for what I didn't do before? A way to get back to a time when, for me and Patrick, all paths seemed possible.

Don't think. Just come back. If you don't come back now, it'll be too late for Patrick. If you don't come back now, it'll be too late for you: You'll never come back.

THE DRIVE FROM ARKANSAS TO Indiana took eight hours. Somewhere in Missouri, I pulled into a service station to fill my tires with air. I could feel my heart beat in my chest.

First I needed to tell the source of my funding: the director of my fellowship, famed for her exacting speech, ironclad memory, and knockout red suits.

I called her.

"I need to see through Patrick's case," I said. She had read the *Times* piece, so I didn't have to explain who he had been to me. "I need enough time to run through his options with him. And I just feel like I've been running away from the Delta and have unfinished business there."

"How much time do you need?"

I didn't know. "Until May," I tried. I was just guessing. May sounded like enough time for me to reconnect but not so much that she would say no.

She calculated. "Seven months? Is that enough time?"

"Yes. Seven months," I repeated, as if I had determined this beforehand.

I called the director of Centro, my organization. She asked, "Are you truly planning to come to California? Otherwise, we need to make preparations."

For a moment I tried to imagine ditching California and staying in Helena permanently. Drinking beer on the porch, gardening alongside the kids, and wearing a big hat—I'd be moral and authentic, physically strong, like Tolstoy's hero Levin in *Anna Karenina*, pushing a wheelbarrow and singing a tune he picked up from the muzhiks. But then I remembered all my drives to Memphis alone when my coupled friends went on vacation, and the old man who accosted me once in a grocery store, saying he fought the Japs in World War II. I couldn't tell if he was expressing alliance or enmity; that depended on what kind of Asian he saw.

"No, no, I'm not going to stay," I said. "I've been practicing my Spanish," I added, hoping she wouldn't say anything in Spanish. Otherwise, I'd say, *Hello, hello?* and hang up. But she continued in English: "Good luck, keep us posted."

Then I had to call Adina about our apartment in San Francisco. She had just helped my mom and me move in, unpacking dishes and lamps. I apologized. I insisted that she keep my security deposit. I said I was flying back to get my stuff.

Last—my parents. Last because I feared them the most. The past couple of years had been rough. I had made the mistake of telling them a first-year associate's salary at a New York law firm. They had no idea that a lawyer made so much. The idea that I would turn it down seemed crazy to them. A family fight ensued. In its dynamic of expectation and disappointment, it reprised the fight we'd had two years before in the Delta. But this time I had learned: Don't ask for permission; stand firm. My brother took my side, which helped. By the time graduation rolled around, my mom and dad had altogether forgotten about the fight. "Come home," they said; they knew I needed a place to study for the bar. "We've always supported what you want," they continued, model revisionist historians.

Home has always been the best place to study. In our house, a person studying is pampered like a king. Nobody interrupts you. I made a hamlet out of their kitchen table, a castle out of books and notes. My dad listened as I recited tedious rules on contracts and torts, occasionally interrupting with, "That's a stupid law; here's why." My mother popped in with fruit and tea. Cutting a mango, she sliced the meatiest parts onto a plate for me and left herself the core to gnaw on.

My best friend was getting married two days before my bar exam, and my parents had looked on dubiously as I packed my suitcase, a dress smashed under a mound of heavy tomes. "I've never heard of anybody going to a wedding before a big test," my dad observed. But he didn't say anything more.

The night before I left, my mother took me aside to tell me that she, too, had had a momentous exam, back in Taiwan. A talented high school student, she wanted to be a doctor. To do so, she had to take a battery of tests at the end of her senior year. In other words, the fulfillment of her professional dream hinged on a test she took as a teenager. It is a trauma-producing system: As in Japan or Korea or China, shortly before or after the exam, suicides could be counted on. On the day of the physics test, she panicked. She failed. She told me her score and looked away. I saw her face before she turned, and in this moment, especially, I loved her deeply.

My mother cooked alone, cleaned alone, and worked full-time. In her late twenties, her big dream was to get a Ph.D. She enrolled at Michigan State. But it was hard with two kids, not to mention her aging in-laws and sister-in-law, all crowded in our house; she dropped out. Like a lot of women of her generation, especially immigrant women, she got little encouragement. Much later, she read an essay I wrote, a seed of this book. She wrote: *I read second time this morning, and I tears, And read again, It is real touched and gave people's feeling that it is real story. Keep writing, write down all your feeling every day.*

When I was growing up, my father had waited outside until my piano lessons finished, but my mother often tried to catch the tail end, captivated by my piano teacher. "How do you make the sound last?" my teacher would ask me, unaware of her question's existential agitation. She'd strike a key. The sound would soar then fade. We'd be quiet. She'd strike again. We'd wait. The sound would last. "Now you try," she'd say. My mother leaned toward my hand, watching. She was not regulating me, not monitoring my learning—in fact, for a precious moment she had forgotten me. She wished to play herself but thought it would be a luxury. The trope was true: She gave me what she wanted. When I practiced, I could hear her humming along in the kitchen. The clear, bright tones of her voice rose above the vegetables being chopped.

Tiger mom has become a shorthand to describe parents, usually Asian, with rigorous discipline. For me the term fails absolutely. It mistakes a person's fragility for her power. My mother was authoritarian about learning because she didn't know how else to be. It was not a choice among pedagogies; it was desperation. Without the success of her children, who would she be?

While I studied for the bar at home, I read *Pnin*, Nabokov's hilarious tale of a Russian émigré in upstate New York. The book opens with bald-headed Pnin on a train, on his way to give a lecture, not knowing that he is on the wrong train. I was thrilled. Pnin! Here was the immigrant of my dreams. Not miserabilist Chinese railroad workers, not the coolies spat upon, not the Japanese unjustly interned. Pnin mastering English phrases—*okey-dokey* and *to make a long story short;* Pnin captivated by the American washing machine, stuffing it with shorts and handkerchiefs, just to watch them tumble endlessly like dolphins; Pnin triumphant after an excruciating tooth surgery, showing off his new treasure—a set of false teeth, which smiled back at him, and which he frequently took in and out of his mouth to show colleagues. Pnin was mocked cruelly behind his back and called a freak. Pnin had no idea. Poor Pnin! Heroic Pnin!

So Pnin was nothing like my parents—they weren't clumsy, had never heard of Pushkin, didn't pronounce *difficulty* as *dzeefeecooltsee*. But weren't they, after all, more like Pnin? Didn't they have Pninian moments? My mother: "Do lots of yogurt," thinking *yoga* and *yogurt* were the same word. Talking about her first years in America and her discovery of the hamburger, she sighed with happiness. My father slurped his noodles in large ghastly gulps of saliva and hunger; his glasses fogged up—he took off his glasses to improve his speed.

My parents put on no airs. They had been shocked by the amount a lawyer made because they didn't know a lawyer. My parents' lack of advice for college, beyond telling me to become a doctor and not to date, was really evidence of how innocuous they turned out to be. So this, after all, explained their dogmatic style of advice—they suspected they couldn't help me beyond what they'd already done: given me a childhood filled with opportunity. It turned out that, just as I knew Pnin was on the wrong train, I had the power to situate my parents in the world, to write them down. I was stronger than they were.

Thoughts of my parents continued to flood my mind as I turned in to their driveway. Pnin was lovable because his trauma was hidden. One never said: Foreign Pnin! Immigrant Pnin! Pnin Burdened by History! Here was the pleasure of Pnin: His failure to comprehend was so consistent, and so stubborn, and so masterful, that you forgot the world that failed him. I thought about my parents, who, like Pnin, were products of forces beyond their control. My dad himself was the child of immigrants: His mother and father had left China for Taiwan in 1949, and, like most in that generation of refugees, never saw their family members again. My parents had grown up under martial law in Taiwan and left before it democratized. Their memories of Taiwan remained frozen in the 1970s, when they left. Perhaps, more than they admitted to themselves, they no longer knew the Taiwan that had reared them. And maybe this was why they often reminded me that they'd lived in America longer than I had. They wanted me to regard them as Americans.

In the garage my parents rushed out to greet me, even though it was chilly, already autumn. My dad reached for my luggage; my mother touched my hair. They hadn't eaten, they'd waited for me.

What would they think of my decision to return to the Delta? I knew they wanted me to get on with my life. They believed I made decisions selfishly, without consideration of them. And they were right: Learning how to disregard their opinions was essential to my life. I hoped they knew I did think of them tenderly.

Over dinner, I tried to speak more Mandarin than usual, something I do whenever I'm attempting to ingratiate myself. I told myself to speak slowly, in short, patient sentences. I'd always spoken English too fast. Though my father could catch most of it, my mother could not. How had we even communicated all these years? What did we talk about? We had needed grades and awards to mediate our relationship. How did the world view me? Did my teachers like me? Was I smart? The grade had answered these questions. The grade had made me legible.

And now that I was done with receiving grades for the rest of my life, it seemed that in place of grades we had only one thing: the story. Could I tell a story that moved them, that made them understand? This was the urgent thing.

Switching between Mandarin and English, I told them I'd seen Patrick. I told them that the jail was like the school where I'd taught. Decrepit and accountable to nobody. I told them that Patrick didn't even know the name of his lawyer. At this, my dad shook his head. Then I said it seemed as if Patrick had forgotten just about everything he'd learned. I had him read out loud. He was scared of getting words wrong. I told them that in spite of everything that happened, Patrick was still sweet. He had thanked me for visiting him. As if he expected me to never show up again. As if he didn't expect anything from anybody. He put everything on himself. I told them I was probably never going to live in the Delta again. "You were right," I said. "I wasn't happy there. But I need to go back for just enough time to make peace with it. So I think I need to stay," I said finally.

I knew from my mother's face that she understood. She was quiet; she wanted to hear more.

My father asked, "How are you going to pay for it?"

I reminded him that, back when I taught, my monthly portion of the rent for a three-bedroom house, with hardwood floors and a fig tree out front, had been a stunning one hundred fifty dollars. If you added that up over a year, it was about a month's rent in San Francisco.

"Yes," he said matter-of-factly. "Because nobody wants to live there."

My mother mourned the labor it would take me to transport my clothes from San Francisco to Arkansas.

Then her face lit up at a thought: We had so many books no one was using, old books from when I was a kid; maybe Patrick would like them?

My father was pleased at the idea that I might clean out the basement.

PART
III

*"No, no!" said the
Queen. "Sentence
first—verdict
afterwards."*

—LEWIS CARROLL,
*Alice's Adventures
in Wonderland*

5

Crime and Punishment

THE CHINESE RESTAURANT IN HELENA WAS A PLACE I usually tried to avoid, entering only on masochistic occasions of extreme desperation. Nonetheless, Aaron, my former student with perfect attendance, wanted to eat here, and so I said yes.

Opening the door, I triggered a hanging bell. Two customers, both white, turned to stare at me. I understood at once: They were observing how I, Asian-looking, would speak to the restaurant owner, also Asian-looking.

I greeted her, speaking in English.

"Hello," I said.

"Hello," she returned.

At this, the men turned back to their food.

Aaron and I approached the buffet. He packed his plate, accepting every option. "I love me some chicken chow mein," he said, beaming.

Aaron was doing well. He had graduated from Central and was getting a degree in environmental science at the community college, while working part-time at McDonald's and supporting his baby boy.

"You hear what happen to Tamir?" he asked, his mouth full of noodles.

My heart jumped at hearing Tamir's name.

"No," I said. "How is he?"

"You won't recognize him," Aaron said. "He don't look like nobody. He got no look to himself. He just blend in."

"Blends in?"

"With the homies on the street." Aaron wiped some grease off his lips, then plunged back into the chicken. "He's in Little Rock; he's a crackhead on the street. Begging for money."

The last time I'd heard Tamir's name was a month after I left the Delta, some three years ago. Tamir's ninth-grade English teacher had left me a voice message. She said she'd asked students to respond to a question, *Who is a person who changed your life?* Tamir had chosen to write about me.

"How can I find him?" I asked, my voice uneven.

Aaron shrugged at the futility of the question. Once off the grid, you stayed off: no phone number, no email address.

I saw something familiar in Aaron's manner, something I recognized from my teaching days. What was it? Schadenfreude? No, I thought; it was less glee than relief, with a tincture of pride: *That could have been me but it isn't.* In Aaron the tone was tempered by his solid sense of worth, but I heard it nonetheless.

"What about Miles?" I asked.

"Miles? He not doing nothing. He'll be another Tamir. Lately Miles been shooting at people."

"You mean with a gun?" I said, nearly choking on my food.

"Yeah, he don't care. Got arrested, got right out. 'Cause his family be rich now, they post bail in a *second*. They got a million something and more, and now they blowing it all away." Aaron was referring to the lawsuit his mother had brought against the flower-shop owner who shot and killed Brandon. It must have gotten settled and paid out. "Yup, they bought a new home, they got five cars, mopeds, truck, Lexus. He used to just have Oldsmobile."

I swallowed my mouthful.

"And Jasmine?"

"Jasmine got a baby now."

"Kayla?"

"She got a baby, too."

"Cassandra?"

"She got two. Would've had three but had a miscarriage."

Aaron finished his plate and I looked at him casually, trying to pretend I wasn't watching him. Why had he graduated and not the others? There was the matter of him being male: The pregnant students almost always dropped out, unless they got help from family. But his family also had better education. His mother worked in administration at the nursing home and, I recalled, had graduated from high school; his grandma owned a sewing and fabric shop downtown, one of only a handful of businesses that had survived the economic downturn. Few other students at Stars had a parent who graduated from high school and held a steady job. Did it just come down to these basic metrics in the end—the family's level of education and quality of employment?

"You ain't eat *nothing*, Ms. Kuo," he said, looking up finally from his plate. "Bet it don't taste like your mama's." He helped himself to some chicken from my plate.

Outside, I asked if he wanted to take a drive through the neighborhood.

"Drive with *you*, Ms. Kuo?" He let out a chortle. "I ain't crazy." Then he got into the front seat.

Unprompted and garrulous, Aaron gestured at our passing landscape and said that he was going to give me a tour of "Hell-Town." As I drove, he pointed down roads where I should turn, neighborhoods to enter.

"That where Miles *used* to stay, before they got rich," he said. "The sheriff, he got that place on curfew." I asked what kind of curfew. "You know, lockdown. Because someone got shot at in daylight."

In reality Aaron had probably forgotten that I'd gone to these neighborhoods often, to drop off Patrick and other students. As if on cue, Aaron said offhandedly that Patrick stayed around here, too.

"You hear about what happen to Patrick, Ms. Kuo?"

Again that tone, the gossipy not-quite schadenfreude—yet now I detected something else, a submerged warmth or regret, a tone more like ersatz detachment, a method to avoid mourning.

We passed by a small green patch near Central. Aaron said, "A little sixteen-year-old got killed the other day, coming home from a football game at Central, the homecoming," he said. "He was beat up, then somebody shot him in his head. They don't even know who did it."

Then the police station, a hundred yards from the county jail: "In July, the day after the Fourth, my cousin, he was killed right over here by the jail, right in front of the sheriff's office. Two or three leftover flowers still there."

He rolled down his window and so I slowed the car. We gazed together at the makeshift memorial, a ragged, colorful hodgepodge of objects. Pink and yellow bits of old petals; framed pictures; a stuffed animal.

He shrugged off my condolences over his cousin and said, "That happen *right* after the sixteen-year-old girl who go to *KIPP* died," he said, emphasizing the name of the school. Knowledge Is Power Program was a charter school that had been built a few years before I'd first arrived in Helena. "Somebody was shooting at her mama's boyfriend, and the boyfriend pushed her in front, like she was a shield. She was shot. Chest, arm, and thigh."

So this was a change. As KIPP expanded into an elementary and high school, its reputation had grown. It was known as a place where students didn't slack.

"And she be going to *KIPP*," he repeated, with a tone of admiration, as if to say she, a studious person, couldn't have been responsible for her death.

Aaron pointed out the county jail. I did not mention I already knew it. He said he knew someone who had escaped by climbing to the roof and jumping off.

"He didn't get hurt?" I asked.

"Naw, he chunky. He ain't hurt himself at all."

Apparently the escapee hung out, saw family, and went back the next day.

As a final act of nostalgia we visited Stars. It was abandoned. We peered through barbed wire. A garbage can was knocked on its side. The grass was uncut, overrun by tall weeds.

We drove away and Aaron dialed a number on his cellphone.

"Gina, guess who in town, guess who I'm on the road with?" Then he said, "*Ms. Kuo,*" and a high-pitched scream burst through the other end. Aaron jerked the phone away from his ear and we both guffawed.

"We got lunch," he continued. "Gina, only thing I can tell you is, 'Thank God for seatbelts.'"

I laughed, easing back to our old rhythm.

"Matter of fact, her driving got worse. You know Helena got all these potholes? Ms. Kuo hit about seventy of them."

He handed me his phone.

"Ms. Gina Gordon!" I said, smiling into the phone. "How are you, my dear?"

She said, "I got a tongue piercing, nose piercing. A little change, not a lot done change."

I HAD MOVED IN WITH Danny and Lucy. Lucy was making granola, and Danny had gotten out the Scrabble. Only their cats seemed unhappy to see me.

They gave me the news about Helena. Good news: There was a new Mexican restaurant and it had margaritas. A new health center featured brand-new treadmills and a yoga class. A new library—from funds Danny had helped raise—would be unveiled at the end of the year. It had a children's section and computer lab. Our Blues Festival, now an annual event, had another successful year. And construction of "Freedom Park," a public space dedicated to black refugees in Helena, would soon begin.

KIPP Delta had among the highest scores on the state math and literacy tests: Black children from the poorest part of Arkansas had gotten higher scores than white kids from private schools in the wealthiest parts of Arkansas. Ten years ago, most policymakers would have laughed at this as impossible. Some white families in Helena now complained about being excluded from the school.

* * *

WHEN I WENT TO SEE Patrick the following morning, there was a new jailer, a Mr. Cousins. He was diminutive and rotund and had a cheerful, almost sinister air.

Again, nobody at the jail wrote down my name or bothered to ask it. My bags were not checked, my cellphone was not taken away; I said merely that I was looking to visit Patrick Browning.

Mr. Cousins looked me up and down. Then he said, smiling, "I ain't gonna let you see him until you give me a hug."

I coughed. "Excuse me?"

"A hug," he said. "You know, an old-fashioned hug."

He leaned in, waiting.

I held my breath. When our bodies touched, he squeezed my back.

Then he pulled away, smirking. We walked side by side.

Sounds of metal clanging grew louder as we neared, and I realized inmates were banging on the cells.

"Guess 'cause they thinking about what they done," he said, chuckling.

In the control room the jailers were chatting, watching *Matlock*, and eating breakfast. The odor was a weird mix of grease and must.

"I'm gonna quit this motherfucking job."

"You ain't gonna quit nothing."

"You watch me."

"Boy, you gone get fired in any other place. That mouth of yours, you know you got it."

"I sure do."

I tried my best to be unobtrusive. But nobody appeared to notice I was there.

Back in the windowless room, I was looking up at the ceiling, searching for the source of a puddle on the floor, when Patrick suddenly appeared in the doorway. Seeing me, he smiled and pulled up his baggy black-and-white-striped jumpsuit.

"Ms. Kuo," Patrick said, walking in, shaking his head, marveling. "You came *back*."

Then he asked, "What you doing here, Ms. Kuo?"

I told him I was going to be around Helena for longer than I'd expected, that I'd missed living here.

"Here?" he said. "That sure crazy." He shook his head again, but he was smiling.

We caught up. I told him I'd just gotten back from seeing my parents in Indiana.

"You got a mom and a daddy?" he asked.

I said I did. I took out my phone to show him pictures.

"You can take pictures on these?" he asked.

Patrick watched the screen carefully as I swiped the screen with my thumb and the next picture appeared.

"See?" I said. "Now you try."

He wiped his hand on the side of his jumpsuit and placed his finger on the screen. Gingerly, he imitated my gesture.

"You look like them," he said.

He seemed interested in the pictures, examining every image thoroughly before proceeding to the next. "What's that?" he'd ask. I had taken pictures of my mother's cooking. Noodle soup, I'd say, or Chinese vegetables—I didn't know the exact name in English. For a few he supplied the answer. "Shrimp," he said to himself.

Then he said, "You been to China, Ms. Kuo?"

"Yes."

"You been to Africa?"

"Yes." I paused. "Do you want to go to any of those places?"

Still looking down at my pictures, he said, "I don't know about all that. I just wanna get out of jail."

He handed me back the phone.

"How are you?" I asked.

Patrick's mood shifted suddenly, as if I'd brought up a forbidden topic. He slouched back in his seat, shoulders sagging.

"Ain't nothing happening here."

"Nothing?"

"Nothing. Just crazy stuff."

He put his hands over his face, then took them off.

"My cousin be here; there be this other dude messing with him. Dude went crazy, threw my cousin's tray against the wall. Then he took the juice jug, threw it up in the air." He paused. "And they be burning plastic."

"Burning what?" I asked, unsure if I'd heard correctly.

"*Plastic*," he said, louder.

I was puzzled.

Patrick tried to be patient. "It cover the windows, you know. They be trying to burn a hole through the windows."

I recalled *The Shawshank Redemption* and Tim Robbins chipping away at the wall.

"Why?" I asked, feeling foolish, wondering if the answer was obvious. "To escape?"

"Naw. To get weed through the windows. Then they sell it to the jailers. Or the *trusties*." At this he scowled.

"Who?"

He explained. The trusties were inmates who lived in separate quarters. The jail outsourced janitorial work to them. "They cook, you know, clean up around here. They mop; they work; they just don't get paid."

"Trusty?" I repeated. I'd never heard the word before.

"Yeah, *trusty*. Like somebody you *supposed* to trust. People who *supposed* to be trustworthy." He grimaced, affronted—he still expected words to mean what they promised to mean.

He opened his mouth to say something but stopped himself. His head dangled lower, a gesture now almost familiar to me.

"Ms. Kuo, I don't—I don't *know* what I got myself *into*."

He laid his head in his hands.

"I can't sleep. I can't help but breathe in all that smoke."

The room was still. I was at a loss.

I heard myself ask, "Can you get a different room—cell?"

His voice came out muffled from under his hands: "If the jailer *let* you."

Then words poured out of him. "And nothing be working here. Like, they got these intercoms. But they don't work. If you need some attention or someone get to fighting, you gotta beat on the window. Like the other day, this guy had a seizure back there. But the jailers only come back when they *feel* like coming back. You gotta beat the window, and they don't know if you serious or not, because people beat the window all the time for nothing." He rubbed his hands over his temples. "Trapped around these niggers all day long."

I reached awkwardly to touch his shoulder, a tentative pat on his back. Yet his body was coiled so tightly that he didn't appear to register my touch.

"Time," he said. "You can't go back in time. Everything that happen is about cause and effect. One day lead to another. And now I'm here."

Patrick covered his face with his hands.

"Hey, Patrick," I said finally, consolingly, wanting to say something. "You're being strong. Keep your chin up."

At this he lifted his chin, as if I'd meant the phrase literally.

THAT AFTERNOON, OUT OF THE blue, Jordan, an old teaching friend, called. Jordan was among that special breed of teacher who had come with Teach for America and decided to stay. He'd started the year before I had, bought a house, married another teacher, had two kids, and was planning to live in Helena permanently. He was a Catholic with religious tattoos and sported the grim persona of a former gang member turned priest.

My students at Stars had had him at Miller and recalled him with a mixture of respect and recoil. Kids never forget a class where they feel expected to succeed at a deep level and are given the means to do so. The memory of feeling smart, even if only for a day or week, doesn't ever go entirely away.

Jordan asked how California was.

I replied nonchalantly. "It's okay. I'm going to do legal aid. I'm excited about that."

Among the dozens or so teachers who had stayed in the Delta, with the exception of Danny and Lucy, I tended to withhold mention of anything that made me look frivolous, likely because I felt exposed around them: They had done what I could not, and more, they'd done it without any apparent agony.

Jordan was now a principal at KIPP. It desperately needed a part-time Spanish teacher, he told me. His full-time teacher, Ms. Alvarado, was overloaded with seven classes. "My Spanish is pretty bad," I began. "I just had two years of college Spanish."

Jordan smiled; in the Delta, that was worth a lot.

"I could teach English," I tried. No, he needed Spanish.

I have never been good at saying no. Also, I wanted Jordan to like me.

"Just two classes," he said. "Freshman Spanish. Can you do just two? You'd have to start Monday."

Maybe this was why I had come back—to teach in a school that was functional, where students were expected to achieve. The tidy row of KIPP students lined up at the bus downtown now warmed my memory; nearly every kid carried a book of some kind, Philip Pullman or *Black Boy*. Besides, a paycheck would be nice—I was living off savings and an IRS return. There was such a dire need for middle-class professionals in this town that within days of coming back, I could have a new job.

"I'm in," I said, resolving to avoid Ms. Alvarado, lest she try to speak to me in Spanish.

I HAD ONLY A FEW days before my job at KIPP would start, and I still needed to meet Patrick's lawyer. I'd promised Patrick that I would figure out when his court date was. This was all he had asked of me. He had been in county jail for over a year, and still there was no trial.

Knowing Helena, I half-expected Patrick's public defender to be wearing sweatpants and chewing tobacco. But Rob looked respectable: sharp canary-yellow tie, tailored black suit. He was black and looked as if he was in his forties. A graduate of the University of Arkansas Law School, Rob had worked at McDonald's to pay his tuition. He had become a public defender because he believed poor people needed access to legal services. But soon he discovered that he needed a private practice in order to stay afloat. There was only one other public defender in Helena, and both worked part-time, because the state of Arkansas declined to pay for anything more. In total, they each received a copy machine and 1,700 copies a year. Postage, long-distance calls, gas, transportation—all these came from their own pockets. They had zero funds for private investigation, including police-misconduct inquiries, psychiatrists, forensics experts. Investigations required money Rob didn't have.

"Have you talked"—I paused, trying to word my question carefully—"gotten a chance to talk to Patrick yet?" I asked.

"I've got over a hundred clients," he responded.

Then, as if conceding my point, he said ruefully, "It's legalized malpractice."

Rob explained that Helena had only four sessions of court in a year. (In contrast, in Massachusetts, criminal court took place every business day of the year.) Each session in Helena was little more than three weeks long. If a trial was held, all the other cases—and there were usually more than a hundred cases on the docket—were pushed to the next session. Cases such as Patrick's were not "priority," and so his case had gotten repeatedly delayed.

"Imperfect self-defense," Rob continued, was probably Patrick's best argument. It meant exactly what it sounded like: Patrick's belief that he was defending himself—he thought Marcus had a weapon—was mistaken, imperfect. This could lower the charge of murder to manslaughter.

I said that in poor communities, where there was a lot of violence and a lot of death, wasn't it safe to assume that most people had a belief about the dangerousness of others? Wasn't this belief the very core of fear—a belief in the possibility of harm that could be based in reality but also could be mistaken? Even if Marcus had turned out not to carry a weapon, was it really such a mistake—an "imperfection"—for Patrick to feel afraid, to think he might be in danger?

Rob appeared amused, and his smile seemed to say, *This is what a Harvard education is worth.*

"That's a good point," he said. "But you can't tell that to the prosecutor. The law's the law."

"What about plain old self-defense?" I laid out the case. "You're eighteen; you're just a kid. A drunk guy shows up on your porch. He's bigger; he's older than you; he's aggressive. And he's got your sister with him. She's just sixteen and she's a little slow, in special-ed classes. You tell him to get off the porch, and he won't get off the porch. He's really drunk and—"

"That really depends on the jury," Rob interrupted. "But it's a risk to take it to the jury."

"If Patrick were white . . ." I tried finally. This was the elephant in the room. It seemed perfectly obvious that a white resident confronted with a drunk black aggressor on his property would not be charged with murder.

Rob's eyes sparkled, bemused. I wondered if he thought I was very stupid. "I agree, I agree," he said. "But there's nothing we can do about that."

I VISITED PATRICK TWICE MORE that week. Even in this short time, conversations had started to blend together. We would speak first of me. "How you be, Ms. Kuo?" he'd ask. (Sometimes, attempting formality, "How *are* you?") Just about any trivial fact caught his attention—a movie, a meal, the weather. The conversation tended to the mundane. *Did it rain? What you been eating? What kind of car you drive?* He would lean forward, not wanting to miss a word. Almost any photo in my phone, no matter the content, captivated him; he studied the image as if it contained an encrypted message from the world. I answered questions, often logistical: What city was this in? How did I get there?

But if we spoke about *him*, we seemed to talk mostly about the jail and how dirty it was. The showers were the worst. Trusties dumped leftover liquids into the drains, and cockroaches crawled out. Patrick thought that the Kool-Aid was the culprit. "I flush my Kool-Aid in the toilet, but people be dumping it everywhere," he said. When he showered, he kept his arms close to his body, afraid that his skin would touch the colorful fungus that grew on the walls.

Broken toilets went unfixed, and the jail smelled terrible no matter how far you got away from them. Trusties put black garbage bags over the ones that they couldn't repair. "We end up using all the same toilet. At the other cell, they was just peeing all over the floor. Ain't no telling, with these guys back here, what disease I be catching."

The cells had no doors, so people wandered in and out of Patrick's. One guy stalked into his cell, spat on the floor, and stalked out. An older guy walked around muttering that he was Martin Luther King, Jr. Patrick's cousin with schizophrenia had been given the wrong meds—another inmate's heart medicine— for two weeks. There was always chatter of who's gonna jump who, who's in for what, and constant fighting, yelling, beating on walls.

The details became repetitive, insistent, dull: The mold grows on the bathroom walls; the cockroach crawls out of the drain. Sometimes Patrick forgot details he had already told me. "I be in the best cell," he said. "Because all the other cells got toilets that don't work."

I told him I'd talked to his lawyer, assuming this would pique his interest. But he had only one question: When was the trial date? He wanted to get it over with. I repeated what Rob told me, that the date again had been postponed—likely no trial until December or maybe even February. At that he lost interest in the law altogether. He didn't want to talk about his defense. Offhandedly I used the phrase *murder charge*, and he winced.

He moved the topic to his past. Maybe he had nothing else to talk about and no other direction to go. In retrospect, all incidents seemed to him connected. When he was twelve or so, he said, he was riding his bike, going to *steal* something. It was a friend's idea. He had never stolen anything before. On his way he got hit by a truck and was knocked off his bike. "That be a *sign*, Ms. Kuo."

"A sign?" I repeated. I'd known he was religious, like most of the kids, but I hadn't known the extent of it.

Yeah, a sign: God was talking to him right then and there. God was saying he shouldn't have been doing what he was doing. Nobody knew him the way God knew him.

Patrick recast important events in his life as premonitions he'd ignored. When he was eleven he was in his backyard, playing with a jug of gasoline. He ended up in the hospital, he missed weeks in school, and he fell behind. That was the same time the twin towers fell. He showed me his burns, darkened blotches on his ankles.

"Yes," I said, "I remember."

"Cause and effect," he repeated to himself, as if this were the reason he was here now, the common phrase assuming theological weight. Patrick appeared trapped in a feedback loop: first self-reproach, then a desire to forget, and then, for wanting to forget, self-reproach.

Each conversation had patterns. He would speak and then break off. He would say something that depressed him and he'd drop his head so far down that his back and neck formed a smooth surface, like the top of a table. There were long stretches of silence in which neither of us spoke. I didn't want to fill the silence with chatter or idle consolation. By not speaking, I thought, I was being honest about who I really was—not the rousing giver of pep talks, not the person who said, *You can do it, I believe in you.* By not speaking I was trying to say, rather, *This is who I really am, a person who doesn't know what to say, lost like you.*

But in the end I usually could not take the silence: He needed to hear good news; he needed a messenger. "Hey, look at me," I'd say. He'd raise his head slightly so that his eyes met mine, and I'd force myself to give him a pep talk. "Who you are isn't what happened one night in your life, Patrick, okay?" Or, "Your family has only kind things to say about you, do you hear me? Only kind things." Or, "Your family loves and misses you." Or, simply, "I'm sorry this happened." And despite the lack of substance or originality of these words, their tonal breakings suggested genuine grief.

If he spoke in reply, it was always an assent: "You right," or "Yes, ma'am," or "Thanks, Ms. Kuo."

Before, school had been a world we shared. In the three years I had been absent, we had not simply lost touch with each other, we had ceased to have anything in common. I had assumed just being together would suffice. But we lived in two distinct worlds. His reality was sensory assault. My reality was apparent in the bright screen of my phone, which he touched with his fingertip, trying not to dirty it. Our bond was that between a former teacher and her former student, and its weakness now seemed exposed.

It was possible that for Patrick our conversations were not so terrible; talking to someone is usually better than having nobody to talk to. But for me our conversations were tedious. The shoddy county jail had appeared to accomplish its purpose: This was a punishment, and he had fixed himself into a state of perpetual confession. He *wanted* to feel guilty; he wanted to suffer. And I wasn't qualified to act as a default priest.

And yet the idea that Patrick was solely guilty for the death of Marcus was nonsense, wasn't it? Charged with murder, Patrick was the opposite of an archetypal murderer. He hadn't covered his tracks. He hadn't invented an alibi. He hadn't rinsed the blood off the weapon and hidden it. He had watched the man he hurt walk away. It didn't occur to him the man would die. He sat on the porch waiting for the police. He cried waiting. He got in the police car, he didn't ask for a lawyer, and he didn't feel like talking about a defense now. He did not blame society or poverty. Just himself. The problem was not that he wouldn't confess but that he had confessed too much; it wasn't far-fetched to think he might spend the rest of his life confessing.

And yet maybe he needed his guilt; otherwise the death would have happened for no reason, a result of senseless collision—of mental states, physical impulses, and coincidences. He needed, for his own sense of meaning, to knit his failures into a story. "Cause and effect," as he put it. The thread was that he messed up by ignoring God.

But I didn't believe the story he told himself. I wanted to break it. For me to do that, we needed to forge a connection. But what did I have that I could share with him?

All I could think of was books. There were other things he liked—he'd tended lovingly to his go-cart and said once that he wanted to be a mechanic. I didn't believe that reading was inherently superior to learning how to fix a car, or that reading makes a person better. But I did love books, and I hadn't yet shared with him anything I myself loved. Had I known how to sing, I would have had us sing.

Thus, at the end of October, about two weeks after I'd arrived, I heard myself say, "Patrick, I'm going to ask you to do something."

Patrick looked at me expectantly.

I said, "I need you to do homework every day."

He emitted a little childlike shriek—the first smile all day. "Ms. Kuo!" He laughed and covered his open mouth. "Naw, it's over with."

"What else are you going to do? Eat? Sit around?"

He was still laughing. "What you mean, *homework*?" He hadn't heard that word in a while and it amused him. Then he went silent. "It's over with," he repeated.

"Come on," I said lightly. My voice sounded too casual.

"Too late, Ms. Kuo." His fingernail scratched the wood. "It's too late."

"What do you mean, too late? Dude, you didn't graduate from *high school*," I said. I cringed at how my words sounded in the air, affecting an ease that we didn't yet share. I already knew he would do whatever I asked of him. Patrick, like Aaron and Gina and Kayla, always took guidance from adults, particularly me.

More gently, I said, "When your daughter sees you and can talk to you, won't it feel good to read to her?"

"Yes, ma'am."

"And you know I'm right."

"Yes, ma'am."

"Then it's settled. Homework every day."

I had no idea what the homework would consist of. What would I teach? How would I check his homework if I was coming only once a week? And what if I only knew how to relate to Patrick by exerting authority over him?

6

The Lion, the Witch and the Wardrobe

ON MONDAY MORNING I WAITED IN THE LOBBY OF THE JAIL, excited to read Patrick's first piece of homework.

This time, nobody was at the front desk. Another woman, also waiting, shrugged at me. I shrugged back.

I had been pleased with my assignment: Write a letter to your daughter. "It'll be good to have her on your mind, don't you think?" I had asked. It would comfort him to think of his daughter and help him understand writing as a direct address to another person.

Patrick had looked scared, but I'd pretended not to notice.

"You want me to write . . . write a letter to Cherry?"

"Yep, exactly."

Patrick had opened his mouth to say something but then stopped himself.

After another good ten minutes of waiting, the woman turned back to me. "They ain't see us," she said. She pointed at a camera. "Power be broke; the video's out." She climbed over the front desk and touched a switch. There was a large buzz and the latch to the security door, which led to the cells, popped open.

She stepped through the door, having broken into the jail.

"Hello?" she called out.

Now Shawn emerged. Untroubled by what, anywhere else, would have amounted to a major breach of security, he waved for us both to follow him.

Just a few days ago, the Helena newspaper had reported an inmate escape. Now I understood how easy it would be. Surprising, really, that more people didn't try.

Shawn gestured for me to go in.

Patrick emerged.

"How are you?" I asked.

"Stressed-out." A guy he knew had come in the night before. Domestic abuse. "He kept saying he love her, even though he hit her. I be telling him you can't mistreat people you love. I try to encourage him, you know. But, really, it stresses me out." He sighed. Then he said, "Hey, Ms. Kuo, you think you could do me a favor?"

"What?" I asked, happy. He hadn't yet asked me for anything beyond getting his court date.

"Get me some cigarettes—you know, tobacco."

"Oh," I said. "I'm not allowed to do that, am I?"

"Naw, it's contraband. But I really need me some cigarettes."

"I can't. If I get caught or—"

"It's all right."

"I wish I could—"

"It's all right."

I felt guilty saying no.

"Let's see your homework," I said, wanting to change the subject and perhaps even cheer us both up.

Now Patrick chuckled. "Naw, Ms. Kuo, I ain't do it."

My face fell; my blood rose. Why was he smiling? Did he think not doing homework was funny? But then I caught myself. Patrick was just being realistic: Homework wouldn't get him out of jail.

Still, my voice was stern. "You aren't taking this seriously."

Patrick turned away, as if I had struck him on his face.

As soon as I arrived, later that day, to teach Spanish at KIPP, I realized it had been a mistake.

A student asked, "Ms. Kuo, how do you say *boat* in Spanish?" He liked boats, he said.

"I'll tell you after you finish your work," I replied, trying to remember.

The student was respectful; they all were. And diligent. And studious. The school had an extraordinary sense of safety—there would be no random violence here. No threats. No bullying. No sly slap. No promise to jump you between classes. Safety, in turn, generated conditions for concentration. I felt within ten minutes what I had longed to feel at Stars for two years: These kids could do anything; they could go anywhere. In the classroom next to mine, an elderly black teacher taught math. She'd grown up in the Delta and liked KIPP's discipline. "Black teachers are harder on students," she said to me, "because we know life will be harder."

The wall was decorated with pendants representing the colleges that teachers had attended: Notre Dame, Colby, University of Arkansas, University of Michigan, Hendrix, Rhodes. The list went on. The colorful felt triangles pointed unanimously in one direction. Nor was the wall perfunctory: I overheard a pair of girls, both in the ninth grade, gazing upward and discussing the benefits of Hendrix, which "got small class size" and wasn't "too far from home."

Surreptitiously, I looked up the Spanish word for *boat* on my phone.

THE NEXT DAY, BEFORE PATRICK and I had even greeted each other, he handed me his assignment, as if to preempt my hostility or disappointment.

"Good, *you* did it," I said. My tone was more gentle. Why, I thought, *should* he care about homework? Homework had mattered to me—had been central to my childhood—because it was the only task my parents had really expected of me. For him, teachers at Stars didn't bother assigning homework, because they didn't expect students to do it. Come to think of it, I hadn't bothered to assign much, either. I bent my head down to examine his paper, asking absently, "How are you?"

It was a shock. The writing looked crazed. The blue ink was heavy and smeared. The cheap ballpoint pen I'd given him didn't help; pressed too hard, it leaked dollops of ink that blotted the page. The letters looked like jagged marks that happened to cross one another, scratching the page. They were arbitrarily sized and haltingly drawn.

I did not recognize his handwriting at all.

Hey cherry i know im not in your life it be my fault. it hurt me i aint there wit you. Here people be argurring about nothing tring my pasiens. Siting here doin nothing but how I messed up an thinking of you.

Love Youre Daddy

I tried to maintain an impassive look. Was it so bad? Yes, it was. Capitals, apostrophes, spelling . . . His English had never been this poor in my class. And beyond its errors, the message was no good for a child. It reminded the child that he, the father, was absent. It stated that he was at fault for the absence, raising the question of what he had done. It alluded not indiscreetly to his pain. This was not a letter that would make a child feel safe.

But wasn't it natural also for a father to want to apologize to his daughter? At least he was honest and loved her. Maybe the problem wasn't the letter itself but the fact that the letters were likely to repeat themselves: *I'm sorry; I wish I were there; I should be there for you but I'm not.* I had thought homework could help him escape from his feeling of failure, but it wasn't enough. We needed something that would help him step outside himself.

"I know there be all them mistakes," he said. "I get confused, Ms. Kuo."

In a casual tone I asked, "How long has it been since you've picked up a pencil?"

"I don't know. A couple years."

Where to start? I had no idea.

I leafed to the back page of a notebook that I had brought, pretending that I knew what I planned to write.

At the center of the page I wrote, GRAMMAR.

And below:

I'm   im

"See," I said. I pointed to *im*. "This is what you've been writing."

Patrick looked, the muscles on his face tensing in thought.

"Do you know what's wrong with this?"

He was silent.

"There are two little things—can you see?" I circled the *I* and the apostrophe.

Patrick nodded.

"What's the difference between your *I* and mine?"

"Yours be capitalized."

"Do you see how you wrote it?"

"Yes, ma'am."

"Can you make it right?"

"Yes, ma'am."

Patrick bent down. His hand was unused to the pen; he gripped it too hard.

He wrote:

I'm Patrick.

"Okay," I said. "Good job."

We worked all afternoon. As I put on my coat and scarf to leave, I said cheerfully, "Ready to do your homework for tomorrow?"

"Yes, ma'am," he said quickly.

Patrick's obedience made me sad, as if I had done something wrong. Who was I in his life—a person whose role it was to widen the world of things to be ashamed about?

"Look," I said, "let's make a deal. You keep doing your homework; I'll bring you those cigarettes you wanted."

At this Patrick lit up, astonished.

"Aw, for real, Ms. Kuo?"

I laughed. "For real."

"You do that for me?" Then, perhaps afraid I'd change my mind, he said, "Get me them Buglers."

"What? Where?"

Now it was his turn to laugh. "You ain't never smoke a ciga-rette, Ms. Kuo?"

"Not really."

"Like tobacco leaves, you know, you roll them. There's a place right next to the Dollar General. Before you get to the Walmart, where my house be. If you go past Walmart, you gone too far."

"Okay. I'll get them. And give them to you. When you do your homework." We smiled at each other.

PATRICK'S CENTRAL HIGH SCHOOL TRANSCRIPT was a white space interrupted by a lone column—F, F, F, D, D, F—that repre-sented, in total, one semester of high school.

I had wanted to see the transcript for myself, because he wouldn't tell me what his grades were. I'd trekked to the school secretary's office, thinking that perhaps he'd exaggerated and maybe even pulled off a B in his English class. Then I thought of all my other students. How, I wondered, had they fared? "Do you have the list of dropouts?" I asked the shrunken secretary, Ms. Smith. "For the year 2006?" This was the year I had left.

The printer was noisy and archaic—dot matrix, not laser. Its paper had perforated vertical ends, which as a kid in the eighties I tore off to form bracelets.

The document was titled STUDENT DROPOUT REPORT. But there was no report—just names. Because the sheets were at-tached to one another, the list unfolded like an accordion that extended to the floor. Unbelievable, really, that this list consti-tuted only a year of dropouts.

Name after name I recognized. Tamir, Miles, Kayla. Wil-liam, Stephanie. My stomach dropped, and I wanted to sit down. It was a shock. Who had lasted? Years ago, these names had been gathered in my grade book, in my handwriting. Now they were in cheap automated type.

Who is a person who changed your life?

Had I changed them? The paper in my hands told me no. My face was warm with shame.

Next to each name was a number that designated the reason for dropping out. Some had been designated as *moved;* others, *lack of attendance.* But the reasons were not correct. The list stated a number of students, including the girls who'd gotten pregnant, as *moved out of state.* Patrick was listed twice: *lack of attendance* (correct) and *moved out of state* (incorrect).

"It gets worse every year," Ms. Smith said in a raspy voice. "I just don't remember anybody dropping out thirty-five years ago. *Nobody* dropped out. You quaked in your boots if you got sent to the principal."

Ms. Smith explained the school procedure on absence. Each morning, teachers got a form where they marked a student's status as *P, T,* or *A:* present, tardy, or absent. Under state law, after ten consecutive days of being absent, the transformation was complete: A student officially became a dropout. Ms. Smith's office sent a memo indicating teachers could delete the student's name from their grade books.

"Who looks at this?" I asked.

"You."

It was terrifying. Students dropped out and that was it, game over. Nobody looked for you; nobody stopped you. Nor, it seemed, did people document, correctly, why you dropped out.

Ms. Smith showed me official reasons permitted for absences:

A doctor's note
An obituary or funeral program for a death in the
    family

A court document
Proof of incarceration
Suspension
School business
A parent note approved by principal

Students were allowed fourteen unexcused absences, she explained. This included parent notes, in addition to any other unexplained absences.

"What a joke. They're allowed *fourteen days* of parent notes—it doesn't matter what reason, what excuse. What are they really doing? Who knows. I think they just don't want to be here."

As if on cue, a mother and her teenage daughter came in. The mother looked sleepy—she was wearing pajamas. "We overslept," the mother said simply.

"You need a note," Ms. Smith said to the daughter, ignoring the mother.

The daughter rolled her eyes.

The mother asked for paper.

Ms. Smith handed her paper.

The mother asked for a pen.

Ms. Smith handed her a pen.

The mother scrawled something and left. The daughter went to class.

Ms. Smith gestured at the clock meaningfully—the school day was nearly half over.

I said, "So if Patrick's parents had written parent notes for those fourteen days, he could have come back to school?"

"Exactly."

I looked stricken, which gratified her.

But we were thinking different things: Whereas Ms. Smith

thought it was ludicrous that Patrick could come back, I thought it was ludicrous that his parents hadn't tried to write a note to get him back in.

Helena employed one person whose job was to contact families and inform them that their child was a truant. But it would have made little difference for Patrick: Everybody in his family knew he'd stopped going.

"LORD ALMIGHTY, IT'S Ms. KUO!" said Ms. Riley as she gave me a hug.

Now that Stars was shut down, she was in charge of ISS—"in-school suspension," all-day detention—at Central. It had been tough to find her: The ISS room was isolated on the other side of a hill, like a hermitage. Ms. Riley was playing a computer game at her desk. The bell had just rung and her students had disappeared.

She motioned for us to go outside and I followed her to her car, so that she could smoke.

"Ms. Kuo," she said, lighting a cigarette and getting straight to the point, "Stars be gone to the dogs. It be worse than a doghouse. They threw everything to the curb, all the new good books you ordered—they just threw it away. Or they left it down there like they was nothing. They just so *wasteful*."

I thought of my students' graffiti inside the covers, how they wanted other kids to know they'd read the books.

"I miss our children," she said.

"What happened to them? It seems like most of them dropped out when they got here."

"This place is a joke. Central is a joke. The teachers are intimidated by the kids, so they don't teach anything. Kids be hollering, howling. I could just cry seeing them, pants hanging down by their butts. When they're outside"—she gestured to the campus—"nobody keeps them or watches them, no teachers or nothing."

Ms. Riley's new tone of bleakness disoriented me. At Stars she had greeted me daily by saying, "God is good, God is good." At Stars she had wielded real power. Incoming teachers like me looked up to her; students behaved for her. What she lacked in teaching certification, she'd made up for in moral authority. Now she'd been exiled along with the students. She was trying to build a fort on quicksand.

"I tell them, 'Don't come in here with no foolishness.' You know me, Ms. Kuo. I got my gospel music, I got my Bible on my desk, I say to the kids, 'Better shut up and hush.' But that village is down; they killed it. Where is that village, where is that village? Ms. Kuo, I remember when I was growing up, you could sleep with your windows up all day *long*—I don't care how low on the ground they were. You could leave food on our stove and say, *Hey, neighbor, hey, Mary, hey, Joanne, I left my neck bone on the stove and got to run off to the store and get some potatoes.* She'd say, *Okay, I got you.* And I tell you, Ms. Kuo—*your food wouldn't burn. Your food wouldn't burn.* That's how close people were."

I told her I'd gone to see Patrick.

"The devil got him, Ms. Kuo," she said. "Once the devil gets you, he don't let go."

She threw away her cigarette. "The things that are happening with our people, the devil just seem to have all the control, all the control."

THE TOBACCO STORE WAS A drive-in, my first. "Buglers?" I asked, unsure if I'd gotten the name right. The woman at the window grinned, showing a gold tooth; when she turned to get the tobacco, her dice earrings rattled. The package was baby blue, with a pretty logo of a man with a trumpet.

The next morning Patrick greeted me enthusiastically. "I did my homework."

"Two days in a row!" I said. "That's great." On cue, I began to scrounge around my bag, signaling that I'd brought his tobacco and made good on my end of the deal. Patrick poked his head out into the hallway, checking for guards. He nodded.

I passed him the package and he deftly made it disappear. The stealth of our exchange and the way he stowed the package inside the folds of his jumpsuit made me distrust him for a second.

From my bag, I retrieved a book: *The Lion, the Witch and the Wardrobe*. "I read this again over the weekend," I said. "It's so good that I almost started crying at the end."

"You, Ms. Kuo?" he said. "Crying?" He shook his head, smiling at the idea.

I handed him the book.

It was a light paperback, but Patrick reached for it with both hands, as if I were handing him something heavy and fragile.

He bent down, examining the colorful illustration on the cover. I was nervous that he'd be offended it was a children's book. Yet he seemed curious. Perhaps he was thinking about his daughter or his own childhood; I didn't know. He traced the illustration's outlines with his fingertips.

"What do you see?"

He stared for a long time. "I see two little girls. Look like they dancing with the lion."

"What does the lion look like to you?"

Patrick hesitated.

"There's no right answer, you know," I said.

"Like a beast, but they having fun in a field. It look like a sunset."

I nodded and then pointed to the page for him to start. Patrick read:

"To Lucy Barfield"

"Who do you think Lucy might be?" I asked.

Patrick looked hard at the words, as if the answer would appear if he stared long enough. He got agitated. "I don't know, Ms. Kuo. I don't know about *none* of this."

"Hey," I said. "My bad, I didn't explain. You're not *supposed* to know. We're just guessing."

In his panic, he didn't seem to hear me.

"My dear Lucy," I began, ignoring him. "Now you read."

My heart pounded. I was afraid he'd refuse to continue. He cleared his throat.

"I wrote this story for you, but when I began it I had not realized that girls grow quicker than books." He continued until he reached the signature: *"Your affectionate Godfather, C. S. Lewis."*

Patrick's reading was awkward. His words rushed together in a flow barely impeded by punctuation.

I asked, "So who do you think Lucy is?"

Patrick leafed to the front cover, checking the name. "It be *his* goddaughter."

"Yes." I nodded emphatically. "That's exactly right."

"So he wrote this for her?" he asked. "Like a gift?"

"Yes. Like a gift."

And then we began to read.

"Once there were four children whose names were Peter, Susan, Edmund and Lucy," I started. *"This story is about . . ."*

The room was just big enough for our purposes, with one table and two chairs. We sat facing each other, each with our own book, and took turns reading aloud. ("See here?" I said.

"This is where the *paragraph* begins. And where the chunk of words ends—see that space?—that's where the *paragraph* ends.") When it was my turn to read, he relaxed, his finger following the words as I spoke, as if assuring himself that each word were properly tended. And as I approached the final sentence of my paragraph, his shoulders stiffened; his turn was coming.

"'*This must be a simply enormous wardrobe!' thought Lucy, going still further in and pushing the soft folds of the coats aside to make room. . . . But instead of feeling the hard, smooth wood of the floor of the wardrobe, she felt something soft and powdery and extremely cold.*"

"Have you seen snow?" I asked. He said he didn't think so.

"Well, you're about to," I said cheerfully. At this Patrick looked perplexed but encouraged.

JAILERS MOVED PATRICK FROM CELL to cell without warning, and I didn't want his homework papers to be scattered, so I had decided that a single composition notebook would be the repository for all his work. Assignments included vocabulary (sentences), a lesson from the day (say, on apostrophes), journaling, and responses to the reading. The reading questions were sometimes specific: *Why do you think the creatures tortured Aslan?* And sometimes open: *Write a letter to Lucy from Edmund.* The journaling was mostly open—observations, for instance, about jail: *What is one thing you've noticed about jail?*

Patrick's homework made me happy and filled my days. Part of it was, of course, teacherly satisfaction: He was being useful; he was doing something with himself. What teacher wouldn't be pleased with his quick grasp of irony: *It is ironic to know Calvin comes back to jail after being released a week earlier.* It takes discipline and patience to use one's mind, and here was tangible proof of both. Part of it, too, was my writerly sadism, which I had always inflicted on others who sent writing my way: I regarded my brutal editing as a sign of care. And so I thrashed through his words, circled errors, barked orders. I battered the page so thoroughly that sometimes it was difficult to see what he had originally written. Sometimes I shouted. (*APOSTROPHE!*) Every forgotten comma was noted (I circled the space where the comma should be and wrote, *What's missing?*), every run-on sentence was marked (*Where should this sentence end?*). If a pattern of mistake emerged—*crying* spelled as *cring*, *trying* as *tring*—I assigned extra homework to eliminate future mistakes. I also tried my best to take note of what he was doing right. If he used *their* correctly, as opposed to *there* or *they're*, I wrote, *Good job, that's the right one!*

The task of correction gave me a peculiar but necessary distance from him and a semblance of control in a situation where I had little. He would write, for instance, a sentence for the word *sunder*. *To sunder me and my family is like cutting my life short.* I drew a smiley face next to the sentence and responded, with the emotional deafness of a robot, *Perfect use of* sunder. *Yes, jail has sundered you and your family.* For the word *profane*, he wrote, *People in jail talk crazy and are profane to each other even elderly folks.* Wanting to repeat the usage of the vocabulary word, I wrote idiotically: *Yes, it's unfortunate that they are profane.* Or he wrote, *It would be figurative if I say I'm dead in jail.* I responded: *Wonderful use of* figurative.

Perhaps this is how all writerly beginnings work: with a focus on mechanics, with the enactment of distance. But there was also a merciless honesty in my corrections. Because Patrick worked quickly to stamp out old errors, I told myself that he craved my corrections in a way that certain people, seeking guidance, trust only that which is most savagely dispensed. For me and perhaps for him, the task of making a sentence perfect had the effect of containment: It kept unbearable emotions at bay.

And, in fact, Patrick was learning with a ferocity I did not remember from the first time around. To keep up with his pace, my visits went from once to twice a week. I instituted Friday quizzes on vocabulary and bought him a pack of index cards. Within a month he would exhaust the supply. He had no rubber band, so the cards were always tumbling out of his notebook or forming a thicket in his hand.

The cigarettes had given Patrick new cachet; he traded them, it appeared, for candy and chips. Often he had some kind of junk food for me. "Here," he'd say casually. A jumbo-sized Snickers bar would appear suddenly from his jumpsuit, in his outstretched palm.

"How are you?" I asked one Monday morning.

"Ain't nothing going on here," he said. "Just drama. What'd *you* do this weekend, Ms. Kuo?"

"I cooked a bean soup with Danny and Lucy," I said casually. "Then we saw a movie."

He was silent, his hand on his chin, as if I'd said something very philosophical.

"How does that sound to you?" I asked brightly.

He said, "Lovely."

Then he said, "They married?"

"Yes."

"Ms. Kuo," Patrick said, "you got a boyfriend?"

I felt an immediate discomfort. To receive male attention is a universal horror for young female teachers in secondary school. On the other hand, I thought, I asked him about his personal life; why couldn't he ask me about mine?

"Yes," I said.

This was a lie.

"What he do?"

I ignored him. "Hey, why don't you start some silent reading while I check your homework."

He returned to his book and I tried to hide my distress. I was just being paranoid, I thought.

I looked at his homework. I had written, *What is the best part of your day?*

In his handwriting: *Thinking back when you ask me whats the best part of my day. I must admit it is when I see your face. Here in Jail theres nothing really going on outside of negativity. When you say yea, I feel you sound very sexy.*

I felt queasy. Why did he have to go and ruin the exercise like this? I felt a rush of nostalgia for my female students. They'd written about boys, breakups, feeling ugly, unrequited love, single moms, hope, flowers, candles. With them I never had to engage in the fearful, self-inspecting review: Was my blouse modest, my skirt long enough? Instinctively now I glanced at my clothes: baggy pants, baggy sweater, muddy sneakers, hair pulled back—yes, I looked like my usual unkempt, androgynous self who caused my poor mother despair. No, I had not encouraged him.

But for the past three years, since dropping out, he had wandered around Helena without any institutional contact and forgotten all its rules. I looked young, I was a woman, and he was surrounded by men. I visited him; I showed compassion.

So why was I mad? Because of what I had to do now: make boundaries clear.

"Patrick."

He looked up from his book.

"This is not okay. It's *inappropriate*." I pointed to the last line of his writing.

My tone surprised me—there it was, the teacher's tone still intact, an affect of no-nonsense irritation.

Patrick looked down. My frankness had humiliated him. He didn't want me to think that he was like creepy Mr. Cousins or shameless Shawn or his trashy jail mates. So much of jail seemed to involve convincing yourself that you were different from those around you.

"Sorry, Ms. Kuo. I ain't mean no disrespect. Really, my mind ain't be clear here, you know. Things be crazy here, jail mates be—" He stopped.

So this was why I was angry, too: Patrick had lowered himself, not knowing any better, and I had caused this lowering by showing up in his life.

"I'm your *teacher*," I said.

Officiously, I pointed to his book, even though he had been reading it dutifully and I had been the one to interrupt.

He never crossed that boundary again.

PATRICK'S HOUSE WAS ON A corner and it had a porch. This was the sum of what I remembered from three years before. I peered out the window into the bright sun, searching for something that would trigger my memory. When I reached a stand of leafy poplars, I doubled back, with the strange feeling that this had all happened before.

Patrick had asked me to pick up cigarettes from his family. It would save me some money, he'd said. This also gave me a chance to talk to his parents. I thought they should know a teacher had started visiting their son in jail. Maybe I could offer them some help. And I was curious about how they made sense of the night of the killing. The only thing Patrick had really told me about his family on that night was that, from the police car, he had seen his mother crying on the porch.

The house I suspected to be Patrick's was small, square, and one story tall. I looked for a doorbell. Finding none, I opened the screen and knocked lightly. I waited. Looking up, I saw that the porch ceiling was very low, a cobweb within arm's reach. A baby magnolia had littered seedpods and leaves across the yard.

The door creaked open. At first, it was as if a ghost had opened the door. I saw only the dark inside. Then I lowered my head and saw a toddler with a head of bountiful curls. Our eyes met. Losing interest, he waddled soundlessly back into the shadows of the house.

Now the dark room lay in view. Yes, this was the right house.

I took a tentative step inside. I put my hand above my eyes so I could see more clearly. The boy had returned to the couch and was poking at something—a man, Patrick's father, I thought. Though supine, he was awake.

His body and face were gaunt. His right leg was disfigured, twig-like.

I introduced myself, still standing. I said I used to be a teacher of Patrick's and that I was reading with him in jail.

"Oh, yeah, yeah. Pat tell me you been visiting him; that's good, that's good."

"I've been giving him homework—helping him keep his mind active," I said.

"Yeah, yeah." His eyes flicked back to the program he was watching.

I cleared my throat. "Patrick—Pat—told me you had some cigarettes to give to me."

Now he looked up, as if seeing me for the first time, and

started to rummage behind the couch. Wordlessly, he passed me the same brand of Buglers that I usually picked up for Patrick.

"He likes this kind," I said, trying to make conversation. Then: "I went to see Rob," I continued, wondering whether it was rude to sit down when he hadn't asked me to. Probably. I stayed standing.

"Who?"

"Patrick's—Pat's lawyer."

"Oh, yeah, yeah." He nodded. "When his court date be?"

Mentioning Rob, I realized, was my way to justify being in his house—he didn't seem to care that I was teaching Patrick, so I offered myself as an intermediary between Rob and the family instead. They had never contacted one another.

"It was supposed to be December," I said. "But it's been postponed until February."

He did not sigh or grimace but seemed used to the vicissitudes of court dates.

I inched closer now and stuck out my hand.

"Ms. Kuo; you can call me Michelle," I said.

"James," he said. "And this be Jamaal, my grandboy." James gestured to the little boy, the son of Patrick's eldest sister. Now he finally motioned for me to sit.

"Were you born here?" I asked.

"Born and raised. Mary, too." Mary must have been Patrick's mother.

"Your mom and dad also from here?"

They were. Were they still around?

"Naw."

"They died—they died here?"

"Yeah."

He took out a cigarette.

After his mother died, he said, as he lit his cigarette, he was sent to his father's place across town. But his dad didn't want him, and he spent his time on the streets. He was kicked out of school in the eighth grade; he thought it was a miracle he'd lasted that long. "I think they tolerated me for as long as they did *because* of my handicap." He pointed to his disfigured leg—polio. (At this I must have had a look of pity on my face, for he then said, "It never affected my trigger finger." He hit his hand on his knee, laughing at his joke. "Just playing.")

"Could you tell me . . ." I hesitated. "Could you tell me what happened the night of the . . . the killing?"

At this he sat up.

"Okay, I hear arguing," he said. "I hear Pat say, 'Get out of my yard, get out of my yard.' I got up to go to the door. That boy Marcus reached in his pocket"—he mimed reaching for his pocket—"kept reaching for something. When I get out the door, Pat was coming in. He say, 'Dad, I had to do it; dude be trying to jump on me.' I said, 'Do what, what you do?' I looked out the door again. Guy had gone up and fell beside the hedge. He was walking out the yard and he done fell out and rolled." A sister called the ambulance. "By the time they got here, boy was dead."

I asked where Pam had been. "She went to a party the guy be at. They was having a get-together in an apartment building over there. We didn't know then. But the woman there *knew* my daughter supposed to be at home." It was a Tuesday night, he continued—a school night.

He lowered his voice, even though no one was home besides Jamaal. "My daughter, she a little slow. That's her nature, she like kids. Her older sister—I mean, her twin—she been *quit* playing with them. But Pam still playing. She play with a lot of *little* kids. You know what I'm saying. You could leave your kids with her; she'd keep 'em all day. She'll talk to anyone. She's eighteen but she act childish."

James lit another cigarette. "But after all that went down" with Patrick, "she just stopped doing it. After school she didn't want to go nowhere. She didn't want to play with no kids. It wasn't like her." He inhaled. "It was a lot going up to see her brother. He was telling her, *It ain't your fault, stay in school,* stuff like that. He real protective of his sisters, especially her—he worry about Pam a lot more than he do the other sisters."

He tapped his cigarette, ash falling. "On just a normal day ain't *no* way in the world he would've done that. He didn't go around fighting people. Never had no trouble like that out of him." He inhaled again, thinking.

I had hoped Patrick's father would help me make sense of the crime, but he seemed bewildered, as well.

"I think him and the guy got into it before. What I heard, Pat backed down from the fight then. Guy had hit him in the face with a shoe, guy tried to make him fight. So maybe Pam being his favorite sister, she the one he look out for the most . . ." His voice trailed off. "Maybe, to see that guy with her that night, maybe he thought the guy was trying to get over on him by getting with his sister in some kind of way."

I didn't know that Marcus and Patrick had known each other. If his dad's speculation was true, maybe Patrick had snapped when he saw Marcus hanging out with his little sister and, blaming himself, overreacted. And maybe he'd also felt he needed to prove he could hold his own.

"How's his mother doing?" I asked. "I know Patrick loves her a lot."

"He crazy about his mama."

"Patrick says he doesn't like to call her, because it upsets her."

"It do kind of upset her when he talk to her. I'm glad she work on the weekends, 'cause then she don't have to go up there and see him. One weekend she didn't have to work, we went up together. She cry a lot. She even go to crying when she talk to him on the phone." He tapped his cigarette again. "Truth is, I think she feel bad because she told him to go and look for his sister. I think she hate she had said that. It do weigh on her."

Meanwhile, Jamaal had wandered to the front door, ready to step out. "Stop it, J-ball!" James yelled. Jamaal turned to look at us, returned. His grandfather opened his arms to the boy, bounced him up on his lap.

"Me," he continued, "I was going up there every weekend the first year, you know, when he first was locked up. Then he told me I didn't need to. Matter of fact, I don't think he wanted me to go up there too much."

"Why?"

"I don't know. Maybe he don't want me to see him locked up. He call, I send him things when he need it. Soap, stuff like that. You know."

Now he released Jamaal from his lap.

"I wasn't good to be around, you know, when he was growing up. I don't know what my son saw—'cause, you know, I kept him with me a lot. We went to a lot of places together. I don't know if he really remember. He was like three or four years old. He might have saw me doing some stuff that I don't want him to see. Kids remember things you think they don't."

"Like what?" I asked.

Now his father looked me squarely in the eye, as if he suspected I was playing stupid. But in truth, I had no idea what he was talking about.

"I don't want to get into that," he said decisively. He bent his head down to light the next cigarette, then stopped. "My younger days, I spent time locked up. Drugs. I wasn't around for some years. When I went in, I went as a certain type of person. You know. I didn't care. I didn't care if I went to jail or not. I didn't want to go, but it wasn't like it was a big deal for me.

"What went down . . ." He made a sound. "I wish I could take his place. I know this all new to him. It's hard for people that feel for others the way he feel to be locked up like that, away from family. Me, I'm not a very emotional man. I think I lost my emotions a long time ago."

Now James held his unlit cigarette, the lighter still burning. He was thinking. "I just want my son to be . . . to not think of me as wrong as I was. In a lot of ways I wish I could have been better. I don't know. If I went to school, I could've gotten a job, even with my handicap. I don't know." Now he inhaled. "Like I said, he was a good kid. A lot better than me." He repeated, "A lot better than me."

I STARTED TO GO TO the jail everyday.

"*Deplorable.*"

"Is it wicked?"

"Yep. Example?"

"Jail be a *deplorable* place."

"Perfect." I nodded briskly. "*Inquisitive.*"

"Lucy," he said immediately. "Because she be curious, looking inside the closet."

"One more."

"Cherish. How she be looking at everything, touching everything, like she want to know what it be."

"*Sarcastic.*"

"If Ms. Kuo ask me how was my day yesterday, and I say, *Great.*" His tone suddenly became exaggerated, imitating bitterness.

"Awesome," I replied. "And we're done. Let's see how you did. How do you think you did?"

"Probably missed a couple," he said casually.

"Better than that," I said. "That's an A in Ms. Kuo's personalized school."

Then we opened up *The Lion, the Witch and the Wardrobe* and started to read.

IN THE SNOWY PLACE LUCY had come upon, she met the Faun. The Faun was half-man, half-goat. The Faun was so surprised to see a little girl that he dropped the parcels he was carrying.

"'Delighted, delighted,' it went on. 'Allow me to introduce myself. My name is Tumnus.'

"'I am very pleased to meet you, Mr. Tumnus,' said Lucy."

At this Patrick laughed. "He a *goat* but she calling him *Mister.*" I laughed, too.

It was cold outside and Mr. Tumnus invited Lucy to tea. He told her she was in Narnia. *"Lucy thought she had never been in a nicer place,"* Patrick read. His voice adopted a strange, singsong tone, exaggerating certain words, as if he was imitating someone he had once heard reading aloud—perhaps me.

Patrick continued, reading about how they ate *"buttered toast, and then toast with honey, and then a sugar-topped cake."*

He stopped at *cake* and I gave him a look; we were both hungry.

Then the Faun's brown eyes filled with tears. They trickled down his cheeks and soon were dribbling off the end of his nose.

"'Mr. Tumnus! Mr. Tumnus!' said Lucy in great distress. 'Don't! Don't! What is the matter? Aren't you well? Dear Mr. Tumnus, do tell me what is wrong.' But the Faun continued sobbing as if its heart

would break. And even when Lucy went over and put her arms round him and lent him her handkerchief, he did not stop—"

"*Sobbing* mean crying, don't it?" Patrick interrupted. I said that was exactly right.

Patrick leaned his head toward the page. He was studying the illustration of the Faun, who laid his head in his hands and slumped back in his chair, with his tail in a loop on the floor.

"That him crying, ain't it?" Patrick said. "That the Faun."

I said it was.

Then Patrick resumed reading.

The Faun confessed to Lucy: He was a kidnapper for the White Witch. The Witch, he explained, was the reason it was always winter in Narnia.

"'*Always winter and never Christmas,*'" Patrick read, his tone as forlorn as that of a self-loathing faun.

The Witch had threatened the Faun. If he didn't obey her, she would cut off his tail, saw off his horns, and pluck out his beard.

Patrick read, "'*And if she is extra and specially angry she'll turn me into stone and I shall be only a statue of a Faun in her horrible house.*'"

He gave his head a baleful shake.

"It's awful, isn't it?" I said. We grimaced in unison. "What do you think he'll do with Lucy?"

"I think . . ." His fingers touched his chin. "I think he be letting her go."

"Why?"

"Because he a good man. Or goat. Or whatever he is. And he crying. He want to do the right thing."

Patrick read on and saw that the Faun did indeed let Lucy go. "'*Then be off home as quick as you can,*' said the Faun, '*and— c-can you ever forgive me for what I meant to do?*'

"*'Why, of course I can,' said Lucy, shaking him heartily by the hand.*"

Patrick, now deeply absorbed, pressed on.

The Faun asked Lucy whether he could keep the handkerchief that she had lent him. She told him yes. And there the chapter ended.

"Your prediction came true," I said.

He glowed, then looked away.

"Why do you think the Faun wanted the handkerchief?"

"Because he know she special," he said. "So he want to remember her." His fingers tapped his chin in thought. "And I think . . . I think he know he did the right thing, letting her go like that. So the *handkerchief*"—he said the word slowly, so as to not stumble over it—"it be like a good memory."

I WENT HOME ECSTATIC. I barely noticed the rain as I drove. A book: Of course this was what came first. Not just any book but a magical book, where the heroes were children, and children on the side of good. In the damp cold jail a book could be a fantasy, a refuge, a separate place.

Patrick continued to gain momentum. For homework, I'd asked him to choose one child from the book whose feelings he related to. It had not occurred to me that Patrick would see himself in Edmund, who betrays his siblings and gets tricked by the Witch. I had imagined he was more like Lucy, who was on a journey, or Peter, who was the eldest and protected everyone.

Lewis had written, *Edmund felt a sensation of mysterious horror.* Patrick wrote:

Every since I had my terrible incedent. Some days I wake up hating to be in Jail. Hopeing it was really a dream to began

*with. Although it was'nt then, as soon as I try to forget or look
around being here. Once I dreamed my mother was sick or had
died. When I awaken the sense was so devastating. My mind
wouldnt let me call home an check right off. Those are a couple
of reasons I chose Edmund.*

Patrick had clearly labored over each letter. Each period was
a circle that he'd carefully closed. Difficult words were correctly
spelled: *awaken, devastating, reasons*. He must have taken the time
to use the dictionary I gave him.

Patrick watched me as I read his work. "It's probably pretty
lousy, because my head was hurting."

I said, "It's not lousy. It's good."

I would correct the apostrophes later.

"I saw your sisters yesterday afternoon," I said, changing the
subject to a more pleasant topic.

Patrick jolted up, excited.

I had started, on a regular basis, to pick up cigarettes from
his house rather than buying them. This time, all three of his
sisters had been home, the picture of pleasing domesticity. The
eldest sister, Willa—this was Jamaal's mother—was attempting
to read some kind of textbook as Jamaal grabbed her hair. She
was taking a class at the community college. Patrick's father and
Pam both seized Jamaal, trying to hold him back, as they competed for his affection. The worn-down couch sank under the
weight of their struggles. Kiera had just woken up, having
napped after a long night shift at the retirement home, where
she worked with her mother.

"Pam be okay?" he said, asking about her first.

"She seems really nice."

At this Patrick grunted. "She *too* nice. People always be trying to put their kids on her, but they don't pay her. These *grown*

people, they already got babies and they trying to put their babies on her. They take advantage 'cause they see she got a good heart. I try to tell her, 'People will use you, they ain't your real friends.' I don't know if she know or if she don't care. That's how she is."

"Pam is very trusting," I agreed. "She and Kiera told me to tell you they're hoping to see you soon."

This was the wrong thing to say. Patrick flinched and brusquely waved his hand in the air. Did he know they'd put off visiting him because coming was too hard? Or did his wave mean that he already understood and forgave them?

Patrick fingered the cover of the book.

"*Narnia,*" Patrick said. "That a real place?"

"Oh," I said, surprised. "I wish it were."

I shook my head to indicate I was sorry that Narnia wasn't real.

"But, Ms. Kuo," he said. His brows, insistent, were ridged with concern. "It got a map right here."

Patrick opened the book, expertly creasing back the spine. He pushed into my view a map of Narnia, its borders designated by hand-drawn lines. "And that a *compass,*" he said, gesturing to the star in the corner. It was apparent that he had already studied the map in earnest.

"I'm guessing the author drew the map, too."

He seemed less disappointed than baffled. "So he made this all up?" He was thinking aloud and didn't appear to expect an answer. Then his face lit up. "Maybe Narnia be like that place he from—where you say he from?"

"England."

"Yeah. Maybe Narnia be like *that.*"

"That's possible," I said. "Though I don't think there are half-men, half-goats there."

At this Patrick gave a little chuckle.

"Ms. Kuo," he said. Distracted, he held his fingers on his chin. "A man once told me you can do one thing that could change the rest of your life. Man locked up in cell *next to me*. He told me that *right in front of my house*."

The man's duplicated proximity to Patrick startled him, as if converting the man's words to prophecy.

"Do you think that one day is going to change the rest of your life?"

"It have already."

"How is it?" I asked finally, hesitant to interrupt him.

"Great."

I had started to carve out time where I just let him read. "Like silent reading," I said, hoping he remembered. While he read, I corrected his homework, but usually I finished before him.

"Which part are you on?"

"Part where the stone table cracked."

"You like that part?"

"Yeah, where they be battling, Edmund and Peter. First they fighting with the Witch, and Edmund's the one that kept them going."

"What do you like about it?"

"Edmund," he said, without hesitating. "He be real smart. He just a young boy, you know. The Witch started turning him into stone and he thought to knock the wand out of her hand when everybody was doing something else. And Edmund be on the *Witch's* side at first."

"Why do you think he was on her side?"

"He be fooled by the Witch. I believe he went along because

he was alone. And because he took that Turkish Delight. And because he wanted to be a king. He be mad at his siblings because they gave him the cold shoulder, wouldn't listen to him."

"How do you think he changed?"

"He became"—here Patrick struggled to find the words he wanted—"a lot *stronger* and *wiser*."

I WAS THERE WHEN HE finished the book. From the corner of my eye I saw him reach the last paragraph, his pinkie finger tracing the words. Disbelieving, he turned the page: It was blank. He turned the book again to the back cover, as if the book were playing a trick on him, as if books did not truly have endings. Then he leafed backward, looking for a chapter he wanted to read again. He continued to read for a bit longer.

Later, I would draw an upward-sloping line. "This is how a story is structured," I would say. "What is the rising action?"

He wrote, *He abandoned his siblings with the beavers and betrayed them for the witch.*

"What goes at the peak?"

He wrote, *Edmund been forgiven and granted a sword.*

I HAD THOUGHT I WAS choosing a fantasy into which Patrick could retreat. But Narnia was real to him. What made the story fantastical for Patrick was that Edmund was able to change.

7

He Wishes for the Cloths of Heaven

> *Deep autumn—*
> *My neighbor*
> *How does he live, I wonder.*
> —Basho

> *New Year's Day—*
> *everything is in blossom!*
> *I feel about average.*
> —Issa

Haiku: This was how my college poetry professor, the poet Jorie Graham, had begun our semester. The essentials of poetry, she insisted, were contained in the three-line form. On the board she wrote one translation: *Sick on a journey / my dreams wander / the withered fields.* Then another: *Sick on a journey / over parched fields / dreams wander on.*

She asked how they were different. I had no idea.

Then she erased the second version—which, without explanation, she said she didn't like—and kept writing, her back turned to us. *Another year gone / hat in hand / sandals on our feet.* And then another. A small eternity passed as the three-line poems proliferated on the board. Our homework, she said, was to choose a few—she was never too specific in her instructions— and rearrange each one ten times.

Back at my dorm, I tried various permutations, each worse than the next. I tried: *I wonder how he lives / My neighbor / In deep autumn.* Then: *In deep autumn / I do not know how / My neighbor lives.* Was this any different? Better or worse? Probably worse. I was not a natural, but something did happen to me as I scratched through the assignment, hating my bad drafts. I had slowed down and focused on just a handful of words. The original text, which initially appeared like something I might have written myself, now seemed untouchable, invulnerable to correction.

Did Patrick know that poems like this existed? We had just finished *The Lion, the Witch and the Wardrobe*, and I didn't know what to teach next. These little poems seemed just right. They were too short to intimidate. Periods and commas appeared optional. Just one or two images; just one or two senses; just one surprise. They could be rewritten in infinite ways. Or, as I learned, they resisted being rewritten. Reading these, there was less potential to feel that one's response was wrong and more opportunity simply to respond.

READING HAIKUS SILENTLY THE NEXT day, Patrick laughed.

"What's funny?" I asked.

> *Don't worry, spiders,*
> *I keep house*
> *Casually.*

"Spider busy, not bothering anybody," he said. "I can relate to that, you know."

I gave him the whole book of haikus and told him to take his time flipping through them on his own. "Mark the ones you like," I said. "There are more than a hundred, so take your time."

Minutes passed. I waited. I occupied myself with an anthology of poetry, marking poems I wanted to read with him.

"Which one's your favorite?" I asked finally.

He studied the poems, comparing them. Then he pointed at this haiku:

> *Blossoms at night,*
> *and the faces of people*
> *moved by music.*

"Probably this one," he said.

That one body of words moved him more distinctly than another—this seemed vital. But why had he chosen it?

"I like that one, too. What do you like about it?"

"That it be real." He shrugged to indicate he was done talking.

"Okay," I said. "What else do you like?"

Patrick chose this:

> *Napped half the day;*
> *No one*
> *punished me!*

"Why do you like this one?" I asked.

"'Cause it be true. I sleep all day here and don't nothing get said about it. Don't nobody punish me for doing *nothing*."

I asked if he meant at home or in jail, and he said both.

Then he pointed to another poem and said, "I like this one, too."

> *The world of dew*
> *Is the world of dew*
> *And yet—and yet*

I said, "That's a good one. He wrote that after his son died."

He nodded—that appeared to make sense to him.

"What kind of feeling do you get reading it?"

Patrick gazed at the page intently. Then he said, "Feeling of accepting. It is what it is."

Now he leaned forward and asked suddenly, "Is it raining, Ms. Kuo?"

I wondered if the dew in the poem had reminded him of rain.

I said it had been raining when I came in. He nodded soberly, as if I'd said something serious about God or politics.

"Man. I miss the rain. I can't tell when it rain. I thought it be raining today. I was gonna ask you if it really raining or a shower from another cell."

"You're never sure?"

"Naw."

The rain now made me remember something I meant to show him. "Oh," I began. "I met this nice old white dude named Douglas."

Patrick guffawed and covered his face. "Ms. Kuo say *old white dude*," he said to himself.

I laughed, too. "What's so funny?"

I had met Douglas a few weeks ago, I said. The man knew every tree in Helena. Patrick's shoulders had loosened. "You like them trees, Ms. Kuo?"

I didn't know much about trees, but I did love the ginkgo. When I'd told Douglas that, he lit up. The ginkgo! He liked the ginkgo, too. It was an old tree, here since the day of Adam and Eve. Its bloom was very short, only a week. A few days after that conversation, I found a bag of tomatoes holding down a piece of paper on my windshield: It was a map of downtown Helena, with an *X* to mark the last blooming ginkgo tree.

"When I saw the tree," I said, "I wished you could see it, too."

I said that a poem has *images*, a fancy word for what he already knew all about: a picture of something that we could see or hear or feel or touch.

He got the hang of it quickly. "What are the *images* here?" I'd ask, pointing.

"*Blossoms*, because you can see them; *music*, because you can hear it."

"What about this one?"

"*Dew*, because you can touch it and smell it," he said, then added after a second, "And sometime see it."

We went through more. Words I normally took for granted were for Patrick a labor of imagination—some described things he had never encountered. "*Mountain*," he read. "I ain't never really seen a mountain, to be honest."

"What about an *ocean*?" I asked.

He wrinkled his eyebrows, a great groove now bisecting his forehead. "Maybe," he said finally, honestly.

"Last poem for the day," I said. "It uses a vocabulary word, *fleeting*. I'm going to tell you how *fleeting* is used and you guess what it means. Ready? Okay. Let's say you hear the sound of a bird but only for a second. Or let's say you have a dream about Cherish at night but it disappears as soon as you have it. We say that the sound is *fleeting*, the dream is *fleeting*. Now, what do you think *fleeting* means?"

Patrick thought. "Brief?" he asked. "Passing by?"

I nodded and then put my hand in my pocket. "Can you guess what's in my hand? Just guess," I urged.

"Some candy?" he asked.

I gave Patrick a golden ginkgo leaf. He ran his fingertip along its veins and then twirled the leaf in his hands, like a make-shift pinwheel.

"This bright gold that you see doesn't last long on the tree. After the leaves turn gold, they'll fall within a week or two. Like, you could say the color blooms in a *fleeting* way, or *fleetingly*." Patrick was still studying the leaf, not listening to me.

"What do you think?" I asked.

"It got some sun in it."

I wasn't sure what Patrick meant by this—whether he meant it was golden, like streaks or spots of sun, or whether he meant it had literally been shone on. So I said, "That's very poetic," and he smiled.

"Okay, last poem for the day," I said again. "Why don't you read it aloud?"

> *How admirable!*
> *to see lightning and not think*
> *life is fleeting.*

"*Lightning*," Patrick said, surprised by the word. "I forgot about lightning."

"What other images," I asked, "could Basho have used?"

Patrick was thinking. "The sunset," he answered. I hadn't heard him use the word since we looked at the cover of *The Lion*, *the Witch and the Wardrobe.* "Because it happen so fast. You *look*, then it *gone*. But it be different than lightning. Because you never know when lightning be striking. But the sunset always come; you always know your day gonna end."

"Which is sadder?"

"The sunset," he said definitively.

Years later, I still associate the ginkgo leaf with sunset.

FOR THAT SUNDAY'S GROCERY SHOPPING, I settled on Food Giant. Walmart was bigger, but I had just gone for a run and was sweating, in shorts and sneakers. I didn't want to see anyone I knew, especially people coming back from church in their fancy hats and floral dresses.

As I picked through Food Giant's yellowing spinach and molding blueberries, I sensed a man staring at me. He was white, middle-aged, well dressed—nobody I knew. Being Asian in the Delta meant getting stared at, so I ignored him.

Now the stranger approached. A woman and man accompanied him, forming a small circle around me that blocked my access to the tomatoes.

"Weren't you in that movie about Helena?" the stranger asked, referring to Richard Wormser's documentary. "I used that in a workshop," he said, "and I got hell for it.

"But it was a striking movie," he continued, "and you were the heart of it." He nodded to himself, remembering. He had led a professional workshop for teachers, the man said, and he was a paid consultant. I could tell that he was not from Helena. If he had led a workshop of any kind, likely he was from Little Rock or Fayetteville, the more urban areas of Arkansas.

"You have a gift for children, a real gift. For speaking with them. And speaking about them."

He paused, waiting for me to respond. I said thank you, inwardly hoping that the other teachers in Helena, especially those who knew that I left, had not seen it.

"I showed it to teachers in a workshop and used it as an example of the key of keys—*care*. The student in the movie, he used that word to talk about you, to explain why you made an impact on him. I told them a teacher's care could change someone."

At this, his friends nodded gravely, as if this were an original thought. I nervously guessed at what was to come next: What kind of consultant session involves showing some film and telling teachers to care? Few teachers like to be told that other teachers care more than they do. And I didn't care more; I had left.

"So then one teacher got offended; she thought I was saying something about *her*." Now the man grew agitated, the conflict surging in his memory. "She said that kid didn't change at all. She said he murdered someone and is in jail now. Then she got up and left the room."

Expectantly, the three faces turned to look at me. They were waiting, I realized, for me to confirm or deny that disgruntled teacher's account. This is what it came down to—true or false. Patrick had either killed someone or he hadn't. Caring could change a person or it couldn't. I thought they were naïve, yet maybe I was no different.

I had not intended to talk or even think about anything that mattered to me this morning. Now, in my gym shorts and silly sweatband, I'd been ambushed in a fluorescent aisle of Food Giant by a stranger who wanted to know *what happened. What happened* was just facts; it was nothing of the inner life, nothing of a person's complex regrets or intentions. But for them, *what happened* was a shorthand for understanding *who he was*.

It is destabilizing to think of a person as X—incapable of killing someone—and then be told he is Y—a killer.

But it wasn't about being right or wrong about a person. This wasn't some final reveal in a story where the violence represents internal evil, a crux to a person's character. This was just life. Anybody exposed to fighting knows it's a matter of degrees. A knife instead of a belt; a fatal cut instead of a shallow one.

I looked straight at the man and said it was true. It was true that the student in the documentary had killed someone and was in jail now. The man's face fell; the others', as well. Now I knew: They weren't from around here. Nobody from here, even the mild and kind elderly folks who fed me pie at the Presbyterian church, would be so shocked, so overtaken by pity.

"It was a fight late at night, you know," I said. "The man who"—I paused, choosing my words carefully—"died, he was older, drunk on his porch, with Patrick's sister. Patrick got scared."

The three shared the same face: stricken and curious, as if they had never heard of a fight gone bad.

I wanted to tell them how Patrick was doing, that he was in pain, indeed agonized by what he had done. And I wanted to tell them Patrick had read *The Lion, the Witch and the Wardrobe*, tell them about his fondness for Lucy, his forgiveness of Edmund. These were ethereal, precious gains.

But it was clear that little of what I wanted to say mattered to them, for they wanted to hear that Patrick hadn't killed anyone. I had nearly forgotten—in fact, I had been glad to forget. Hadn't forgetting been the very point of reading together? Hadn't it been a way of detaching us from the past?

I started to panic. No matter what he did for the rest of his life, Patrick would never escape that question: What happened? The question of his inner life would always be overshadowed by fact. I thought of the lines concentrated around Patrick's jaw as he wrote, his eyes squinting as he searched for a word: the way you could see on his face the silence, the private labor, the proof of feeling, the evidence of thinking.

"It's been a pleasure," I said, and pushed my cart of dismal produce away from them.

"You pass that test?" Patrick greeted me.

"The test?" I said. "Oh! The bar. Yes!"

He had remembered that my results had come out over the weekend.

"I was in Memphis with Danny and Lucy when I found out. They took me out to celebrate."

He grinned, happy for me. "That's great, Ms. Kuo. Really, I ain't surprised, you real smart. Where you go to eat?" I said Mexican food.

He wanted to know about Mexican food, or he was trying to procrastinate. Obligingly, I explained the tortilla and the enchilada.

Then we returned to poetry. His eyes got wide at the sight of my *Norton Anthology of Poetry:* "Ms. Kuo, that be bigger than the Bible."

I found the Tennyson poem I wanted to talk about: *He clasps the crag with crooked hands; / Close to the sun in lonely lands, / Ringed with the azure world, he stands.*

"What words sound alike? Don't worry about what they mean."

Patrick repeated the lines to himself, trying to hear their sound.

"Maybe *crooked* and *crag*."

"Good. You've already got the heart of this lesson, and we haven't even started. Any other sounds that sound alike?"

"*Clasps* and *crag*," he concluded, after some thinking and muttering to himself.

"Exactly. Do you remember what vowels are?" At once I cringed at my wording: *Do you remember.* Bad pedagogy: It framed learning in terms of what he had failed to retain.

"*A*," I said hastily.

Patrick blurted out, "*E, I, O, U.*"

He learned assonance quickly. "Could be *close* and *lonely*," he said. And consonance, as well. "*Lonely lands,*" he said.

And then meter.

"Syllables. How many *syllables* are in your name? *Patrick.*"

He looked at me questioningly—he was about to apologize. "*Patrick,*" I interrupted, cutting him off. "Two. *Pat*"—I put up my thumb to indicate the first syllable—"and *rick*." Now both my thumb and index finger were in the air. "See, two syllables."

For an hour we practiced trochees and iambs. Trochees were long–short, I explained; iambs were short–long. I spouted off a list of arbitrary words and names. *Patrick, Pam, tiger, belong.* "Iamb or trochee?" His answers were sometimes haphazard, pure guesses. "Say it to yourself," I advised. "*Tiger, tiger,*" he'd repeat. Eventually he got the hang of it. "That be long–short, ain't it."

Now I leafed through the *Norton* and found a poem by Yeats, "He Wishes for the Cloths of Heaven."

> *Had I the heavens' embroidered cloths,*
> *Enwrought with golden and silver light,*
> *The blue and the dim and the dark cloths*
> *Of night and light and the half-light,*
> *I would spread the cloths under your feet:*
> *But I, being poor, have only my dreams;*
> *I have spread my dreams under your feet;*
> *Tread softly because you tread on my dreams.*

"*Had I the heavens' embroidered cloths,*" Patrick began. "*En-wrought,*" he said next. I hadn't taught *enwrought,* not seeing a point, and so his forehead now settled into quizzical lines. But the lines vanished when he reached the colors, *golden and silver,* which came so effortlessly that these words seemed like a re-prieve, an oasis.

Patrick's voice now relaxed. "*Of night and light and the half-light.*"

"What's your favorite line?" I asked him. I didn't want to bludgeon him with questions about theme or meaning.

He clasped his hands, thinking carefully.

I said, "There's no right answer."

His eyes followed the lines. Finally he decided. "*The blue and the dim and the dark cloths.*"

I was surprised. I realized I had expected that he would choose *But I, being poor, have only my dreams.* How stupid. Which line he loved—what moved him—I couldn't know.

I asked, "Why is this your favorite line?"

"I don't know, Ms. Kuo."

I waited.

"Because it make me think about the sky. How it looks at night."

"That's lovely."

He was squinting now.

"Yeah. Before it get dark."

"See what the last words of each line are?"

"*Feet,*" he muttered. "*Dreams,*" he continued. "*Feet . . .*" Then, suddenly realizing the pattern, he laughed to himself.

"Why do you think he chooses to repeat those words?"

"'Cause it's all he has."

It was a wonderful answer. I simply nodded.

"Okay," I announced. "I think you're ready."

Patrick looked up, expectant.

"Let's memorize this."

"Right now?"

"Yes. Right now."

"Ms. Kuo, you crazy."

For the next hour we practiced. *"Of night and light and half-light,"* he tried, not looking at the page. I said, "You're missing a little word, one little syllable," and he counted on his fingers. Yes, he'd forgotten: *the half-light.* Then he said, *"I would spread the cloth,"* and I stopped him and said, "Just one cloth?" And swiftly he corrected himself and said, *"Cloths."*

AFTER JAIL IN THE MORNING, I drove straight to KIPP and taught. By the time I got back to Danny and Lucy's house, I was exhausted. On their couch, I read Patrick's homework. I had run out of time during jail that day to read it. ("Can I take this home?" I asked, holding his notebook. "Does that mean I don't have homework tonight?" he responded.)

To my beautiful baby Cherish. I remember when you were born you weighted only four pounds an three ounces. So tiny I was afraid of holding you. Danielle told me how fragile you would be. Also this look you gave me of a constant stare. When ever you was awake. More like the same mezmorized sensation I had for you. The humble smile you had at first. Im picturing it laughs whenever I hear you over the phone. Now that you're a year an Five months old. Missing you crawl an take yo first steps. Has been a disappointment for the both of us I know ... See you soon. We will catch up. Love yo Daddy.

It was better, wasn't it? *So tiny I was afraid of holding you.* The word *fragile.* The *same mezmorized sensation.* I knew exactly, I thought, where he had picked up the word *sensation*—from the line *Edmund felt a sensation of mysterious horror*—but he had improved its context. And I loved how he pictured her laughing; we had talked about picturing people, picturing mountains, picturing oceans. There was the allusion to his *disappointment*—but at least it was spelled correctly.

It was already time for bed, but I still needed to grade my pile of Spanish tests—there were sixty in total, on verb conjugations of *estudiar* and *hablar.* Why in the world had I agreed to teach a language I didn't know? I wished I had more time in jail to talk to Patrick about his work. What I really wanted to do in the Delta was becoming clear: teach Patrick. It was a utilitarian's nightmare—Patrick was one, the KIPP kids were many. The likelihood of improving the odds of the younger, motivated, fresh-faced students at an institution hell-bent on getting them to college far eclipsed that of reversing the fate of a lone adult in a county jail.

I switched back to Patrick's letter. I marked it up. I circled the *an* and wrote *and.* I wrote, *Sweet, tender detail!*

MY EMAIL TO JORDAN LOOKED like a breakup note: *I have something I need to talk to you about.*

I felt like I'd written a lot of these notes lately. I was turning into a real flake.

Jordan was nice about it. Who knows what he really thought.

Soon the only student I would have left was Patrick.

BY MID-DECEMBER, PATRICK AND I had a ritual: We began each morning by reciting a poem.

"You go first, Ms. Kuo," he'd say, teasing, gesturing with his hands, as if permitting me to walk through a door first. This was part of the ritual, too—neither of us wanted to go first.

"Had I the heavens' embroidered cloths . . ." I'd begin.

Patrick would turn serious, assuming a grave air, nodding encouragingly, as if I were a child. He knew this poem almost by heart, and he'd wait anxiously for each right word.

"Enwrought with silver and golden light—no." I'd furrow my brow, I'd stop, I'd search . . . *"Golden,"* I'd try, mangling the line. *"Golden and silver?"*

I'd check Patrick's expression for assurance: Now his brow was yanking inward; he didn't want me to fail.

I'd continue: *"Of night and light and the half-light,"* I'd say. *"I would spread the cloths . . ."*

Patrick would shake his head, interrupting me in a mild voice. "You be skipping a line, Ms. Kuo."

"Are you sure?" I was buying time.

He'd wait.

"Give me a hint." Stumped, I'd give him my best expression of mock despair.

Another student would have burst out loud with the answer, showing off the fact that he knew. Perhaps I was that kind of student. Patrick was quiet; he hoped I would figure it out.

"Oh!" I'd remember. He was right; I had skipped a line. *"The dim and the blue and the dark cloths,"* I'd try.

"Closer," he would say. He didn't want me to win by cheating.

I'd look at him blankly.

Finally, he would relent. "The *blue* come before the *dim*," he'd say. "Like life."

8

Narrative of the Life of Frederick Douglass

What's a brook?
A little river.

Meadows parching—if parch means dried up, what will happen?
No more brook.
So what will happen?
No more peace inside.

He likes these lines of Yusef K. (my favorite, too!) *This
man / who stole roses and hyacinth / for his yard, would
stand there / with eyes closed & fists balled*

His assonance homework, lovely:
long, strong, bone
bee, tree, leaf

when we memorize he always gets this line right: *And like
a thunderbolt he falls*

—Notes about Patrick from my journal, 2009

WHEN I DECIDED TO COME BACK TO THE DELTA, I WANTED TO do what I viewed as the moral opposite of publishing a piece of writing about my past experiences in *The New York Times Magazine*. Instead of remembering the Delta inside my room at a far remove, I would talk to people. Instead of fixing Patrick to the page, mourning him as if his life were over, I would help get his life started again. If I did continue writing, I would permit it under certain conditions: It would not be a "personal essay"—*personal* meant *indulgent*—but rather a sweeping history or sociology, which had scope and ambition. These were the books I read in college that had equipped me with an understanding of race and poverty and pushed me to come to the Delta in the first place.

But the contents of my notebook betrayed me. It told me what I really cared about. It was about Patrick, just Patrick: about his handwriting, about the crazy way it looked at first; about how he stared at the picture of the Faun crying; about memorizing poems and why it seemed to mean so much; about how hard it was to teach, how easy it was to regress, what it was like to learn. My relationship with Patrick—wasn't this the core of it all? Until I saw him in jail, it had never occurred to me that a student could regress or that we could resurrect roles in which we'd previously failed.

"THINK OF IT AS A very little guy," I said.

I was speaking about the apostrophe. "It's not nice to forget him just because he's so little. Don't be a mean friend."

Patrick laughed.

"Ms. Kuo, I bet you got a lot of friends."

"I have a few good ones," I said carefully, "which is all you need." This was a lie. I had more than a few.

"Danny and Lucy, you know them from college?"

"No, from teaching. Danny was my first friend here."

"He be a good teacher?"

"The best." Then I asked, "What about you?"

His mood shifted. *"Friend,"* he said, emphasizing the word with an ironic tone. "Are they friends if they get you killed?"

We were quiet.

"I got you," he said. "And I got my mama and my sisters. That all I need.

"Ms. Kuo," he said suddenly—something else was on his mind. "Do me a favor and get me some more cigarettes from my daddy today?"

Even though I wanted to be there for him, I was feeling pressed. I had told Jordan I would finish out the semester at KIPP, so I still had packed days. "I have work."

"When you get off work?" he asked.

"Six," I said, though it was five.

I WENT TO PATRICK'S HOUSE later that evening to get the cigarettes. Patrick's mother came to the door and knew at once who I was. She waved for me to come in. I'd hoped she would be home. I was filled with curiosity about her, because Patrick loved her most of all. In a letter he had written to her, he'd said: *I miss you too much to keep writing.*

In her arms was a child: Patrick's daughter. Cherish. It had to be her. She had big cheeks, a big jaw, and resembled Patrick. Her braids dangled prettily, framing her face, tied at the ends with pink and blue beads.

"It's Mary, right?" I said. "And Cherish."

She nodded and smiled as if she was about to cry.

"You know when Pat's court date be?" she asked.

Patrick was still in legal limbo—arrested, charged, and in jail, but with no trial date. I told her the delay was terrible, that it wouldn't be allowed in big cities. "It was supposed to be last month, in November, you know. But now they say it's going to be in February."

She nodded as Patrick's father had, accustomed to the legal system.

"Patrick's doing well," I said.

Hearing this, she at once relaxed.

"Patrick say you an angel watching over him," she said. "I do believe God is helping us, I do believe that."

"I've been giving him homework; he's been reading every day, working on his own mind, you know," I said.

Now her attention strayed. I took out some of Patrick's homework to show her.

Mary looked absently at the page, not seeming to realize I wanted her to read the actual words.

Pam emerged suddenly from the back of the house and went straight to her niece, stealing her from her grandma, sweeping up the baby so that they touched noses.

"She know a lot of words now, Ms. Kuo." Pam was bragging. "*Quit, no, chair.*"

The two disappeared to play.

"I heard you're a cook at the retirement home," I began.

"I fry a lot of fries, chicken, and fish; that's what they love. Older people love that fried chicken and fish."

Mary was open. This wasn't the proverbial gregariousness of a Delta storyteller but rather a person without defenses, without secrets, whom it was easy to ask much of. I asked if she liked working there.

Mary said, "My boss, he's real sweet. He's real quiet. He walk around with his head down, but he smiles. He's from Helena, go to Tennessee, come back. He gave us a two-dollar raise."

"He sounds nice," I said.

"These women I be working with, they sixty, seventy years old, they been working a low-class job twenty or thirty years, barely making forty cent over minimum wage—and this man came along, he give them a two-dollar raise, and they treat him like—" She shook her head. "It's weird. If you ain't treat people the way they used to, they ain't trust you."

"They treat him how?" I guessed that this man was white.

"Like, there be another boss, she be calling them the *N* word, then they sit up straight and say, *Yes, ma'am, yes, ma'am, yes, ma'am*. That's what these folks respect around here: They want someone to treat them like dogs, like that the only way to get them to bark right."

"She just said . . . said the *N* word openly?"

"When I started there, she be planning a Christmas party and be asking them about music. One woman, about sixty-five, she say, 'I got some music,' and the manager say, 'We don't need no nigger music,' and the woman say, 'Yes, ma'am.'"

Mary started laughing uncontrollably, a strange mirthless laughter.

"Oh, my God," she hiccupped, finally getting a word out. "Every now and then the word come out of her mouth and people sit up straight. Ms. Rollins be her name; yes, Ms. Rollins."

Like her husband, Mary had been born and raised in Helena. She was born in 1969, the same year that DeSoto was chartered to circumvent integration. Her mother had worked at the Helena hospital, and her dad worked at an electrical company on Highway 20 that closed not long after Mohawk shut down in

1979. After that, he started to drink more. He drank himself to death.

Mary met Patrick's father at Eliza Miller, the same middle school that Patrick and my other students had attended before getting kicked out. She fell in love with him because he was fearless. The gym teacher was white and racist; he called students *niggers*. James wasn't afraid. He talked back. "He'd cuss the teacher out; he ain't afraid of *nothing*." Mary shook her head, still admiring after all their years together. She made it to Central High, but she got pregnant and dropped out. "I got myself in deep trouble. We brought up during a time when you didn't talk about sex. A young girl didn't mess with a boy till she got married." Her parents kicked her out of the house. Her mother died of kidney failure; she drank too many sodas, Mary said.

She kept working: at the casino, at Pizza Hut. "I like the night shift better. I take care of the children; I left them with Daddy at night, three or four times a week. It was nice. When he went to jail, he got three years or something. So I keep working."

"You stuck by him," I said.

"I tried to."

"How come?"

"I don't know. I guess we was always told do unto others what you want others do unto you. If I went to jail, I'd probably want him to wait on me." She clasped her hands, unclasped them, scratched her head. "I loved him, I did. I still love him."

At the age of thirty-four, she discovered she had diabetes. Her blood sugar was over 200. She tried to walk more and switched to sugar-free sodas. "Sometimes I don't be speaking clear, I can't remember too much of nothing," she went on. "It's because of my diabetes. I get stressed; I get seizures. I think it be all the stress I'm under. I talk to God all day, yes, I do. I ask him a lot of *why* questions."

She looked up silently at the ceiling, as if she actually was talking to God. I waited for what seemed like a long minute.

"How . . ." I managed finally, "how did you feel after what happened with Patrick?"

"I ain't sleep; I ain't sleep for weeks. I keep wondering about that other boy and who his mom be. I be thinking about the two of them together. Then I ask God to put me in a room with her." She smiled faintly. "And he did."

She had asked around at work to see if anybody knew Marcus's mom. "Someone told me her name, Ms. Carly. I looked her up in the phone book, and I just call her. She picked up the phone, just picked it up, and told me to come over. She lived two, four blocks down from where we live."

Mary had been nervous. She worried it was a trap. "I thought something bad was gonna happen when I meet her, I swear to God I did. I thought a cousin or brother or somebody was gonna do something to me, I sure did."

But Marcus's mother answered the door and was alone.

"She looked kind of like one of my aunties: short, dark-skinned. She got this little smile on her face—it let me know everything. I thought she was gonna be mad with me, but she say she ain't surprised that it happen. She said he used to jump *her*, his own mama, when he got to drinking. It was all crazy there; we be crying and hugging. She was more sorry about it than I was. I had more tears on me than she did."

Mary touched her face in a remembering way. "When I say my prayers, I ask God to forgive me, to let me start a new day. I be praying all the time. I wake up in the morning, I ask God why this, why that. All day long I talk to him."

"Do you feel like God responds?"

"He do, he do."

She went quiet. I said eventually, "Did it surprise you, what happened that night?"

"Pat, what he did . . . it surprised everybody. He never do physical fighting, he just don't do it. I believe . . ." She paused. "I believe he was trying to impress his father."

Impress his father? I must have looked confused, because then she explained, "His dad love to see that type of stuff. His dad ain't scared of nobody, you know. So I believe Pat didn't know what to do but he didn't want to back down. I try to tell him, 'You were protecting your sister, not killing nobody.'"

It dawned on me how different Patrick was from his father. The crippled leg had misled me. He had a much stronger street mentality than Patrick, embodying a male code fundamental to surviving: Meet a blow with a blow, defend your honor. A Stars student had told me: "My dad told me if someone lays his hand once, you walk away, but the second time, you got to hit back."

Just because Patrick himself generally avoided fighting didn't mean that the code didn't rule him. His dad wanted him to be tougher, to fight back. Maybe Patrick was unused to fighting, to the point of responding with too much force. Had he grabbed the knife because he wasn't skilled with his fists? There were two different stories about where the knife came from: The police wrote that he'd gone into the house, but he said it had already been sitting on the porch. I did not want to confront him. I didn't know what to believe, but I did believe he had been scared.

"I try to tell him that things happen for a reason. That boy's death . . . maybe that be what it took for Patrick to separate himself. He been hanging on with that boy Harrison; they family all do heroin. So . . ." She clasped her hands and looked down.

Inwardly, I was trying to decide if she was being crazy: Did someone have to die in order for her son to stave off a potential drug addiction? But I remembered that Patrick had told me that his uncle had killed his great-aunt. Given these circumstances, her thought was just utilitarian. Prison was better than addiction.

As if on cue, she said that her brother was in prison for life, out at the maximum-security prison. Patrick had been nine when he went away.

"I guess yesterday is gone," she continued. "I can't change it. I try to live one day at a time. I just wish I know what was gonna happen next."

I didn't know whether she was speaking in spiritual terms or about Patrick's trial date.

"I'll go see Rob," I said.

"Who?"

"His lawyer."

She nodded, still playing with her hands.

I said I should probably get going.

"GOOD NEWS: MARCUS *WAS* DRUNK," Rob said. "Very drunk." His blood alcohol level was 0.26, more than three times the legally permissible level.

It had taken more than a year for the coroner's lab in Little Rock to send back the autopsy. ("Helena doesn't have anyone to do the autopsy?" I asked. Rob laughed.)

"How can I help?" I asked.

"Matter of fact, you could go to the police station and pick up Marcus's record. Character assassination," he continued. "If the victim is an undesirable, we'll have a better case."

Undesirable? I wondered.

Then, as an afterthought, he said, "Maybe I'll even have you do some case research." He winked, suggesting that case research wasn't something public defenders in rural areas did.

At the station, where a pile of homemade DVDs titled *Jesus* sat in a basket, free for the taking, I got Marcus's reports. I managed to restrain myself from reading them until I got into the car. Was Marcus a sociopath? A rapist? Did he have a record of violent felonies? I hoped that the record was bad. I began to read, struggling to make sense of the poorly written police reports. The year before, in May 2007, he was charged for contributing to the delinquency of a minor. A girl was cutting school and hiding out at his house. *Ms Rowan call to the school and found that her daughter was not at school. Mr Rowan neibhor that lives next to informed Ms. Rowan that Marcus was inside the house with two other kids. Ms Rowan call the police . . .*

In May 2008, four months before he ended up on Patrick's porch, police were dispatched because he was drunk. *On 05/06/08 unit were dispatched to 871 Chicago for a disturbance upon my arrival spoke to a Rhonda Sampson who stated her boyfriend [Marcus] Williamson was drunk and cause problems. He had already been into a fight with several unknown people. Mr. Williamson walked out of the house cursing with a bat in his right hand. He was told to drop the bad twice. Which he did not due.* The report ended: *Mr. Williamson had a strong odor of intoxicants coming off his breath.*

On another morning that same month, at 5:02 A.M., the police were dispatched *in reference to a unwanted male subject.* Another disorderly. He was pepper-sprayed after trying to kick out the windows of the police car. Marcus went to county jail for a week.

The earliest charge, eight years prior, was made when he was seventeen. He had broken into a person's house and stolen a pair of shoes and a box of cassette tapes.

In sum, his charges included second-degree reckless destruction of property; disorderly conduct; public intoxication; and resisting arrest. No infraction had been serious enough to send him to state prison.

It seemed clear that Marcus was, at worst, an alcoholic who could get aggressive. By the look of it, he was not so much dangerous as unlucky. He had been drunk on the wrong night and shown up on the wrong porch.

"So what do you think?" I asked Rob, ferrying the reports back to him the next day, hoping he would find something nefarious where I had not.

Rob was unimpressed. Swiftly, he leafed through the pages.

"I do know this name," he said. "Williamson, Williamson . . ." He searched back in his memory. "Matter of fact, I defended *her*; the mother. Sure did. She was robbing a house with one of her sons. Police found her hiding out in the bushes." She and another son had stolen a DVD player.

He clapped his hands, celebrating the strength of his memory.

BUILDING A LEGAL CASE WAS fundamentally contrary to grieving. You showed no respect for the dead. You mounted evidence of his poor character, implying that he helped cause his own demise. I found myself trying to assert Patrick's innocence in terms of Marcus's guilt.

"Good news," I said the next Monday, trying to channel Rob's ease. "Marcus was drunk."

I knew the words came out wrong, because Patrick winced.

"We got Marcus's autopsy," I said hurriedly.

At the word *autopsy*, Patrick looked down.

"How do it . . . how do it look?"

He played with the edge of his notebook.

Then he blurted out, "Ms. Kuo, he just *came* at me, talking crazy. I kept telling him, 'Get out of my yard, get out of my yard.'"

"Did you think . . ." I hesitated. "Did you think about calling the police?"

Apparently this was an absurd question. "Naw, naw, ain't no one call the police. The police here ain't no *police*. They out smoking weed and dealing drugs. How they gonna come to your house?" He paused. "Besides, they know my daddy—they gonna think I started something."

AFTER KIPP CLOSED FOR THE winter holiday, I went to my parents' house in Indiana. I turned twenty-eight. My brother baked me a strawberry shortcake for my birthday. My parents gave me, among other things, a card with a sizable handwritten message that had oddly encouraging words. "Do you like it?" they kept asking. Apparently they'd spent hours in an aisle dedicated to Hallmark cards, trying to find the card that matched what they wanted to say. The winner, though, had an ugly picture, so they copied the message onto scrap paper and purchased a prettier blank card.

"I love it," I said, feeling suddenly crazy with love for them.

Satisfied, they returned to the usual topic of conversation: why I was not married.

"She's not mysterious," my mother said.

"She'll spill her guts to anybody," my dad agreed.

"I'm right here," I said.

BACK AT THE COUNTY JAIL, the New Year had passed and the rain bucket needed emptying.

"It's raining, ain't it?" asked Patrick.

"Yeah."

"Man. I be missing all of it."

"What've you been up to?"

"Nothing. The food's better on Christmas."

"There was this MLK Day parade in Helena yesterday," I said. It had been a cold day in Helena, with light rain. One store had put up a sign that read: CLOSED FOR MARTIN LUTHER KING AND ROBERT E. LEE'S BIRTHDAY. Twenty-five years earlier, the Arkansas state legislature had passed a law to combine both commemorative days into one state holiday.

"What's that?"

"MLK," I said. "Martin Luther King."

"Oh, yeah."

I asked, "Do you know what he did?"

"He died."

Patrick spoke matter-of-factly, without hesitation or emotion. I had thrown him an easy pass and he'd given me a satisfactory answer.

"Anything else?"

He thought for a moment. "He kind of like Jesus."

I wasn't sure what he meant. "Because he died?" I offered.

Patrick nodded. "So we can live."

I felt a little sick. For Patrick, King was a religious martyr, a lone man braver than the rest of us, transcendent and detached from history. Erased, in this account, was the collective moral power in being black, in the ordinary people who risked their lives and helped lead *him*.

The next day, I brought in Frederick Douglass's autobiography. I'd always regarded *Narrative of the Life of Frederick Douglass* as a rich artifact. I'd read it in high school and wasn't particularly excited by the idea of reading it again. But it seemed like an important thing to offer Patrick. It spelled out the place of slavery in American history, and it showed the genius of one of the people who'd risen up to fight it. "Do you know who Frederick Douglass is?"

"He made something; he invented something."

"Close, kind of," I said. I directed him to the title page:

NARRATIVE

of

the life of

FREDERICK
DOUGLASS

A Modern Day
Slave

WRITTEN BY HIMSELF

Published in Boston

1845

Patrick read the title page, including the date, out loud.

"Do you remember—did you learn when the Civil War started?" I asked.

"1940?"

He saw my face and said quickly, "1900?"

I gave him the answer.

"Civil War the one when they fought over slaves?"

"Good," I said. "Why do you think there was slavery to begin with?"

"Money," he said. "Things be cheaper for them. We can do all the work; they get paid for it."

"Yes, money was a big reason," I said. "Smart response."

"So he wrote this before we got free?"

"Yes. That's exactly right."

William Lloyd Garrison had written the preface. I told Patrick that Garrison and Douglass had been *abolitionists*. He didn't know the word, and I spelled it slowly so that he could write it down. I talked about them. Patrick took notes on what I said. He wrote in his journal:

> *Abolitionists—people who get rit of slavery*
> *William Garrison—white man*

He drew a little curve between the two lines to indicate that Garrison was an abolitionist.

We skipped most of the preface and landed here:

> *A slaveholder's profession of Christianity is a palpable imposture.*

"I'll give you a hint. This word"—I pointed to *imposture*—"is related to the word *impostor*, a person who pretends to be something he's not."

Patrick nodded. "So according to Garrison," I continued, "what isn't this slaveholder?"

"A man of God."

I nodded, and Patrick read on.

> *He is a felon of the highest grade. He is a man-stealer. It is of no importance what you put in the other scale.*

I asked, "How would you say this in your own words?"

Without faltering, he said, "He the biggest crook of them all."

Then he pointed to the name Wm. Lloyd Garrison at the bottom.

"Ms. Kuo," he said, with incredulity bordering on apprehension, "you say this be a *white* dude?"

I laughed.

"Damn," he said. "I mean, shoot."

And so we began *Narrative of the Life of Frederick Douglass, written by himself.*

> *By far the larger part of the slaves know as little of their ages as horses know of theirs, and it is the wish of most masters within my knowledge to keep their slaves thus ignorant.*

Patrick's voice gathered force when he read and lingered on the word *ignorant*.

"Shoot. We ain't know how old we be." He paused. "White children know, but we ain't."

He continued:

> *I never saw my mother, to know her as such, more than four or five times in my life; and each of these times was very short in duration, and at night.*

Patrick stumbled over the word *duration*—yet he didn't wait for me to correct him. He kept going.

> *She was hired by a Mr. Stewart, who lived about twelve miles from my home.*

He stopped. "Twelve miles," he repeated, recognizing how far this was. Anxiety creased his forehead.

I asked, "Why would it be advantageous for slaveholders to separate mothers from children?"

"What?"

"I mean, why would it be useful?"

Patrick's words came in a torrent. "To keep him from helping her," he burst out. "He gonna try to take care of her, and now he ain't able to. And Mama—she gonna try to *teach* him to do the right thing; she know a little more than him. She probably try to help him escape—she wouldn't want him to be no slave. And if you that boy, you see your mama working as a slave, you ain't *plum dumb*, you know what they doing."

Patrick stopped to catch a breath and then kept talking.

"Everybody's mama love them. Like my mama, she do anything for me; if I'm right or wrong, she do *anything*. She be there, like right now, my situation. That's why it be good to know *your* mother; she gonna have affection for you *regardless*. But if you a child, you don't know all that. He probably think his mother hated him, because she never around. He ain't able to know about affection; he probably never gonna get to know his mother." He shuddered at the thought.

Then he resumed reading.

By the time I checked my watch, we had read the bulk of the first chapter aloud. It was already six. I nearly jumped. "Sorry," I said; I was late to meet Danny and Lucy for dinner.

Hearing the sound of my voice, Patrick started, as well; he'd been lost in the book.

I had feared that he would be bored by Douglass, that its language would sound antiquated and dull, but I was wrong: The book was alive, full of blood for Patrick.

"Hey," I said. "You don't need to stop just because I'm leaving. Keep going."

At this Patrick looked surprised. He asked, "I can keep it?"

Then, answering his own question, he said, "Naw, Ms. Kuo, I can't keep it."

I nodded encouragingly. "I have my own, see?" I held up the second copy.

He returned his gaze to his own book, looking at it uncertainly.

"I give it back," he allowed.

Within a week Patrick had read half the Douglass on his own, sitting on the third step of an unlit concrete stairway. He'd gone to the stairs, he told me, because he couldn't concentrate in his cell. "They be bothering me *specially* when I reading," he said. "Like they want me to get mad. I can't get no peace here."

Patrick was chapters ahead of me.

I reviewed his homework. "What surprises you when you read Frederick Douglass?" I had asked.

He wrote: *It is amazing that Mr. Douglass knows all these big words cause I dont.*

"What would you change about yourself?" I had asked next.

He wrote: *If I could change something it would be me not dropping out of school.*

And last I was startled to discover this list:

Ways im like a slave

Me being ignorant
haveing things deprived from me
    cause im in jail
having a master or jailer
Being a black man Its more favor for white men
I will have to work for white men

If a black person is killed its not much fuss or nothing
    really said about
A nigger most likely not being successful in America.
Commonly said Im only promised to be dead or in jail

I had not assigned a question to prompt such a comparison. He had written it on his own. He must have looked up the word *ignorant* in the dictionary or checked it against the Douglass text—it was spelled perfectly.

Soon we started the famous passage where Douglass is introduced to the alphabet:

> *Very soon after I went to live with Mr. and Mrs. Auld, she very kindly commenced to teach me the A, B, C. After I had learned this, she assisted me in learning to spell words of three or four letters.*

Patrick gave me a mischievous look and said, "I know someone like that." We laughed and he read on. Mr. Auld found out that Frederick was learning. He told his wife to stop: [It] *was unlawful, as well as unsafe, to teach a slave to read. . . . "Now," said he, "if you teach that nigger (speaking of myself) how to read, there would be no keeping him. It would forever unfit him to be a slave. He would at once become unmanageable, and of no value to his master. As to himself, it could do him no good, but a great deal of harm. It would make him discontented and unhappy."*

"How would you put this in your words?" I asked.

"He not gonna be a slave anymore when he knows what's going on. Ain't gonna be a slave all right."

Under her husband's influence, Mrs. Auld changed. *"The tender heart became stone,"* Patrick read. He looked up and said, unprompted, "She gonna stop teaching him, and he gonna have to teach himself." And Patrick was right: Soon Douglass was found with a newspaper, and Mrs. Auld rushed toward him in fury, snatching it from him.

So Mrs. Auld had stopped teaching Douglass, but it was too late. At the shipyard, Douglass watched carpenters write letters using chalk. The larboard was marked *L.*; the starboard, *S.*; the larboard aft, *L.A.* He copied the letters to practice.

After that, when I met with any boy who I knew could write, I would tell him I could write as well as he. The next word would be, "I don't believe you. Let me see you try it." . . . [M]y copybook was the board fence, brick wall, and pavement; my pen and ink was a lump of chalk. With these, I learned mainly how to write.

Suddenly, Patrick flipped to the front cover of his book to stare at the indubitable Mr. Douglass, venerable and black, a thick mane of white set against his dark skin. Patrick studied the picture as he had studied that of the Faun, so carefully and gravely that his expression resembled a frown.

"Hey," I said, bundling up to go. "I picked up some cigarettes for you from the store. Because you've been working so hard." I handed him the package.

"Thanks, Ms. Kuo," he said. "But I got one at the house. Can you get it for me?"

There was something unnatural in Patrick's tone—at once urgent and uncomfortable.

"You've got this one already. Why do you—"

"Naw, my dad got it for me." He looked away.

I was suspicious.

"Is there something you want to tell me?" I said.

"Ma'am?"

"What makes his different from mine?"

"See, my mama got it for me." I hesitated; hadn't he just told me his dad got it? "I don't want her to feel bad," he continued. "It make her happy to give me things, you know."

I looked him in the eye. He couldn't hold my gaze.

"Okay," I relented.

As I PULLED UP TO Patrick's house, I was nervous. Heroin? Coke? Weed? His dad must have put something in the package. But Patrick wasn't using any of them, was he? No, his homework was too good.

The yard was steeped with water; it had been a rainy January. In the large ditch, leaves and pinecones floated on top.

I trudged to the door and saw his dad immediately—he knew why I was there. I wiped off my sneakers while he poked his head under the couch.

Now I was sure something was wrong. Why would tobacco be hidden? I started to back away. "I'll come back later," I lied.

"Naw, I don't want you to leave empty-handed."

He gave me what looked like a typical package of tobacco leaves. But for the first time I noticed Scotch tape on the front. It had been opened and sealed again. How many other packages, I realized with dread, had also been opened? How many of these had I given to Patrick from the house—three, four, five? I'd lost count.

Back at Danny and Lucy's house, I parked in their driveway, relieved that the dark of the rain shielded my windows. I broke the tape open. Some leaves flitted out like confetti, and there it was—weed.

I felt like a fool. Patrick had lied to me, and so had his father.

Over dinner, Danny fumed. "Do you know how fucked-up it is that his dad is giving this to him? That it might get his son *more* in trouble with the law? And to put you, the *teacher*, a lawyer, in that position?"

I didn't say anything.

"What if it had been worse than pot? Heroin? Cocaine?"

"But it wasn't."

I didn't tell Danny what I was worrying about myself—that I was in the process of filling out the "moral application" for my bar. If the California Bar Association caught wind, it would hurt my chances of getting admitted.

"Why do you think you have been giving him those cigarettes?"

"I don't know."

"To reward him," he said, supplying my answer. "But you reward him with your presence, with your teaching, by showing up."

I hung my head.

Danny said, "Stay away from the father. And destroy the package."

THE NEXT DAY, PATRICK STRETCHED out his arm to hand me his notebook.

I didn't reach for it. Confused, he pulled the notebook back toward his chest.

"I know about your cigarettes," I said impassively.

Patrick froze.

"This isn't the first time, is it?"

He shook his head.

"Why?" I said. My anger swelled, remembering the lie about his mother. "Why? Why would you risk it?"

Quickly he asked, "What'd you do with it?"

That this was the first thing he said made me even angrier. "I threw it away."

He cringed. "Ms. Kuo," he protested.

"Do you know how fucked-up this is?"

Patrick flinched. I rarely cursed in front of him. "Having your teacher sneak in weed to the jail? Your teacher who's going to be sworn in to be a lawyer? Who's trying to help you? Letting your dad give the drugs to her? What do you think your dad was thinking?"

"I don't look at it that way. It's up to me; I make my own decisions."

"If *I* were your parent," I began, a perilous phrase. "If I were a parent and I had a child in jail—"

"I ain't a child," Patrick burst out.

"You sure are acting like one," I said.

Patrick jumped back as if I'd slapped him. Then he covered his face.

"Take those hands off," I said.

He didn't obey.

"I know you heard what I said. Look at me. I'm not perfect; you're not perfect. But let our trust be perfect."

At this he let out a small sound.

"What were you doing with it? Selling it? Smoking it?"

Now Patrick got evasive.

"It ain't matter—it make no difference."

"Patrick," I said, now more quietly. "What the hell were you thinking?"

He didn't answer. He just said, "If I weren't in jail—none, *none* this would happen. I don't know—I don't know how to get better."

I got up and left, leaving his homework on the table.

* * *

WHAT, REALLY, WAS I so mad about? Was it just the basic fact that nobody—nobody—likes being used? Few emotions are as universal as this. In the end he was just a kid trying to get some pot.

The next morning, Patrick walked in, carrying his notebook and his books. He held out his notebook tentatively.

I reached for it—a gesture of reconciliation.

"What's been on your mind?" I asked.

"Wrong stuff. Bullcrap."

He avoided eye contact—he was still afraid of me. Maybe he thought I was going to curse again or raise my voice.

He had written down some things that were not assigned. One paragraph in particular was really a note to me.

My family are getting old and I'm sitting in here wasting time. My momma is waiting on me to come home. This place is ruining me more than I already am. It's like I need help, but I can do bad on my own. Sorry for my mistakes. Thank you for tring to help me.

My voice was low, almost tender. "I'm sorry I lost my temper yesterday. I can't know how stressful things are in here, I really can't. Only you know."

Patrick didn't say anything. He was watching me, testing my sincerity.

"And I'm sorry I said those things about your dad. I guess I just don't . . . I don't relate. I thought I could, but I guess I can't. My dad taught me math just about every night growing up; he didn't let me—"

"It ain't like that with my daddy," he burst in. "Really, I got to help *him* with his times table."

He cleared his throat and paused, weighing his words.

"When I was little, we all stayed in Helena. But my daddy had another house where he was selling dope out of. I was living there and I be thinking to myself, I five years old and it a *dope house*. My dad, he's like a professional at selling drugs; he strict about how he handles business. He don't sell to anybody he don't trust. He used to teach me how to sell. Teach me things like, don't never call them crackheads. Teach me that it better to deal with people who work, like who fix pipes or got a job. Teach me that at nighttime it got to be a different price, like the price need to go up." After a few years, his dad was arrested. "He was out on a bond and the night before he went in, we rode around. He was buying me stuff, buying me everything, buying toys. Just spending time together. The next morning I saw the sheriff's car outside."

His dad was in prison for two years, came back, then got caught again shortly before Patrick was sent to Stars.

Patrick stopped himself. "My daddy was good, he *was*, he a good person, he a good person to me, I'm glad I got him. He was there. A lot of fathers, you know, ain't there, at home. And *his* daddy weren't there. He had to learn how to hustle. He the one who showed me how to fix my go-cart. He be real good with his hands; he know how to fix stuff. And how to draw, he can draw."

"Drawing?"

"When he was in jail, he sent a lot of letters home with drawings. And he know how to sew, stitch up clothes and stuff. When I got holes in my pants, he stitch them up. Though he's the *strongest* in my family, it really—it really tore him up I'm here."

My neck was burning. I hadn't helped Patrick by casting judgment on his father.

He paused. "Like what I say in there"—he gestured to his notebook—"it's true. Really. Thank you for trying."

We were back to where we'd started, the dynamic in which he thanked me and felt as if he'd let me down. How much of this dynamic had I myself created? I wished he would associate me with feeling successful. Of course we were not on a level playing field, but I wished he knew we were equals.

"You start," I said. "Then I'll go."

He looked at me blankly.

"Yeats or Dickinson?"

"Emily," he said. He referred to her by her first name; sometimes he called Douglass "Frederick."

"*Have you got a brook in your little heart,*" he began. He closed his eyes to remember the next line. "Your turn," he said, when he was finished.

I stopped giving Patrick cigarettes, and he didn't ask for them again.

We kept reading Frederick.

"*The more I read, the more I was led to abhor and detest my enslavers,*" Patrick read. I asked what he thought *abhor* meant, and he said, "To hate," and kept going. "*I could regard them in no other light than a band of successful robbers, who had left their homes, and gone to Africa, and stolen us from our homes.*"

His reading was improving: He read now with a steady pace. Words fell from his lips with control, not too fast, like arrows aimed at a target. Gone was the hesitation, which had hidden the depth of his voice. Perhaps the marijuana incident had cleared the air, permitted us both to be less than perfect.

"*. . . learning to read had been a curse rather than a blessing. It* *had given me a view of my wretched condition without the remedy,"* he read.

"How do you think Douglass is feeling?" I asked, though I already knew what he thought from the way he read.

"Hopeless," Patrick said. He was tense, keen-eyed. "Because freedom, opportunity, all the things that he missing out on, that all be"—he paused, searching for the right word—*"weighing* on him. He learning to read *depressing* him. What the master said is coming true." He looked back at the words. "And the pit"—he was referring to the line *It opened my eyes to the horrible pit, but to no ladder upon which to get out*—"that be a *metaphor* or whatever for how he be feeling, because he can't leave."

Without waiting for me to respond, knowing that he had answered my questions, Patrick continued reading. *"In moments of agony, I envied my fellow-slaves for their stupidity. I have often wished myself a beast. I preferred the condition of the meanest reptile to my own. Any thing, no matter what, to get rid of thinking! It was this everlasting thinking of my condition that tormented me. There was no getting rid of it."*

Patrick grimaced, perhaps shocked by the passage's direct applicability to him.

I asked, "How do you think he relates to the other slaves?"

Patrick shook his head, as if I had already answered the question by asking it. "What Frederick mean here," he said, "is that slaves be like beasts or dogs who got nothing to worry about. And he jealous of them 'cause they ain't know any better. They be in pain but not the *mental* kind, you know. They ain't worried the way *he* be worried. Like my jail mates. They be spitting and cursing all day. They make all that noise, everybody moaning and groaning, a thousand noises; I hate that sound. So Frederick, he don't got nobody to relate to. He be a little smarter now, he know about *the past and the present*," he said, with an emphasis that made me recall the way he had said *cause and effect.* "For him to know how to read—that change everything."

We kept going. We read how, over the holidays, the masters gave slaves gin, knowing the slaves would get very drunk. This was a way to disgust slaves with their freedom. Slaves would return to the fields sick and staggering and so conclude that freedom did not suit them, that they could not handle freedom.

Reading this, Patrick moaned out loud.

And quickly he swallowed his sounds, then kept reading. He didn't look up; he didn't stop. He did not wish to undo or unlearn the feeling most painful to him. To keep reading was urgent—in fact, not a choice at all.

If what Patrick felt in reading Douglass was recognition and aching clarification, I felt something different.

I had imagined that reading Douglass would bring Patrick and me together, in shared contempt for slavery, but now I felt more separate from Patrick than when we had first started to read it. When I was growing up, *Narrative of the Life of Frederick Douglass* had been synonymous with aspiration—literacy was a means to freedom; literacy had freed him. That is the trope of the slave narrative: Reading and writing ignite self-awareness, creating both the practical and spiritual conditions for escape.

But I did not anticipate the visceral psychic feelings that Douglass seemed to trigger in Patrick—the panic and dread and shock. And depression. Kafka wrote that we must read books that wound, that *affect us like disaster,* that act as an *ax for the frozen sea inside us.* For Patrick, Frederick Douglass was that ax, and it broke him apart.

Douglass had written from the standpoint of having made it. Douglass had taught himself, even after Mrs. Auld repudiated him. If books were a source of illumination for Douglass, they reminded Patrick of his failure. He looked up words. He wasn't sure if he understood their meaning. He was goaded to do his homework with cigarettes. He had duped his teacher into smuggling in pot. He was in jail.

Patrick could not know—or would not accept—how much he seemed like Douglass to me. How he read in county jail, without table or light, how he wrenched self-discipline out of himself among inmates who were waiting for him to crack.

9

I Have Read Everything on This Paper
(The Guilty Plea)

"I think speaking Latin is a betrayal of the poor because in lawsuits the poor do not know what is being said and are crushed; and if they want to say four words they need a lawyer."
—MENOCCHIO, a sixteenth-century miller,
from Carlo Ginzburg, *The Cheese and the Worms*

DRESS CODE FOR COURT

NO SHORT PANTS
NO SAGGING PANTS
NO HATS OR CAPS ON MEN
NO VULGAR T-SHIRTS
NO HALTER TOPS
NO MUSCLE SHIRTS
NO FLIP-FLOPS
NO HOUSE SHOES

* * *

As I pushed open the door to the courtroom, I noticed, with surprise, that every word on the sign was spelled correctly.

Inside, a pair of American flags flanked a balding white judge. His head was bent over his papers. To his left sat a row of young black inmates, dressed in either fat-zebra-stripe or garish-orange jumpsuits. To his right was an empty jury box, that hypothetical congregation of the community.

I had gotten a phone call from Rob. "It's time."

"Time for what?"

"Court!" he barked.

"Okay," I said, as if it were perfectly normal for a state court system, after nearly a year and a half of delay, to administer a case with less than a day's notice. Rob said that Patrick had to show up today but he was near the bottom of the list, so the judge might not get to him.

Sitting in the back, I searched for Patrick and we found each other at the same time. Then he looked down and started to fidget with his sandal straps, self-conscious in his oversize jumpsuit, its black and white stripes now on public display.

Rob's counterpart, the other Phillips County public defender, approached an inmate. In a millisecond that young man's posture utterly transformed: Taut, alert, he leaned forward, trying to catch the lawyer's every word. I realized it was likely the first time the lawyer had seen his client. Even from where I was sitting, halfway across the courtroom, I could discern his desperate attentiveness.

The judge called the courtroom to order.

He read the first inmate's name.

A man shuffled to the center.

The judge asked, "How old are you?"

"Twenty-five."

And then: "How far did you make it in school?"

"Ninth grade."

These were not questions judges typically asked defendants, and this judge didn't appear surprised by the man's answer or even interested in it. Perhaps, I speculated, the judge had once asked these questions to humanize the defendant, but over time they'd become perfunctory.

The prosecutor stated the charges: residential burglary. "A plea bargain has been made, Your Honor."

And then, the judge: "Do you understand that you have a constitutional right to a trial by jury? Do you understand that by entering a plea of guilty to the charges you are waiving your constitutional right to appeal of issues in the charges against you? Have you discussed all possible defenses with your lawyer?"

The judge spoke in a flat, efficient monotone. The man's answers were barely audible, recognizable only by their percussive rhythm: *Yes. Yes. Yes.*

The judge said, "The record will show that the defendant knowingly, intelligently, and voluntarily understood the charges against him."

Thus commenced the tedium.

The defendants' ages ranged from sixteen to sixty, they were all black, and their education generally fell somewhere between the fifth and tenth grades. No one spoke to what we all saw happen; no one said, *No, I just met my lawyer five minutes ago.* To me, the procedure was farcical, but nobody around me laughed or looked aggrieved.

It would have been pleasing to witness a crisis, anything to shake up the malaise of bored power and powerlessness. But the judge and bailiff seemed sleepy. The court was not efficient enough to be called machinery, not organized enough to be called bureaucracy, not malicious enough to be called dehumanizing. Sitting there, waiting for something interesting to happen, I felt within me the absence of rage, an inarticulable nothingness in the spacious courtroom, which Patrick later described as "full of fresh air."

RECESS WAS CALLED. ROB SHOWED me where Patrick's name was on the docket to explain why it hadn't been called yet. It was a long list, and a bunch of the cases, he explained, had already been delayed and wouldn't be heard until spring. Some were out on bail, and others had already been sent back to jail to wait, as Patrick had waited, for another trial date.

Every third or fourth name I recognized as that of a former student—sometimes, two in a row. Each name triggered a wave of associations. *Samuel Toggins*. He wrote in light, nearly imperceptible cursive. *William Batts*. William had been stealing with Brandon the day Brandon died. He'd gone to jail for robbery. "How can they put him in jail?" someone had said. "His best friend dying is punishment." He must have served his sentence, gotten out, and then returned. *Jemarcus Lane*. Face round and flushed, like a valentine; had a learning disability. *Cameron Storey*. Another learning disability; could not spell *dog*; kept asking me if I had a boyfriend. Ms. Jasper had paddled him. Later I would ask a jailer what Cameron was in for. She said, "I ain't sure. Probably for getting mad. Or stealing little things. I tell you one thing, it sure ain't for selling drugs. He ain't got a mind for that." She chuckled to herself.

The names went on. *Ray Reed*. The fifteen-year-old who'd stolen my Picasso poster. *Malik Jones*. Hot-tempered; surprisingly toothy smile. Wrote a paper that began: *The hardest thing in my life is not growing up with a father.*

I tried to count the number of black males of my sixty-something students over two years who had at some point gone to jail, and I ran out of fingers. The docket was the coda to the STUDENT DROPOUT REPORT—the county jail was where the dropouts landed. There were no jobs in Helena. They had no skills. Most had a disability or an emotional or mental disorder. Where else had I thought they would go?

THE JUDGE LOOKED UP FROM his papers and swiveled his head toward an inmate at the far end of the wall. "Now, who are you, sir?"

Unaware, the inmate stared emptily at his lap.

"You," the judge repeated.

The inmate jerked up, gestured toward himself questioningly.

The judge asked, "Who's your lawyer?"

The people in the courtroom turned toward him expectantly, and the inmate opened his mouth but no words came out. "Garvin," he finally stammered.

The prosecutor and judge started to shuffle through papers.

"Mr. Garvin has withdrawn," said the judge to the prosecutor. "We need to find who this man's lawyer is."

The judge shifted more papers in front of him. The prosecutor made a slight shrug, apparently unsurprised that a man whose fate hung partially in his hands had no counsel.

The judge finally said, "Come up."

The inmate now walked to the front. He tried to straighten his shoulders, but they remained hunched.

"How long have you been here?"

"Eight months."

The judge looked down, made some marking with a pen, and said, "A public defender will be appointed for you tomorrow morning."

It was obvious that the judge was done with the man, but the man continued to stand, back facing us, apparently waiting for permission to leave.

The rest of the courtroom said nothing, pitying the inmate. I looked over at Patrick. He had grown used to being seen and now sat slumped, like the others.

The judge finally spoke. "That's the last case we'll be hearing today." I looked at my watch; it wasn't yet three-thirty. No wonder there was such a backlog. Patrick would have to wait until tomorrow. The gavel sounded, the judge stood, and Patrick was taken away as we, like an obedient flock, rose in unison.

PATRICK WAS BARELY RECOGNIZABLE ON his second day in court, in a collared shirt with baby-blue stripes and freshly ironed khakis. Kiera had brought him clothes from home.

Today was the big day: the day of "closure," the termination of legal limbo, the final conclusion to a night of September 2008.

Kiera waved to me as I walked into the private alcove in the courthouse. Her red nails flew in the air. Mary sat next to Kiera, resting her hands on her thighs. They had all been waiting for me to arrive. Rob had disappeared already; he was talking to the prosecutor.

"Your lips be chapped, Ms. Kuo," said Kiera. "Want my lip gloss?"

I declined. "You look cute," I said. She had a nice blouse and wore tall brown boots with laces on the sides.

"I wanted to wear me some blue earrings, but I thought that'd be too much. You know, ghetto."

She turned to Patrick. "You like the clothes I picked for you?"

She beamed; it was not meant to be a question. Then she sighed: She'd caught sight of his broken sandal. "I sure wish I knew about them shoes. I didn't know they got you wearing flip-flops."

He wore the same broken sandal he'd been so self-conscious about when I first visited him in prison. Scraps of orange plastic now hung from the flap.

"I got a string," he said. "Tied it together."

We all looked at it in silence. Then Kiera announced, "I'm gonna get you some nice shoes. Some clean Nikes for you to take back there."

Patrick waved his hand. "Naw, they just gone throw it away."

Then he asked, "How Cherry?"

"She look just like you, man," Kiera said.

Patrick looked pleased at this. No matter how many times someone said it to him, he always lit up.

"Well, you looking good, Pat. Your skin got lighter. You got some pretty skin." She paused. "But you still got ugly feet."

We laughed.

Kiera disappeared, looking for a bathroom. Patrick said to his mother, "Kiera, she got a boyfriend now, ain't she?"

"She got a *couple* boyfriends," Mary said, and let out a sigh. She began rocking back and forth. "I just be praying every night." She squeezed her eyes shut, as if she was praying here.

"Don't worry about me, Ma," he said.

Mary opened her eyes but stared ahead, still rocking. She wrapped her arms around herself.

"You set aside your prayers and take your medicine."

"I don't eat no sugar, and my sugar still be high. It's stress. Got to be stress. At work, at home."

"You still be cooking that gravy and biscuits?"

"It been a long time." Now she turned to look at her son. "Kiera's sure right. You do look nice in those clothes."

I asked if they'd like a picture together. A picture was something I could give them.

They glanced in unison at the guard. He nodded, giving permission.

At once Mary and Patrick leaned closer, having reason now to touch each other. She hugged him sideways. They smiled, then, inexplicably, broke into near laughter.

I put down my camera phone and Mary took her arm away. But Patrick still held on to her, his arm hanging over her shoulder.

"Want to see it?"

They leaned forward, heads touching, and quietly studied the image of themselves.

A sound: The door opened to Rob in his sharp black suit and bright-yellow tie.

Patrick and Mary jumped away from each other.

Unconcerned, cradling a stack of files to his chest, Rob announced, "I got a pretty good offer." He motioned for them to come sit at a table, and they obeyed.

"Is there really going to be a trial?" Kiera came back into the room. "Twelve strangers? From here? With *your* name? Patrick *Browning*? Naw," she said definitively. She made a clucking sound. "They know your daddy," she said.

Patrick said, "I ain't going to no trial."

I was surprised. Patrick's family assumed that jurors would be prejudiced against him because of his father's record. But the prosecutor's charge—first-degree murder—seemed quite clearly an overcharge. A jury would likely lower that charge.

"Isn't there good evidence for a self-defense strategy?" I asked. "Marcus was drunk and aggressive, on *your* porch. And Marcus got—" I stopped myself. "Marcus's death happened because Patrick got scared, and Marcus was really drunk. I just think, you know, the real story we could tell is that Patrick was protecting his younger sister, who's a little slow." I was relieved Pam wasn't here. "And the jury might think that the guy on the porch was—"

"There's some material here for character assassination," Rob said carefully.

Rob was an old hand. He understood there was no need to pressure a client into a deal: They were ready to take the plea even before they knew the terms.

Impossible assumptions of human behavior were embedded in the plea bargain: It envisioned a self-possessed rational actor who would assess his choices, argue, push back, calculate the risk of a trial. But Patrick and his family didn't think the justice system could help them. Nor had their lives provided evidence that they might have any power over a trial's outcome.

Nobody in Patrick's family wanted to fight. Even now, sixteen months later, it was too painful to speak about what had happened that night or to parse out fault. Patrick's mother had cried with Marcus's mother, and that had been, for her at least, enough of a resolution. So instead of a trial, which might have forced everyone to ask questions and attempt to answer them, the family took the deal. Patrick would sign the plea.

Now Rob spoke, not hiding his tone of triumph. "I got the charge reduced from first degree to manslaughter," he said. "That means anywhere between three to ten years. I think you can get out before five. The prisons are overcrowded; I got clients serving five who are out in three." Rob added, "This is one of the best deals I've gotten."

Rob's assurance sealed their decision.

I tried to understand why I felt so troubled. It was a good deal, yes. But what was the relationship between a "good deal" and justice? Had Patrick gotten what he deserved? Or—and more unnerving to consider—what if he had somehow cheated the system, getting away with something even "better" than what he deserved? The law wouldn't tell us. Afraid to condemn Patrick, none of us dared to ask this question out loud.

Rob put a piece of paper in front of Patrick. Its litany of questions included: *Do you fully understand that you have a constitutional right to a trial by jury on the charges against you and that by entering a plea of guilty to the charges you are waiving your constitutional right to an appeal of issues involved in the charges placed against you? Have you discussed all possible defenses with your lawyer?*

Rob read these aloud.

I could tell Patrick was not listening or reading. Usually he used his index or pinkie finger to follow along. But the language was too technical. It wasn't meant to be read by an ordinary person. This was a language spoken primarily by those who paid to learn it.

Patrick waited politely as Rob read, knowing he couldn't sign until Rob reached the end.

The last line:

I HAVE READ EVERYTHING ON THIS PAPER. I UNDERSTAND WHAT IS BEING TOLD TO ME, WHAT MY RIGHTS ARE AND THE QUESTIONS THAT HAVE BEEN ASKED. MY ANSWER IS "YES" TO ALL

7 QUESTIONS, I KNOW WHAT I AM DOING AND
AM VOLUNTARILY PLEADING GUILTY.

Now Patrick turned to me. "Ms. Kuo," he said urgently,
"you sure they know I already served sixteen months?"

"It's automatic," I said. "By law."

"They gone forget; that how they is." I knew his suspicion
was justified; you never knew in Helena. "You gone make sure I
get credit for serving the sixteen months? Don't forget."

Rob handed him the pen and Patrick took it. Patrick signed
his name.

Then Rob shuffled the paper into a folder, shook everyone's
hand, and left. After that day, none of us spoke to him again.

MURDER IS DISTINCT FROM MANSLAUGHTER because the murderer has a "guilty mind." The guilty mind deliberates and plans.
The more thinking one does, the more culpable one is. A gun is
purchased; an alibi is arranged; the killing is plotted.

What is the opposite of the guilty-mind charge? A situation
driven primarily by chance. A crime with a plausible alternate
reality. Manslaughter is a death that occurs *nearly* accidentally.
Manslaughter is killing without intent to kill.

Manslaughter presents a meditation on chance. If the timing
and day had been different. If certain people hadn't crossed
paths. If X's mother hadn't asked him to look for Z, his younger
sister. If X's mother felt that Z was safe in the hands of neighbors. If Z, a minor enrolled in special-education classes, hadn't
been at a party where alcohol was being served and older men
were present.

If a particular kind of ethics did not rule X's neighborhood, so that he didn't feel he had to win fights, or to fight at all. If someone had called the police; if someone had reason to believe the police would show up. If the knife had nicked rather than sliced through the vital organ. If the knife had nicked a place *below* a vital organ, missing it: the spleen but not the ventricle. If the ambulance had not been slow.

But because *X* and *Y* crossed paths, because *Y* was drunk and walking *Z* home, because *X* told *Y* to get off the porch, because *X* had a knife—what was a boys' fight is now a classifiable legal entity. *Y* is now a person who has completed the process of dying—i.e., *the decedent.*

Misfortune can present people with moral tests they simply cannot pass, writes philosopher Nir Eisikovits. The basic premise of criminal law is that you are guilty only if you're responsible. Yet factors that contribute to the crime are pure accident—here, the misfortune of being born in Helena, on the intersection of Garland and 4th. Those who do not grow up here do not get presented with certain tests. Patrick was tested, and he failed.

Patrick turned to Kiera. "What time you got work?"

"Two. I got to change."

He looked sorry. He didn't want her to miss work because of him. "Y'all can go home," he said. "Thanks for bringing those clothes." Then, as if he couldn't help himself, he added, "You can tell Daddy I'm mad at him. For not coming."

Everybody got quiet.

"He watching the kids," Kiera said finally. Then she changed the subject. "I just mad you got those flip-flops. You sure you don't want me to get you a nice pair of shoes?"

Patrick repeated, "Y'all can go home."

But nobody moved.

"I want to know what's gone happen," Kiera said.

"Y'all *know* what's gone happen."

At this, even Kiera fell silent. She went outside to smoke a cigarette and then came back.

THE TRIAL HAS DISAPPEARED FROM courtrooms, existing mostly on television. The jury, inherited from the English legal system, was uniquely American by its aspiration to be made of the defendant's "neighbors and peers," the community that bore the cost of the crime. In the 1700s and early 1800s, American juries were entrusted not merely with making a legal evaluation but a moral decision. The statistics were telling: Overwhelmingly, in murder cases, juries refused to convict. At the turn of the nineteenth century, more than *three-quarters* of Chicago homicides, for instance, led to no punishment. As criminal-law professor William Stuntz writes, *One historian's study of Chicago homicide cases in that period reads like a compendium of bar fights that got out of hand, nearly all of which took place in front of witnesses and most of which ended in defense victories.*

This bygone, more democratic incarnation of criminal justice applied only to the urban North. Lynching—that *ultimate rejection of legal procedure*, as Stuntz puts it—was the most prevalent form of "justice" in the Delta. Lynchings and mob violence were sanctioned, and often abetted, by state power. During the Elaine massacre, the local police, with the aid of federal troops, rounded up over a thousand black people. At the Helena jail, the police beat, tortured, and electrocuted them. "The Negroes were whipped unmercifully. Every time the strap was applied it would bring blood," a white police officer later testified. "We whipped them to make them tell what we wanted them to tell. We wanted them to tell facts that would convict themselves and others under arrest." He also stated that at least one of the white men who had died might, in fact, have been accidentally killed by other whites: He recalled hearing one of the men in his posse shout, "Look out! We are shooting our own men!"

Eventually, based on confessions that were mostly coerced, the prosecutors indicted 122 black people and charged 73 for first-degree murder. Twelve men were put on death row. In each of these twelve trials, the all-white jury returned a verdict in less than ten minutes as armed whites surrounded the courthouse. The Supreme Court reversed six of these convictions. But locally, there was little public reckoning. Over four decades after the massacre, two residents of Phillips County would write an article that set out, as they explained, to list some "facts." *All those accused of complicity in the Elaine riot were given fair trials*, wrote the local historians. *No mob violence was attempted. . . . Phillips County had always, before this riot, and has since, enjoyed the reputation of having peaceful relations between the races.* The account was printed in the *Arkansas Historical Quarterly* in 1961. Thirty-five years passed, and in 1996, the *Phillips County Historical Quarterly* printed the same article again.

Still, as barbaric as the history of criminal justice is in the South, the number of lynchings declined after the first two decades of the twentieth century: In 1900 there were, on average, one hundred lynchings a year. By the eve of *Brown v. Board of Education*, lynchings had essentially ended. Grassroots movements in the South—not federal intervention—from communist radicals to local NAACP branch members made the difference. They organized, they spoke out, they dramatically changed public consciousness, to the point where white Southern elites were embarrassed by lynchings. By the time of the Civil Rights Movement, new leaders such as King placed the burden of change on the federal government, demanding that it intervene in the Southern states on behalf of black people. And in many ways, these leaders succeeded: The Civil Rights Act of 1965 was a sweeping piece of legislation that dismantled the South's Jim Crow laws.

But pinning one's hopes on the federal government is dangerous: What if the federal government turns on you? This was what happened after the passing of the Civil Rights Act. The hoped-for knight in shining armor instituted a series of measures targeted at the black poor. Policymakers began to distance themselves from the basic idea that poverty was a root cause of crime. *Education, employment, and housing programs, although sometimes defended on their own terms, were increasingly framed as having nothing to do with lowering crime*, writes the historian Elizabeth Hinton. Overt racism was less palatable, but "crime" became the strategic, and politically acceptable, way for politicians to make statements about race: Crime was, as it is today, a code word for what poor black people do.

The story of criminal justice, from the viewpoint of the rural South, is also one of Northern hypocrisy: Attacking the Jim Crow South had been the focus and fulcrum of the progressive moment in the 1950s and 1960s. Segregation was seen as a *Southern* problem, not a Northern one. Yet once massive numbers of black migrants from the South entered the Northerner's backyard, and deindustrialization created a large jobless population in urban centers, punitive policies were devised and carried out. It was not just former segregationists who advocated for a war on crime, but rather a *bipartisan consensus of policymakers*, as Hinton writes, *acting in closed circles or as part of a larger coalition*. Federal agencies distributed millions of dollars to states, mandating them to control crime; state governments pursued convictions; the massive number of cases junked up the system, making the jury trial a pipe dream. Among these punitive policies were the long sentences for drug-related crimes that would incarcerate Patrick's father and uncle. Mass incarceration is the most *damaging manifestation of the backlash against the Civil Rights Movement*, writes civil rights attorney and professor Michelle Alexander. It was out of these years that the plea bargain was born and bloomed.

Most public debate about the plea bargain has focused on urban areas. But its effect on the rural South was, and is, disastrous. Public defenders lack the most basic resources to investigate cases. Professional standards are lower; relationships between the state and defense are more informal and less tolerant of adversarial tactics. The shortage of lawyers in rural areas is as dramatic as the shortage of teachers. Young law graduates do not want to live here. Advocacy and social service programs—mental health, drug rehabilitation, reentry, basic legal aid—are nonexistent, so convicts are trapped in a punishing cycle of plea bargains, poverty, and incarceration.

In both the South and the North today, the plea bargain now dominates: It accounts for 98 percent of the criminal cases in the country. Much has been said about the plea bargain as an assault on justice. How can a person's rights—to a fair trial, to liberty, to the presumption of innocence—be negotiated, bartered, haggled over, like something at a market? The plea said to Marcus's family: *Your case isn't worth it to us.* It said: *This is clogging up our system; we're trying to get rid of it.* For Marcus's family, a trial could have meant public vindication. Should a drunk person on the wrong porch get stabbed to death? Should he die because he walked a girl home?

Even as forms of justice have changed, one characteristic has remained the same: Crimes within all-black communities remain lowest on the priority list. *Like many social disasters, crime afflicts African-Americans with a special vengeance*, writes law professor Randall Kennedy, *for they are more likely to be raped, robbed, assaulted, and murdered than their white counterparts.* In the Delta, this is especially true. *The Delta,* wrote one progressive Southern newspaper editor in the early 1900s, *unfortunately, has never considered the killing of one negro by another seriously.* Another editor wrote, in 1903: *One nigger cuts another's throat . . . and that is the last heard of it. It is like dog chewing on dog and the white people are not interested in the matter. Only another dead nigger—that's all.*

Studying homicides in Mississippi in 1933, Hortense Powdermaker argued that homicides among black people occurred in part because the police consistently turned a blind eye. The local officials had, in turn, taken their cue from other citizens in power: Planters regularly bailed out tenants who had broken the law, even those who committed violent crimes. Black people were induced *to take the law into his own hands. . . . Since he can hope for no justice and no defense from legal institutions, he must settle his own difficulties, and often he knows only one way.*

A trial implies a public reckoning; it is meant to be an effort toward a shared meaning of what happened on a night that changed everything. Yet in the haphazard administration of the plea, the justice system signals that the case's meaning has already been decided. A fight happened in an all-black neighborhood, between two undesirables. As was true for more than a hundred years, killings of black people by black people are considered a routine spectacle, at once invisible and self-evident.

"PATRICK BROWNING," THE JUDGE CALLED.

Patrick stood. His hands leapt to the waist of his pants to pull them up, forgetting that he was wearing a clean pair of khakis that fit properly.

Nearby, Mary began to rock back and forth.

Patrick now stood in front of the judge. He looked alone up there, like a diver on a high board. The prosecutor and defender sat at their tables, far away, like spectators.

As for the three of us, we saw only his back and his hands, which he had clasped behind him. An observer at the rear of the courtroom might think Patrick was handcuffed; in fact, he was trying to be courteous.

Only the judge had a square view of Patrick's face, but his head was bent toward his papers.

Finally he spoke, without looking up.

"For the record, are you Patrick Browning?"

We heard no sound. Beside me, Mary began to heave. Her legs were set several feet apart, left hand on left knee, right hand on right.

"You'll have to speak up," the judge said.

Patrick must have said something, because now the judge had gone to his next question: "How old are you?"

Again silence.

The judge repeated, "You'll have to speak up. You have a quiet voice."

I leaned forward and so did Kiera.

Finally a sound, very low.

"Twenty, sir."

"How far did you get in school?"

"Tenth grade, sir."

"Do you understand you're being charged for a Class D felony?"

"Yes, sir."

Patrick's mother took her hands off her knees and drew them up to clutch her chest.

Rob said, "For the record, he's served five hundred six days."

"Counsel, do you agree?"

The judge turned to look at the prosecutor.

"I haven't made any calculation. But, yes"—here he appeared to look at the ceiling, calculating—"I agree."

The judge commenced a now-familiar torrent of questions, his head still down. He read at a rapid-fire pace, scarcely waiting for the answer. Among the questions:

"Do you fully understand that you have a constitutional right to a trial by jury?"

"Yes, sir."

"Do you fully understand that by entering a plea of guilty to the charges you are waiving your constitutional right to appeal of issues in the charges against you?"

"Yes, sir."

"Are you entering your plea of guilty of your own free will without any promises or threats?"

"Yes, sir."

The judge wrapped up the questions and slapped the gavel.

It was done. Patrick had been convicted. Now he had a violent felony on his record, which could not be erased.

Near me, rustling sounds—Kiera was gathering her things. We nodded at each other and she hurried out, late to work.

Already the next inmate had shuffled to the center of the courtroom, the same one who met his lawyer the day before, having likely waited months for that single exchange. Yesterday I had taken an interest in him. Now I turned my eyes away, focusing my attention on the departing figure of Patrick, as if my disregard for the nameless inmate was justified by my loyalty to Patrick. Patrick needed my partiality.

Patrick had returned to the row with the others, his face again hidden—he was looking down.

The judge was back at the questions. *How old are you? How far did you get in school?*

Beside me, Mary's eyes were closed and her hands were now clenched in a single fist. Possibly she was praying, unaware that the ordeal was already over.

I WENT TO SEE PATRICK after he took the plea.

He handed me his notebook—he'd done his homework.

It was almost like any other day, but we knew it wasn't. So I didn't touch the notebook.

Moments earlier I'd called a friend from law school. "Congratulations," he had said; three to ten years for manslaughter was "a good deal." When I paused, he added impatiently, "For God sakes, he killed somebody."

My friend was trying to shock me out of my unhappiness and in this way comfort me.

"Patrick can be out by the time he's twenty-five," he continued. "And then he can start all over."

It was true, as my friend suggested, that I had lost all perspective: A short sentence is better than a longer one. But it didn't feel good. When Patrick got out, he would have a criminal record. He would be marked as a felon; he'd have trouble getting a job; he would look at himself differently for the rest of his life. He could not start over as if he'd woken up from a nightmare and taken a shower.

"Hey," I said to Patrick, "how'd you feel up there?"

He reached down to touch the flap of his shoe.

"Not knowing what to say," he said finally. "Only knowing"—he swallowed—"only knowing it gonna be guilty."

"Do you *feel* guilty?"

"I *know* I guilty."

He put his head in his hands.

I wanted to tell him: *It's not your fault alone. It's society's fault.*

Bad schools, bad neighborhood, family, history, racism, a now-obsolete economy that had for a century depended on black labor and then discarded it.

But how to explain this?

Would that be saying, *You are not the agent of your own actions?*

Would it be saying, *You cannot change yourself; you cannot change your future?*

I remembered a January day, when I was working at the homeless shelter in Massachusetts. It was the coldest day of the year; there was snow up to my knees. A man outside the shelter was begging me to let him in, but I couldn't, because all the beds were taken. He smelled like alcohol, and all his words were slurred. I kept saying, "I'm sorry, there just aren't any beds left." He kept begging. I kept thinking, Why should I, or anybody, have power over him?

Patrick's head was down; I couldn't see his face.

He said, "Ms. Kuo, I did what I did."

I felt an uprising in my throat; I felt water in my eyes.

He looked up and saw.

"It's okay, Ms. Kuo. Don't cry."

On a day like this, I didn't know what I could teach him. But I knew I couldn't leave.

"I want you to do something," I said. I told him to write a letter to Marcus's mother.

Now he seemed fearful.

"Right now?"

I said, yes, right now. I said I knew he wanted to do it. I said he'd already done it a thousand times in his head, when he prayed. I said if he wanted forgiveness he really had to ask for it. I said I knew he was thinking about her and avoiding thinking about her. Anything was better than what we were doing now. We hadn't learned anything from the law, had we? It hadn't helped him make sense of how he felt and what happened that night, had it?

"You gonna give it to her?"

"If I can find her."

"My handwriting ain't good."

"You know that's not true."

"I'll write it, but you write it over again."

"No."

He wrote her. He wanted her to know that before he went to sleep every night he talked to Marcus and asked Marcus to let him into his heart. He wrote her that he asked God time and time again for mercy upon his and Marcus's souls. He wrote that it was hard for him to talk to her and he had no way to explain away her pain and grief. He wrote he was sorry and that this was only the beginning; there was a heaven. Marcus was there and watched over all of them. It was a better place for them to join and be happy. And at the end of the letter he wrote: *Forgive me Mama*.

Then he folded the letter into an envelope. Two creases.

I asked, "Why do you call her mama?"

"Because he's my brother."

"Why is he your brother?"

"He ain't just another nigger."

He didn't say, *Because he's black*. He didn't say, *Because he's my neighbor*.

Kinship was an assertion. Against the loneliness of feeling degraded, against the way the world sees you. Against its judgment that you must have done something wrong to end up where you are.

10

To Paula in Late Spring

H IS HANDWRITING HAD CHANGED. HIS LETTERS WERE SMALL, consistent, and delicate. I could draw a smooth horizontal line tracing their tops. There were no darkened blotches of ink, no trace of the ballpoint pressed too hard; he had gained control of his pen.

Every day he wrote. Every day we recited poems.

We read Anna Akhmatova, Walt Whitman, Yusef Komunyakaa. We read Derek Walcott, Elizabeth Bishop, Rita Dove, Czeslaw Milosz, Li-Young Lee. We read Du Fu's songs of autumn rain and Richard Wright's haikus. Patrick noticed things, made connections. Richard Wright's line *I am nobody* recalled Emily Dickinson's *I'm Nobody! Who are you?* He knew when the meter of a poem was manipulated and guessed why. I found myself working alongside him, reading poems as if for the first time, and trying to understand what made a line work. Every evening I searched for a poem to bring the next day. I'd never read so much poetry in my life.

Each day I lugged the books into the prison in two large tote bags, one for each shoulder, and stacked them on top of one another so that the dimly lit interrogation room became a little library of picture books and guidebooks, anthologies and dictionaries. When I'd leave, Patrick would look sorrowfully at my bags, asking if they were heavy. It was April and my visits had started getting longer. In the previous fall I usually left the jail after an hour, in a rush to teach Spanish; now one visit might last a whole afternoon or morning. Conversations digressed. In one day we might have discussed the origins of comets, Hitler, and the atomic bomb.

We looked at all kinds of pictures for reference. I'd bring a random pamphlet, like "Arkansas Backyard Birds"; examining the hummingbird, Patrick wrote, *It wings beat a hundred times a second.* He studied the solar system in Bill Bryson's illustrated history of the earth and took notes: *Saturn is the sixth planet from the sun. It rings maybe iridescent gold and blue and gray. It looks like a fishing hat or a sheriff's hat.*

In one day, so much happened in Patrick's notebooks.

Each morning, he imitated a poem. The goal was to listen for the voice, meter, and sound and try to replicate each.

Philip Larkin wrote, *Yet still the unresting castles thresh / In fullgrown thickness every May.*

Patrick wrote, *Some pity these leaves are gone in fall / Another season again it's golden.*

Dylan Thomas wrote, *Do not go gentle into that good night.*

Patrick wrote, *Break down the hill and build a house to live.*

Pablo Neruda wrote, *I do not want to go on being a root in the dark, / hesitating, stretched out, shivering with dreams / downwards, in the wet tripe of the earth, / soaking it up and thinking, eating every day.*

Patrick wrote, *I do not wish to be a dream in a grave / A guitar untuned whining at night / Howling, with the inflection of a wolf, / Complaining, of things that won't be heard.*

Every poem took a long time.

He would count syllables using his thumb, tapping it once on each fingertip.

First his left hand, then his right.

He would frown, lean back down.

He would crack his neck, rotate it.

Then the process would start over.

After, as I read his work, he massaged his hands as if they were sore.

I had been taken aback by Patrick's interest in some of these poems. He loved Whitman. He loved lines about the delight in the carpenter nailing a plank and the mother singing to her child. He loved: *STRANGER! If you, passing, meet me, and desire to speak to me, why should you not speak to me? And why should I not speak to you?* Patrick didn't deride any of it—he wanted to be a part of it. Whitman was fun and easy to imitate: exclamation points, bursts of feeling, clear line breaks. *You, Patrick Browning! What widens within you?* And: *O take my hand Patrick Browning! As the world moves! So vivid and quaking!* And another: *I hear the amazing drippings of a waterfall from huge cliffs or mountains / I hear leaves shaking as the storm rattles the tree branches.* When you wrote a line about waterfalls, cliffs, mountains, storms, leaves, you made that beauty a part of you. You built an inner world that moved and amazed you.

But perhaps of all the poems we studied, he knew W. S. Merwin's "To Paula in Late Spring" the best.

Let me imagine that we will come again / when we want to and it will be spring, Merwin wrote to his wife.

Patrick wrote a version for his daughter. *Let me imagine that I am there with you / when you need me even if a little late*

Then he wrote one for his mother. *Let me imagine that we are high in the mountains*

We recited the Merwin at the beginning of each session; we knew it so well that it nearly bored us.

I HAD RETURNED TO POETRY out of desperation, after a series of failed lessons with prose. We would get halfway through a novel or play and we would quit: a Walter Dean Myers story (he said it reminded him too much of his life), a Shakespeare play (it was taking too long), the Book of Job (he said God must have had a reason to punish Job, and I couldn't persuade him otherwise), *The Things They Carried* (he said it was too violent and that he didn't like not knowing what was made up). So poetry arose from a process of elimination.

"I think you'll like this poet." It was George Herbert. "He was a pastor. And he writes in a simple, natural voice."

The poem was an old favorite: "Love (III)," in which Love exhorts the speaker to eat at his table.

"What's your favorite line?"

Patrick thought. *"But quick-eyed Love, observing me grow slack,"* he decided.

"Like me—maybe I got a little dust on me, maybe my ways be kinda crooked. But Love, because it eye be quick, it watch him fall away. People that don't love you ain't telling you that you falling away. But Love *do*. Love observe you, then Love tell you. What *your* favorite line, Ms. Kuo?"

I told him I liked the last two lines. "*'You must sit down,' says Love, 'and taste my meat.' / So I did sit and eat.*"

He agreed they were good ones. "It's God," he said. "It's God inviting you to dinner. It's God saying, *We straight.*"

Then he asked, "Yesterday wasn't Easter, was it, Ms. Kuo?"

"It was."

"Only reason I knew 'cause yesterday morning time they had given us some eggs. They usually give us plain grits. Somebody was like, it's the first Sunday of the month; it's Easter."

"Do you usually celebrate Easter?"

"My mama, she cook or whatever. But not really. What happen on Easter, anyway, Ms. Kuo?"

He leaned forward.

I began: "So you know how Jesus is killed the Friday before Easter?"

He blinked, suggesting he didn't know. Kids were religious here, but their knowledge of Bible stories was selective.

"So on Sunday," I continued, "Mary Magdalene goes with a friend to visit his tomb."

At the sudden sound of his mother's name, Patrick beamed.

"But on the way to the tomb, they keep worrying about it. Because it's blocked by a big stone. They keep asking, *Who's going to roll the stone for us? How are we going to get in?* But when they get to the tomb, the big stone isn't there. And somebody says, *The tomb is empty!* Jesus isn't there, because he's been—"

"Raised," Patrick concluded. "An Easter—that the day he be born again?"

"Yes, that's right. Everybody is so excited but also terrified, because they can't believe it."

I had not grown up with much religion, but in college I had accompanied friends to services and found myself at a small prayer group for the first time. People prayed about all sorts of things, opening themselves up (it seemed to me) to the criticism that their innermost cares were trivial. What could I say? To be honest, I was doing pretty well. My turn came. "Help me, God," I began, tentatively, awkwardly, wanting to laugh at myself, not believing I was speaking to anybody. "Help me, God . . ." And when I repeated that weird phrase, the repetition softened its strangeness, and I thought it was not such a bad thing to have the structure of address decided for me, so I could focus on content. And indeed the supplicatory posture released the worries I had been holding in: About a friend suffering from the first episode of major depression in her life, a new territory for us both. About a guest at the homeless shelter, his life's belongings, including a picture of his grandchild, in a garbage bag. His two weeks were up, and he wanted to store his bag in our locker, but he worried that the staff would get rid of it, and I locked the bag away. "Help me, God, help me sit still with my friend. Help me, God, to concentrate on things that matter."

I told Patrick all this. He was listening, concentrating. He wanted me to believe in God. And he was happy to hear me explain Easter. It meant something to him that I knew the story. And this in turn made the story mean something to me.

It was almost May, and in the mail I got keys to my place for the summer. It was an apartment in northern Oakland, where, my subletter promised, there was excellent Lebanese, Ethiopian, and Korean food all on one block. I was going to drive, and I decided on the route I'd take. A friend from law school would meet me in Albuquerque and help me drive from there to California. We would stop at the Grand Canyon, see cacti, take pictures. I toyed with the idea of staying longer in the Delta, but now I knew that it was time to leave.

"I'M WRITING THIS IN PART to tell you that if you ever wonder what you've done in your life, and everyone does wonder sooner or later," Patrick read. He paused, curiosity seeping into his voice: Perhaps he was wondering about himself. *"You have been God's grace to me, a miracle, something more than a miracle."*

Patrick paused at the word *miracle*, to think.

Patrick's deep spiritual belief, his ability to recognize tonal joy and grief, his poetry and sense of sound—all of these led me back to *Gilead*, Marilynne Robinson's novel that I had first read at the end of my two years in Helena. An aging pastor writes a letter to his young son. For me the book had been about different ideals of love and how we strive and fall short. There was not enough time now to read all of it together, but I would treat the passages like poems, and Patrick could imitate them as he had done before.

When we reached the end of the page, I told Patrick, "You know what I'm going to ask."

Patrick read his favorite line: *"You may not remember me very well at all, and it may seem to you to be no great thing to have been the good child of an old man in a shabby little town you will no doubt leave behind."*

"How would you describe the tone?"

"Jubilant. Peaceful. Hopeful."

He said the words in quick succession, as if the words themselves formed a poem he'd memorized.

I told him his assignment. "It's just like your imitation of Merwin," I said. "Same thing. Just sentences, not lines."

An hour passed.

Again the motions repeated themselves.

He would frown.

He would crack his neck, rotate it.

He would leaf through his notes, then a book of pictures, hunting for images.

Then the process would start over.

Finally, Patrick passed me his letter.

Do you remember when me, you and your mother went fishing at Bear Creek? I know you do, you were so happy. And yes, I will take you back there again. Down by the bank where I was sitting you came running, calling, "Daddy, look." There near some bamboo you showed me some bright pink flowers. They were pink peonies with many petals that you described as more beautiful than a rose. You pulled one and said, "Take this, Daddy," and I put its stem in my mouth. That made the biggest smile on your face so I picked you up and kissed your nose with the peony still hanging from my mouth. After I let you down, you asked can we come back again one day and I said, of course, yes.

I held the thin, torn-out notebook paper. I could not believe he had written it. It was more than I had expected. It was better than what I had taught him.

I had been searching all along for a form in which Patrick could write. I had thought it was poetry, but now I had really found it: the letter. This was the medium that captivated him even more. And why wouldn't it? In his life he had already done it a thousand times—for what was prayer but a letter to God? He had been writing letters all along: to Cherish, to Marcus's mother. The letter injected writing with purpose, it was a plea to be heard, it was one person addressing another. The choice of *Gilead* clarified itself. It explored love between friends, between spouses, between whites and blacks, between God and his supplicants, between a professional and those to whom he is entrusted—but, above all, it dealt with a parent's love for a child. How to express to a child what you know, what you wish for her? What could you say that is worth keeping?

"Cherry will read this someday and know that she's the center of your life," I said. "You've come so far. Do you remember what your letter was like back then?"

He waited for me to describe it.

"A repetition of *I'm sorry—I'm sorry for not being here, for dropping out of school. Don't be like me; don't do what I did.* This is the first time that you don't seem afraid of her. Because before, what you wrote—that's a weight on a child, don't you think? How would she have felt if she'd read those letters from seven months ago?"

He paused. "Just as lost as I was. Like her daddy don't know too much."

By May he'd written dozens of letters to Cherish, one each day. Today's letter was about canoeing. I'd shown Patrick pictures of my own canoeing trip down the Mississippi during high-water season: Rain flooded the area, trees stood in water, and, in certain channels, the river was transformed into an underwater forest that appeared to admit only animals that could swim or fly. "You canoe *around* the trees?" Patrick asked, studying a picture, surprised. I explained each picture, sharing the names I had learned. "These are Virginia creepers, and these are

cottonwoods, and those are mulberries." And I pointed to a
small green clump and said, "That's a turtle on a log. You can't
really see it, but it's hanging out in the sun."

He worked for an hour. Then he showed me what he'd
written:

*You and I are canoeing down the Mississippi River. There are
so many trees, bunched together in the water like bushes. The
river is shadowy in some places, but the light shines through
cracks of the trees. Near the bank there is a great blue heron,
standing still, searching for fish. And as we are passing, a silver
carp surfaces as if it is jewelry in the water. You say, "Dad look
a snake." I say, "Where" and you say, "No it's just a vine." We
hear splashes, the fish jumping or the frogs croaking. The white
light glitters on the muddy water, which you say looks like
coffee.*

*When we approach the thicket of cottonwoods and cypress,
we can hear an inflection of birds. On some low branches hang
plenty of mulberries. You stretch your arm straight out to grab
some. They are white because they are not ripe yet, but the edi-
ble ones are bluish-black. You eat one and it stains your shirt.
As we row away, I tell you that whenever we are at home and
you take a nap, I think of you as a sleeping berry.*

*It's amazing to see trees grow out of the water, in so many
different shapes. Some have a Y-shape, and others are lying
down. The willow trees are so tall that you can hear our necks
cracking while we are looking for the top. To the left is a float-
ing log and suddenly I see it has two turtles on it. We watch the
turtles until they jump off. You want to feel the water, too, so
you put your foot outside the canoe and into the river. I can see
it dangling under the surface like a little fish.*

I am sitting at the bow, with my hands behind my head,

mesmerized. If the wind blows and the trees leaves shake, it
sounds like rattling paper.

My chest pounded with astonishment. Where had he gotten these ideas? I could trace the mulberries and the turtles, the cottonwoods and the willows. But we never talked about the blue heron, the silver carp, or the nickname for his daughter (a sleeping berry!). Nor the frog croaking, the muddy water, the necks cracking below the trees.

I read the letter a second time. I was searching for myself, for deposits of our conversations, memories he'd shared or words I taught him. But I was barely there. Each word felt like a tiny impulsive root, proof of a mysterious force that exceeded me.

"Remember what you said about Lucy?"

Patrick looked at me blankly. He did not remember.

"How you said the book was like a gift to her from C. S. Lewis? Now your letter is your gift. Someday you'll take Cherish on this trip, and you'll tell her you'd planned it a long time ago."

AND FINALLY WE READ BALDWIN's letter to his nephew, printed in *The Fire Next Time.*

I'd sent him the book when I first learned he was in jail. But he hadn't read it. "I tried," he'd said to me simply when I asked about it. I didn't inquire further.

As I looked at Baldwin's letter again, the strangest thing happened: I heard Patrick's voice as I read it.

I have begun this letter five times and torn it up five times.

I keep seeing your face, which is also the face of your father and my brother.

I tell you this because I love you, and please don't you ever forget it.

And now you must survive because we love you, and for the sake of your children and your children's children.

Baldwin wrote the letter in 1962, at the heart of the Civil Rights Movement. In its brief pages, it told a story of how American history tested your capacity to love. How it made you love less, hate more. How hate made you lose your sense of self. Hate worsened and deepened your feeling that you did not belong. But you did belong: *For this is your home, my friend. Do not be driven from it. . . . you come from sturdy, peasant stock, men who picked cotton and dammed rivers and built railroads, and, in the teeth of the most terrifying odds, achieved an unassailable and monumental dignity.*

I showed Patrick the letter we would read in a few days.

"What's the title?" I asked him.

He read, "'My Dungeon Shook: Letter to My Nephew on the One Hundredth Anniversary of the Emancipation.'"

"And what's emancipation again?" I quizzed.

"Getting rid of slavery," he said, and I nodded swiftly.

"And what do you think black people most wanted after emancipation?"

Patrick guessed easily. "Power, money, respect, land."

"Yes, yes, yes, yes. Land, especially. Do you think they got it?" I asked.

He knew the answer. "No."

I set aside the next couple of days to talk about history.

"After the Civil War," I said, "the U.S. government set up this law where you could apply for land at an office in Little Rock. What do you think might have gone wrong?"

Patrick guessed again, this time answering in the form of questions: "How you going to get all the way to Little Rock? How you going to know about the land if don't no one tell you? They probably don't believe it; it's a trick. And that land's valuable, people going to steal it."

I agreed. "You needed to own a horse or to pay for a ride. There was corruption, and people took bribes to give it away." In the end, only about 250 black families in all of Arkansas got land.

Guiltily, I skipped through major world events of the next hundred years. I wanted him to examine a book that had large black-and-white photographs of the Civil Rights Movement. I said we needed to figure out what was happening in 1962, the year Baldwin wrote the letter to his nephew. Baldwin had been in a different country, in France, but the Civil Rights Movement had brought him back to the United States. He'd wanted to visit the South.

Patrick examined the pictures. In Mississippi, white mobs at Ole Miss were burning and breaking everything in sight. They were angry because they didn't want this guy—I pointed to James Meredith—in their classes at law school. We digressed about Meredith. He wasn't afraid. He pledged to walk a hundred miles across the Delta, starting in Memphis and ending in Vicksburg. He started the walk. A sniper got him on the second day.

"Did he die?"

"No. He was struck; he fell down. But he didn't die. And he got to law school eventually."

He paused. "You say James Baldwin came here?"

"Yes. Well, not Helena exactly. But parts of the South."

"He came back to see his family?"

"No, he'd never lived in the South before."

Patrick looked incredulous.

"I wouldn't do that," he said.

"Maybe you would."

"No." He shook his head.

"Well." I gave him his homework: to read Baldwin's letter.

PATRICK WALKED THROUGH THE DOORWAY, holding up the book in the air as if it were a medal he'd won. "It's real," he said. My heart surged: So finally it could be this easy. You give the person a book, he reads it, he's moved; after a certain point you can just be a delivery woman, a conduit.

Patrick sat down and immediately, without bothering to wait for me to ask how he was doing, wanted to show me his favorite line.

"You must accept them and accept them with love," he read. He explained what it meant to me, in an authoritative, almost didactic way. "This mean that after slavery and segregation I got to put my pride aside and say it's okay. James, he be talking about *real* love. Real love be like a mother has for a child. She don't love you because of who you are; she loves you because she loves you. He want that kind of love to be everywhere; he know that love grow when you give it. We got to be bigger, we got to be greater.

"This real, Ms. Kuo," he repeated. "He be writing to a nephew—I got a nephew, too. Really, it just make me feel better about, you know, being black."

I felt like celebrating at his expression of racial solidarity. I nodded eagerly, not hiding my pleasure.

"What's your favorite line?" Patrick now asked me.

"It is the innocence which constitutes the crime. . . . For these innocent people have no other hope. They are, in effect, still trapped in a

history which they do not understand; and until they understand it, they cannot be released from it."

He agreed it was a good line. "What does this mean to you?" I asked.

"It's deep, it's no joke. I think what it means is, white people don't know our history. Or don't understand. It's deep—he don't just say white people be evil, that they be lying. He just saying they don't know because they don't want to know, so they ain't going to know. Maybe this is why a lot of black folks give up in life."

"And why is that a crime?" I pushed. "To not know?"

"It's like we black people are kinda left behind. So for them not to know, not want to know, that be coldhearted. Because when James say, *For this is your home, my friend, do not be driven from it,* that remind me of Douglass, how Douglass say this be our home, too. So thank God for Frederick Douglass; thank God for people like them protesters. Thank God he fought; thank God they fought."

At this Patrick halted, doubting himself. "But the truth is that even when we be thanking them, they be *stressful* to think about it. People don't *want* to think about it. Like when James talk about white people, how they be *fleeing from reality*. For me, it ain't just about them, it about us. Drinking, getting lost, getting high, trying to forget, being confused—we want to forget, because we don't want to know about slavery, about our history. It real; it painful; it stressful. It unbelievable. But the only way we gonna overcome it is by thinking about it.

"I don't know nothing about slavery, Ms. Kuo, but I can tell you about my life. I really got so many problems. I can kind of figure out that my life is hard, but I just don't know how hard. I only know what I know. I can compare it to yours and say, *Oh, this be harder than yours.* But compared to a slave, my life is easy.

And compared to white people, I don't know, because I don't know really anybody white, so how can I talk about them?"

His voice had grown soft so gradually that the silence now didn't seem strange.

"Sometimes I feel . . ." he began, deliberating. "Sometimes I feel like I want to switch places with Marcus, give him life back. Take his place."

I swallowed. How had we come back to Marcus?

"Maybe I'm just talking," Patrick said, equivocating. "This"— he gestured toward the cells with his hand—"this just what we all go through. It's anguish; it's pain; nobody want to feel pain."

He asked whether we could take a little break.

FOR A MOMENT HIS MOOD had lifted. For a moment the Baldwin had carried him to a clearing, a precipice. Baldwin seemed to give him a new point of view—that of Herbert's Love, whose quick eye observes the people going slack, who forgives by telling them to sit and taste the meat.

Then as he remembered Marcus, the mood had vanished. No sooner had he felt the powerful freedom of historical perspective than he was compelled to look back at himself.

It took work to build an inner warmth toward yourself; without it, you could not see yourself in others, in heroes.

It was through reading Baldwin with Patrick that something clicked in me. This was why I loved Baldwin: He talked openly about the struggle to feel warmth toward oneself. He'd written that questions of race operated *to hide the graver question of the self*. It wasn't that he denied the existence of racial inequality. But the harder task was to figure *out who one was* because and in spite of it. So this was why I had done the "I Am" poems, the pictures of ourselves, the classroom exercises when I first got to the Delta. I had not expected to do any of that. I had wanted, instead, to teach directly about politics and history. I wanted to rile them up with Martin Luther King and Malcolm X, and I hoped they would connect with Obama. For the same reasons, it occurred to me now, I had introduced Frederick Douglass to Patrick. I had wanted to feed students with their examples. I had wanted Douglass's very spirit to merge with Patrick's. But, I was learning, you can't try to fill someone up with stories about the people you think he ought to contain. You first have to work with his sense of himself.

Douglass, King, Malcolm, and Obama were all black men who attained a measure of freedom through the act of writing about their lives. But my students had no stories about the Delta, no frame strong enough to hold these great men. *Is there no context for our lives? No song, no literature, no poem full of vitamins, no history connected to experience that you can pass along to help us start strong?* wrote Toni Morrison. The absence of stories was itself the violence that I had missed.

Baldwin's book lay on the table between us, his portrait on the back cover. His famous eyes looked straight at the camera.

"He always thought he was ugly," I said.

Patrick said, "He ain't ugly."

CHERISH WADDLED TO THE FRONT door of her family's house and looked through the screen. A school bus stopped in front. Children teetered out, wearing backpacks and filling the street with chatter.

"Don't she look just like her father?" Mary said. "I broke down crying when I first saw her, she look so much like him."

I was leaving the next day and saying goodbye. Pam, Kiera, and Willa each gave me a hug. Then Pam swooped Cherish in the air and they all took her outside to look at the school bus.

"If you ever need anything," I said to Mary, "you can call. You have my number."

She nodded, but I knew she wouldn't.

Mary was quiet for a moment, and then she said, "Pat, he see his mistakes. He don't blame nobody for his mistakes. I think that's a good thing about him. He think he burdening us. . . . Hopefully when all this over with, he be able to forget yesterday and start his life over."

"Do you think he can?"

"I believe he can. I talk to God every day, all day. Yes, I do." She started to nod, as if listening to a sermon, and then she clasped her hands. I realized that she was stealing a moment of prayer.

"I always tell him he can come back, this always be his home. But I believe it be time for him to get away from here, find somewhere to live." She swallowed. "Wherever I'm at, my children always coming back."

Mary had stuck by her family, and now they wanted to stick by her. When her husband went to prison the first time and got out, she took him in. When he went to prison a second time, she took him back a second time. When her brother got a life sentence for killing their aunt during a drug high, she didn't forsake him. When her eldest child, Willa, got pregnant, moved away, came back, and had no place to stay, she took Willa and her baby grandson in, no hesitation. When Kiera dropped out of school, she did the same. Everyone would have a home with Mary. The entire time, she never stopped working. At work, as a cook, she stood for hours on her feet, not complaining. She got seizures from her diabetes, she had a string of minor strokes, but she kept going to work. Her boss used to say *nigger this, nigger that*, and others got mad, but she didn't mess with any of them. *He who guards his mouth and his tongue guards his soul from troubles*, she quoted to me. She did live by those words. She liked night shifts because she liked the quiet.

I wondered how many among those who stayed in the Delta had done so to satisfy obligations to people they couldn't bear to leave behind. They couldn't leave their loved ones even for the chance to live a new and different life. With a pang I thought about my parents, how I was constantly moving from one place to the next, never home. They wanted this for me, just as Mary wanted it for her kids. But Mary was in poor health. Her children must have known how fragile she was and wanted to watch over her.

"Maybe I should've left already. I be ready to get out of this town myself. I ain't never live nowhere." Now she began to nod to herself again. "No, ma'am, nowhere else but here."

"You all packed?"

"Yeah."

Patrick gave me his homework. "Didn't want you to get all mad on your last day," he said, smiling. "How many states do you go through to get to California?" he continued.

I rummaged through my bag, got out my atlas, and handed it to him.

I started to read his homework. He had done it all.

To Cherish: *A poem written by W. S. Merwin that I love is called "To Paula in Late Spring." I know it by heart and I would love for you to know it, too. Close your eyes and listen to the sounds of the words. Where is he coming to? What makes him want to come again? What makes him imagine? . . .*

He wrote: *The line I find most mysterious, Cherish, is the line with the phrase "worn griefs." It's full of questions. He never says what his worn griefs are but I wonder. I think of clothes and shoes as worn but grief? What has he been through?*

He wrote: *The last line is "of our long evenings and astonishments." Do you notice the word* our? *I wonder where you and I will be standing. What will astonish us?*

Then I turned to his imitation of W. G. Sebald, a diary entry from *The Emigrants*, from a man who had left his native Germany. Patrick had been studying it patiently.

He could do anything at this point. It was both the right and wrong time to leave.

I moved on to an essay—we still called it a free write—he'd composed about stress.

The first time I encountered stress here in jail is when Ms. Kuo first came to see me. I cried after the visit was over inside of the visiting room. A dude was in there said "you are the one who threw your life away." It is the thought that somebody cares about me that's stressful because I stress them. There are responsibilities that I have to meet the standard of, he wrote. Then later: *I cried because somebody cared for me.*

I hadn't expected to hear that I was the first source of stress in jail—I'd meant to be its relief. I didn't know he cried after he saw me. I didn't know he was caught crying and was told it was his fault. Did it always circle back to this, to one's culpability?

I tried to remember the first day I had come to jail. Yet, like his memory, mine centered not on the visit itself but on what happened afterward: the sudden warmth of dusty air when I stepped outside, the shock and confusion of being seen by someone who knew me formerly. Was this why I had come back? To be known that way, to live up to that memory?

"Did I tell you that I went back to Stars with Aaron . . . ?" I began.

Patrick looked up. He had started to leaf through the pages of the atlas one at a time.

Oklahoma, Oregon.

"It's all fallen apart. Everything's still there, trash cans in the yard. But the gate's all locked up, so we had to look through barbed wire."

"They didn't bulldoze the place or nothing?"

"No. That would've taken them—"

"Too much work."

Patrick grunted in recognition, able to picture the school abandoned and in decay.

"Let's be honest. You went to crappy schools. What would have happened to you if you hadn't?"

"But I had you."

"That's not enough."

"It is for me."

I shook my head.

He looked down at his sandals, now neatly tied with string.

I was worried about Patrick's life after jail. What would he do in Helena? What employer would take him? Would he wander the streets again, sit on his porch? I couldn't imagine his future.

"You with Danny and Lucy last night?" he asked.

"They asked me to be the godmother of their son," I said, beaming a little.

"Aww, Ms. Kuo. Bet you wish you around for the baby birth."

"I know. Lucy is so big now." I made a gesture.

He smiled.

"You were there for Cherish's?" I asked.

"Yeah." He named the date without thinking, in June.

I jotted it down. "Danny and Lucy, they showed me the ultrasound picture."

"The what?"

"It's a picture of the baby before it's born. Did you get to see one?"

"Naw."

"You can see the head."

He squinted, as if he was trying to imagine the picture.

"What was it like holding Cherish for the first time?"

"It felt—amazing, really. To have a daughter, a baby—my own baby. She be real tiny, four pounds and three ounces, like a little pink pig. Her eyes look real big, like—real *bright* on her face. I just remember her eyes looking into my eyes. And I be thinking, this . . . this my *daughter* . . ." He faltered.

Now his voice deepened. "I wasn't ready to have no baby. I wasn't doing nothing. I just looking into her big eyes and thinking I don't got no degree, no job . . ."

His voice choked and he turned away.

I looked at his homework.

Dear Cherish,

I dreamt of us yesterday. In the dream you and I are crossing a rushing white mountain stream. The family in the farmhouse cooks for us fresh water salmon and the most delicious potatoes. Night is nearing. You point out the cabin lodge just above the hill. I say, "Yes, that's where we will sleep." The hike up the mountains is a six hour walk in length and a two hour walk in width, and is one of the most marvelous sights in the world. The trees are a gorgeous evergreen. The mountains are smoke gray with snow covered tops and jagged edges. The climate is always cool even in the summer. In the stream the water flows so rapidly, forming white bubbles like a Jacuzzi, and it runs into a beautiful waterfall. There is also a mysterious ditch the people have dug like a moat. It runs the length of the one farm and cabin. No further. The family told us that this is some of the most pure water in the country. We make our way along the mountain trail where blue birds, bald eagles, and sunbirds rest on low branches.

We see a flower called stargazer lily and it had pink and white polka dots. In the evening, when we are sitting by the stream, you say, Once we leave there will never be another place like this.

I am still awake in the middle of the night, amazed of the land. You roll over and look up at me. Suddenly a lizard, perhaps alone in the night, comes through the window and hides in a corner, as if it couldn't have found a better place. You say it looks like a snake on little legs. At daybreak, when you awaken, it is already gone. Across the stream, above the hills, the smoke gray mountains of paradisal lines are clear in the sunlight.

He had come so far, but what struck me then and for many years afterward was how little I had done for him. I don't mean this in the way of false modesty. I mean that it frightens me that so little was required for him to develop intellectually—a quiet room, a pile of books, and some adult guidance. And yet these things were rarely supplied.

Patrick had collected himself and turned back toward me.

"Can I keep this?" I held up his notebook.

He shrugged casually. Then he saw my face: It must have betrayed my disappointment. His notebooks, now nearly sacred objects to me, were not sacred to him.

Swiftly, he explained, "I be transferred in a month; they might not let me bring them. They get lost. You keep them, Ms. Kuo."

I agreed. "Somebody might take them."

At this he corrected me. "Ain't nobody want *that*." He chuckled to himself.

Maybe a record of someone's private thoughts is worthless anywhere. Certainly in jail—contraband is worth more. But I wondered if it was especially worthless in the Delta, where a calm place to read was hard to come by; where there wasn't a bookstore for a hundred miles and families couldn't afford a book, anyhow; and where a teacher had once burst into my classroom to scold me for having the kids write about the death of a classmate, not wanting them to feel sympathy for him.

Patrick returned to the atlas, studying the legend as if it were a poem he was decoding. An inch represented a hundred miles.

"Ms. Kuo, where you from again? Massachusetts?"

"No. Michigan."

He found Michigan. I showed him the county where I'd been born, Kalamazoo. "It was a good place to grow up," I said, and he nodded soberly, as if my comment was profound and explained a lot about me.

Then he found Arkansas and, tracing the river, Helena.

Then: LITTLE ROCK, FAYETTEVILLE. He pointed at BATESVILLE and announced, "I be looking *here*."

Batesville was small but still bigger than Helena.

"Making my escape route," he joked. "I just need my getaway car."

"Okay. Name the date, I'll be there."

We laughed.

"You gotta get going, Ms. Kuo?"

I checked the time.

"Yeah."

I was thinking of the Merwin poem, and how he knew it by

heart, and how he had written to his daughter, *I know it by heart and I would love for you to know it, too.*

Thinking to buy time, I said, "Let's recite it again."

The words came to us easily; they were a formality, a rite.

> *Let me imagine that we will come again*
> *when we want to and it will be spring*
> *we will be no older than we ever were*
> *the worn griefs will have eased like the early cloud*
> *through which morning slowly comes to itself*
> *and the ancient defenses against the dead*
> *will be done with and left to the dead at last*
> *the light will be as it is now in the garden*
> *that we have made here these years together*
> *of our long evenings and astonishment.*

We made it to the end without a hitch. "It's a bit like singing to yourself, isn't it?" I said. The words made sounds and the sounds kept thought away. After a while you stopped wondering what it all meant, because it's become a part of you.

But even as I said this I could remember the first time we'd read it together, and I tried to make sense of it. It was back in March, five or so months into my time in Helena, and I'd asked him for his favorite line. Answering this question had just started to become important to him.

"We will be no older than we ever were," he had said finally.

I asked why.

"Because whenever you go to this one place, it's like—it's like this place that last forever. It's like this be a place where"— Patrick made a small sound in his throat—"where time don't matter no more. Where time be just stopping."

This place that last forever.
Where time be just stopping.
A place where time don't matter no more.

I thought about all the time he felt he'd lost—no, not lost, wasted—by being in jail, and how this feeling had made him think, in turn, of all the time he felt he'd wasted during his life. For his vocabulary sentence he'd used the word *oblivion* to write: *My teenage years were an oblivion.*

"Do you have a place like that?" I now asked. "Where time lasts forever?"

Without hesitating, he said, "My mama."

I blinked. I felt I was on the threshold of some kind of understanding.

No trick, no magic, no God could reverse the past, undo what happened: un-kill a man, bring life back, or give Patrick the chance to live his teenage years again. But poetry, or this poem, had brought him closer to a feeling, to a presence, to an immensity that could swallow death and do away with time. As supernatural as it all felt, it was just the memory of love: his mother waiting for him to come home.

There were moments when I was reading with Patrick that he appeared to me anew, as a person I was just beginning to know. In these brief moments, there seemed to exist between us a mystical and radical and improbable equality. This was what reading could do: It could make you, however fleetingly, unpredictable. You were not someone about whom another can say, *You are this kind of person*, but rather a person for whom nothing is predetermined. I had given him the books, I had taught him the mechanics, and still the words had moved us separately, as if we had heard the same bird singing and the song entered each of us, changed.

It was time to go. "I need you to do one last thing," I said.

He picked up his pen.

I told him to put it down.

"You won't have to write about this. You just need to relax."

I told him to close his eyes, and he squeezed them shut. I told him to imagine a place he wanted to go. What did he see? He saw water, he said, and then, sand.

"Any sign of life?" I asked.

"A crab, all by itself."

"Any human beings?" His eyelashes flickered, his mouth twitched.

"*Cherish*," he said. I waited. "She's squatting," he continued. "Looking at the crab. She's saying that it has little legs." But, he said, his mouth in a faint smile, "her legs be little, too."

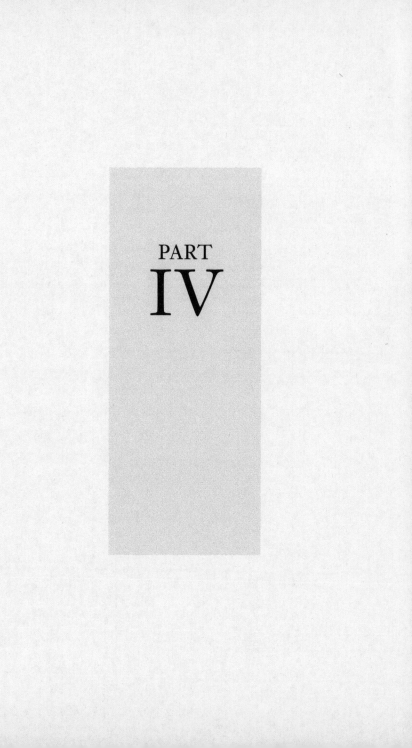

PART

IV

11

Easter Morning

It is to his grave I most
frequently return and return
to ask what is wrong, what was
wrong, to see it all by
the light of a different necessity
but the grave will not heal
and the child,
stirring, must share my grave
with me, an old man . . .
—A. R. AMMONS, "Easter Morning"

I LIVE IN OAKLAND, CALIFORNIA, AND WORK AT A NONPROFIT organization in the district of Fruitvale. One morning a pigeon flies into an open window at work and shits everywhere. This becomes a badge of honor I share with my fellow lawyers. On Thursday evenings we hold "clinics" for clients, mostly undocumented Mexican immigrants: day laborers, gardeners, dishwashers, construction workers, nannies, all either stiffed out of wages or facing eviction.

At the end of the day, we lock up the office and get drinks—a lot of drinks. They christen me with Spanish names: Michelada, Michelina. I am happier than I can remember. *Fondo fondo fondo. Bottoms up.* I am learning Spanish. Within a month, I meet someone at a bar, also a "public interest lawyer," as we're called. I can hardly believe I am already dating someone.

THEN I GET A LETTER from Patrick.

Not just one, but several at once.

He was transferred from the county jail to prison after prison, until he ended up at Calico Rock in northern Arkansas. He tells me that he got my letters and fills me in on his days.

But I have trouble focusing on what he writes, because I'm distracted by the "how." Words are misspelled, apostrophes forgotten. His letters are larger, rounder. Where is the writing from just three months before, tiny and nearly calligraphic, which could pass as a kind of artisanal typeface? That handwriting was proof to me that I had not imagined his progress.

Be realistic, be generous, I exhort myself. Education isn't like business or accounting—present loss of skill doesn't diminish the value of the hours put in. Besides, Patrick reports good news: He's taking advantage of programs at the state prison. He has the best scores in his GED classes. In October, he sends me a copy of his high school diploma in the mail.

In a letter he asks, *Do you have a couple dollars to spare?* He had to borrow money for a stamp.

I begin to worry. Not about Patrick, but about me. I begin to think that those seven months didn't really happen, that I had imagined the mystical silences we shared while Patrick wrote. I must have dreamed the poems we memorized, because I cannot remember the lines anymore. On the way to work, holding the metal bar of a subway, I wonder what it was all for and consider the idea that once you stop thinking about something, it disappears.

STILL, I SEND PATRICK POSTCARDS. One is a picture of sequoia trees—I'd gone to a park in California with friends. *How are you?* I ask. *Look at these trees! They are the biggest and oldest in the world.*

I MOVE AGAIN; THE LEASE is up. I like my neighborhood but I want to try a new one. This time, Oakland Chinatown. My building is ugly, but in the mornings, from my window, I can see children walking to school. A hunched-over Chinese grandpa holds the hand of a little girl in pigtails; she is faster than he is, dragging him along. In the evening as I walk home, I pass by a store that says SINCERE HARDWARE. Good old Chinese.

I meet my family in Taiwan for the winter holidays. We four bike along rice paddies and wildflowers, near the island's eastern coast. Though the view here is nothing like the flat inland of the Delta, the breeze and the blue of the water remind me of driving with the kids across the bridge, our windows rolled down. Meanwhile, my mother has lost the ability to ride her bike. She teeters; she clatters; she falls. We help her get up; she is cheerful and tries again. The mountains are blanketed in verdant forests, but in the heavy mist all we see is blue and then gray and then blue again. There are mountains everywhere, behind and ahead of us, so that it feels as if we are never moving away from them.

I remember one of Patrick's poems. *My mother is around the mountains*, it began. *The cliffs lift me up to see / Her voice is in the air*. It has a lovely sound; I can hear it now: *air* and *around*, *lift* and *cliffs*. But especially wonderful is *mother* and *mountain*, two things he wanted to see; his writing gave them a home together.

Patrick calls.

"I'm out. The prisons be overcrowded, so they let me go."

Just like that.

"You're out?" I repeat. "Where are you?"

"Home."

He had served two and a half years. "I got paroled; I got good behavior."

"That's great," I say. "How is it?"

"It ain't real, Ms. Kuo." I can see him grinning.

I put down the phone. What happens now?

For Patrick, nothing and everything happens. He returns home. His mother greets him on the porch. Then, nine months later, his mother dies. She is forty-three.

Mary was taking a shower when she had the final seizure in a stream of diabetic seizures that had been occurring daily. She hit her head against the tub and died. Kiera found her body.

There was no wake. "That what she wanted," Patrick tells me over the phone, soon after the death. "She had it all planned. She wanted to be cremated. She didn't want make no big deal out of it. She didn't want people crying too much or nothing."

A month later he calls again.

I am at work and a client sits in my office.

"You don't got no two dollars to spare?"

He's insistent. Something in his voice, his breathing, his uncharacteristic pushiness, disturbs me. He is not himself. I think maybe he is on something. Is it drugs? Is it alcohol?

I am torn.

"I can't. I'm sorry."

At first I think he's hung up. But I hear him breathing.

"You there?"

"Yeah. It's okay, Ms. Kuo. I understand."

More silence. I feel trapped. I try to change the subject.

"How's the job search?"

"I be trying, Ms. Kuo. But there's nothing in Helena. I walk down the street and there's nothing."

Still waiting, my client is polite, pretending not to listen, surely trying to determine whether this is a personal or professional call and therefore gauge the extent of my rudeness. A bank has nailed an eviction notice to her door. Her emergency reassures me, as if canceling out Patrick's.

"I've got to go now. I'll try you later," I say. Then I hang up.

I don't hear from him for six months.

A FRIEND TELLS ME ABOUT the Prison University Project at San Quentin Prison, the only program in California that grants college degrees in a state prison. "You can volunteer there," she said. "Teach."

I join, and I am one of hundreds; we pour in during the evenings from organizations and universities scattered across the Bay Area. The disparity between the resources at San Quentin in California and those at the county jail in Arkansas could be measured in light-years.

At the prison I encounter the most motivated students I have ever met in my life. "On the fifth reading of this, I finally understood something," a student would begin nonchalantly.

Fifth reading? I try not to look surprised, because none of the students do. Nor is it the case, as people have surmised, that they have "nothing else to do." For most, the day begins at around six in the morning, with manual labor—upholstery, carpentry, or other jobs for which they are paid roughly two dollars an hour. After that, group meetings, drug rehab, Alcoholics Anonymous, religious meetings, counseling. Somehow they manage to fit in homework.

I meet another teacher. In a sea of white and black teachers, he is one of the few East Asian teachers, my age. He's the only one who looks somewhat like me. He's speaking animatedly to a student. Not being immune to stereotypes, I assume he is teaching math. I eavesdrop. Greek tragedy, it sounds like. *Antigone*; no, *Oedipus*? These are the only Greek plays that I have read—a gap of mine. "So he gouges his eyes out. And the story's about this: Can you change your fate?" Then the Not Math Tutor stops talking and pushes up his glasses. "What do you think?" he asks, smiling. He has a sunny disposition despite his choice of topic.

The joke is on me. There are too many English teachers at the prison, and, that evening, I end up teaching math.

MONTHS LATER, PATRICK CALLS AND says, unprompted, he's sobered up.

"I'm better now," he offers, before I even ask how he is. Inside, I swell with relief. I realize how tense I am when we talk.

"I just call to tell you I'm okay. I know you be getting all worried." He has found work, he continues, at a tombstone store in Helena, on Plaza.

"I know exactly where that is," I say, able to picture it. It's on the same block as three funeral homes, where Brandon was shot and killed at the flower shop.

I ask him what his work is like. He says that his boss puts all the dates and names onto the stones, then Patrick loads them into a truck and hauls them to cemeteries across the county. He digs plots and sets the stones. "It be good work," he says. "It be good to be outside, you know." I remember a poem he wrote: *Under scorching heat / A man is calmly working / Humming to himself.*

He tells me his family has moved to a cheaper place. Without his mother's salary they can't afford the rent. Another family has moved into his old house, and another death occurs on the porch, also of a black man in his twenties. He is shot in the face. Patrick doesn't know details beyond that.

"The same place," Patrick says, and repeats that phrase again, with emphasis. *"The same place."*

After we hang up I reach under my bed and pull out my box of loose-leaf papers from Arkansas. A poem drifts out: A. R. Ammons's "Easter Morning." Maybe I had planned to share it with Patrick but ran out of time. After months immersed in affidavits, spreadsheets, briefs, and letterhead, my eye tries to adjust to the empty space on the page, as an eye adjusts to light.

The poem is in seven parts, a memory of a single experience: When the poet is four, his infant brother dies. *I have a life that did not become, / that turned aside and stopped,* it begins. *It is to his grave I most / frequently return and return.* He wants to ask what is wrong, what went wrong, what might finally put the child to rest. But the child will not rest. *And the child, / stirring, must share my grave / with me, an old man . . .*

I tape the poem to my wall. I start to write about Patrick.

THE NOT MATH TUTOR TURNS out to be Taiwanese American like me. A graduate student at Berkeley, he studies religion and German history.

"You speak German?" I ask.

"Yes, but—"

"Say something in German," I command.

He is shy and refuses.

"You probably don't actually speak German," I tell him.

I begin to date the Not Math Tutor, whose name is Albert.

PATRICK TAKES A BUS FROM Arkansas to California, to visit a friend in San Francisco whom he met through Job Corps. He has just graduated from the program with a certificate in carpentry and plumbing.

Its huge and beautiful, he texts me about California, somewhere between Los Angeles and San Francisco.

My mother and father are in town. Albert and I have just gotten married.

Patrick comes to visit. Everyone shakes hands with him. Mortifying me, my dad reaches out to touch Patrick's giant Afro; Patrick is good-natured about it.

We take a walk alone in Crissy Field, an unfolding sheet of green that overlooks the bay and, farther out, the ocean. We watch a dog gallop past us.

I tell Patrick I am still writing about him, about us, about reading in jail, about Arkansas. "Is this okay?" I ask. "I won't use your name."

"You can use my name," he says. "I believe in testimony; I believe in God."

I feel relieved. But I am thinking to myself, This is not his testimony; it is mine.

I ask Patrick what he wants to do with his life, if he could do anything he wanted. He says, "Truck driving." He wants to handle big eighteen-wheelers and see the whole country.

Later, I will say to my parents, "I always imagined him being, I don't know, an English teacher or something," and they will snicker.

"Truck driving is good," they will burst out. "Good benefits."

My mom: "He'll make more money than you did as a teacher."

My dad, pointedly: "And lawyer."

I tell Patrick I will look into truck driving for him.

He shakes his head. "I already know my felony gonna be a problem."

We talk some more. I tell him I am sorry about his mother.

He says she was sick and under a lot of stress. She was having seizures every day. She had high blood sugar levels. "Water," he says suddenly. "I don't remember her drinking no water." This strikes him, a new clue, and he turns it over in his mind.

I am thinking about how when we read together, he loved water, images and words relating to water. *Rain, river, stream, brook, dew.* For the vocabulary word *assuage*, he wrote: *Rain assuage the earth.*

I say, "You know she loved you very much."

"I talk to her every night."

"That's good."

"I talk to Marcus, too. Every night, too."

"Do they respond?"

"They do, they do." I remember his mother talking about God. Does he respond to you? *He do, he do.*

We are approaching the horizon, blue sky mixing with blue water. For a moment we don't speak, lost in our own thoughts.

Once, I had asked Patrick, "Why do you think Marcus is in heaven?"

"I just think people who be . . . murdered or whatever, they go to heaven."

"Do you think you're going to heaven?"

"I don't know. If there is a place in heaven for people like me."

"People like you?"

"People who have made mistakes or whatever."

The majestic, swooping red arc of the Golden Gate Bridge disappears into fog. I had once showed him a photograph of the bridge, and now we take a long look at it together. It is getting late, we realize, and we don't have time to cross it.

THE IDEA THAT YOU CAN change somebody's life for the better is powerful. It looms, in particular, over the debate about teachers. Are they good or bad, cheats or saints, unfairly demonized or blindly exalted? Underpinning these opposed portraits is the debate over the nature of the student. One side of the argument claims the student is an impressionable blank slate, a tabula rasa onto which teachers—if they're good enough, smart enough, and they care enough—can effectively imprint their passions and knowledge. The other side argues that the student is already permanently formed by his conditions—by violence, by neglect, by poverty. No teacher can change his life. Neither side can be completely true.

I met Patrick when he was fifteen. He'd watched dope deals at age five, accidentally set himself on fire at eleven, and seen a lot that I can't know. It may seem crazy to believe that I, or any educator, could have decisively reversed his fate. In the complex portrait of a person's life, it's possible that a teacher is just a speck.

And yet to know a person as a student is to know him always as a student: to sense deeply his striving and in his striving to sense your own. It is to watch, and then have difficulty forgetting, a student wrench himself into shape, like a character from Ovid, his body twisting and contorting, from one creature to another, submitting, finally, to the task of a full transformation. Why? Because he trusts you; because he prefers the feel of this newer self; because he hopes you will help make this change last.

Now TWENTY-FIVE, PATRICK IS THE same age as Marcus was when he died.

Patrick's daughter, Cherish, now six, attends KIPP, in Helena. Together, Patrick and I visit her classroom. Kids sit on a large colorful patchwork rug made of squares and animals. Cherish is happy to see her dad. He gives her a book about a panda who likes haiku. She hugs the book close to her chest, not wanting to part with it. "Your daddy got that for you?" another child asks, not without jealousy. Cherish nods.

Patrick wanted to stay in Little Rock because there were more jobs there. But he couldn't find one. He applied to a warehouse, but the felony was a problem. He thought about trucking, but the felony was a problem. In Helena the options were even fewer. He applied to the casino. No, the felony. He applied to KFC and Dollar General. No, they didn't have openings. He has no car, no computer.

I drive Patrick to Phillips Community College. I have been pushing Patrick to take a class there.

The lady at the desk says, "You have to take a placement test."

"I took it already, ma'am," he says.

I look at Patrick quizzically. He hadn't told me this. Had he enrolled and then dropped out?

She checks the file. "Your English scores are very good," she says, sounding surprised. "Very good."

I look at Patrick. He is looking at me.

We get back in the car. I ask what happened at the college. He says he took some welding classes, but he dropped out. When was that? I ask. Before he got to Job Corps, he says. I think to myself that this was when his mother died.

The library is next. We have heard that a chemical plant will be opening in Helena. It is a solid lead. He needs a résumé, so I give him a ride to the library. The library is brand-new, clean, and airy.

Inside the library's new computer lab, where there are ten or so computers and a printer, Patrick and I type his résumé and cover letter. Patrick doesn't know how to write in a Word document or open one. I show him how. *There's no work beneath me*, he types, pecking at the keyboard with his index fingers. "That's good," I say. "Why don't you add that you take pride in your work? Because you do."

He adds the line.

I show him how to attach a document to his email, in case he needs to send applications electronically.

I print out twenty copies of the résumé, another twenty of the cover letter. Each piece of paper costs me a quarter. I hand cash to the lady at the desk, and Patrick seems sorry to see money being spent on paper.

The plant is on the outskirts of the western part of Helena, away from the river. We drive through flat fields that stretch for miles under clear blue skies, tens of thousands of acres owned by investors of large corporations. The only signs of habitation are the colossal machines that fertilize the crops. Few of the owners live in the Delta or need human labor.

On the ride, I hand him the book of Merwin's poetry we'd worked from while he was in prison. He touches the thick gray cover. He hasn't held a book for adults in a long time, I'm guessing. I feel a pang but hide it.

"Let's see how many lines you remember," I say.

"Aww, Ms. Kuo," he says, laughing the way he did when I first asked him to do homework in jail.

"You can test me, too."

He flips to the right page; he tries. I try, too. Certain lines come back to us easily.

"Have you been writing at all?" I ask, and without waiting for an answer, afraid that I already know it, I hasten to say, "Sometimes a little diary or whatever, you know, helps let out stuff. It helps. At least, it helps me . . ." I trail off.

He has turned to look out the window. "It's hard . . . to make yourself. You know."

I remember a passage he'd underlined in a Baldwin essay. *And they didn't even read; depressed populations don't have the time or energy to spare.* He said he "related."

At the plant, the boss is red-faced and chewing on something, maybe tobacco. He has a manner that is freehanded, patronizing.

"The most important thing," the man intones, still chewing, "is to be clean."

"Yes, sir."

"Are you clean, young man?"

"Yes, sir. I am."

"Could you take a drug test right now?"

"Yes, sir."

Until now, I had thought of Patrick's crime and imprisonment as the culmination of his pain: In his life it was the worst thing that had happened so far, but, I thought, at least things could not get any worse once he got out.

Now I wondered if I had misunderstood totally. His attempt to reenter the Delta—to find a job, to feel at home, to "make something" of himself—was a new battle, excruciating, and, unlike incarceration, with no end date. If school and then prison had, minimally, taken responsibility for him, now he had no one, not even an institution, to claim him.

Back in my room in California, I search for his letters. I do not even know where I have tucked them away. I want—I need—to read them.

Envelopes of Patrick's letters—the ones he wrote from prison after I left—spill out of a yellow folder. No rubber band binds them, and they're arranged in no particular order. Before today, the envelopes have been opened just once, the letters read just once.

I begin to read.

Once I begin, I cannot stop.

He writes: *The "Sequoia Park" must be the one of those giant trees on the postcard. That's good you got to go there and visit. California must be one of the best places in the U.S. and I bet the air there is very pure.*

He writes: *I'm sending my favorite poem I've read so far by Langston Hughes. We go to the library every other day and I look for books.*

He writes: *I'm still gladly recieving your letters. I really don't like you having a cold and I hope you get better soon.*

He writes: *I write my mom but she doesn't respond. She is busy I know supporting the family. You know I'm not social but I listen to the stories people tell. When you get time write me. I miss and love you dearly.*

He writes: *Last week I passed the pre-test. Next week I'll take the GED test. Also they put my picture on their board because I'm a distinctive student.*

He writes: *Yea, I passed the GED test. In English and writing I made 600. On the essay I made a 4. "The best scores," they say.*

He writes: *Hey! I got the postcards. My friends admired how enormous that church is in Spain. I love it. It's great you were able to travel to Spain and Taiwan that's special. I'm in peace because you are safe.*

When I first received Patrick's letters, I wanted them to represent his progress. I wanted the letters to be my evidence of Patrick's total, radical change. But to see them that way was to miss the hidden work. What is a letter but a stab at the void, an admission of need and of friendship, an expressed desire for a place in the world of human relationships? You give an account of yourself that you hope is worth reading. It is like deciding to look into a mirror while burnishing it.

He writes: *I want to share this from Ecclesiastes. "There is nothing better for people in this world but eat, drink and enjoy life. That way they will experience some happiness along with all the hard work God gives them under the sun."*

He writes: *You are the person who brought me out of my depth. Whatever you do I'm with it to the end.*

And the letter of Patrick's that I love most of all: *I found the "Mysteries, Yes" poem by Mary Oliver fascinating. Really, I laughed when reading grass being nourishing, in the mouths of lambs. Isn't that cool. My favorite line is, "How people come, from delight or the scars of damage, to the comfort of a poem." This line reminds me of you know, everything. Whats your favorite line.*

I'M MOVING AGAIN. I UNTAPE the poem "Easter Morning" from my wall, in the process ripping off a corner. I read it and find myself sitting down.

The poem ends like this: The narrator takes a walk. On this

walk he sees *two great birds, maybe eagles, blackwinged, whitenecked.* They fly, they coast, one swoops away then circles back. *It is a picture-book, letter-perfect Easter morning.* It's about twos, about doubles, about pairs, about converging and diverging. Two birds make up one pattern and forever they move in relation to the other. One merges, veers away, and returns. So two meet in a dream, two share a grave, two break in flight.

It seems to me that once you decide to find doubles, you find them everywhere.

How does a single human mind come to be divided into two beings, into a life that "does not become" and a life that does? In one, life stops, ceases to exist. In the other, life keeps going, like a tree that flowers against its will, enduring.

So Patrick talks to Marcus at night, keeping him alive, as if the man he killed never died. So Patrick talks to his mother before he goes to sleep, placing her next to him, at his bedside, the person he loved most in life, whom he believes he abandoned, now ash.

For Ammons, of all the places in the world, the place where his brother died is *the dearest and the worst* to him. He cannot leave this place. Here he *must stand and fail.* Does everybody have such a moment, a juncture or place to which they return, to which they say, *Come back to life,* so that we go on with our lives, sustaining our shadow selves, spirit-beings who talk to us and also punish us?

Here is my life that did not become, a place to which I return and return.

I am back in the Delta. It is 2006, and I've decided to tough it out. Just a few more years, long enough for me to watch my first batch of eighth graders graduate from high school. I get a dog to ease the loneliness, and this dog is spectacular. On a Delta kind of night, sun setting late and stars visible, my dog scratches at his mosquito bites, and I sip a beer. I call my parents; I tell them I'm going to stay. When I speak, my voice does not tremble: I know who they are, and though they are disappointed now, I know that they will come not only to accept but also to understand.

Because Stars had been shut down and I've started teaching at Central, I see Patrick roaming the halls. When he tires of crowds or noise, he visits my class. He steps in through my doorway, wanting to say hi. I am erasing stuff on the chalkboard, distracted, tired out of my mind. He shows me a poem or rap he's written on a crumpled piece of paper from his pocket.

But it's a chaotic school with regular fighting, and Patrick starts to go absent. I do not notice at first, of course—a new crop of students keeps me occupied—but another teacher mentions it to me. *Didn't you have Patrick Browning? He hasn't been showing up.*

I get groceries at Walmart, and, stepping out into the parking lot with my cart, I remember—his house is just a few blocks away. I knock on his door. Nobody answers and it is dark inside, but I know his father is lying on the couch; I know to wait. Patrick emerges.

Out on the porch we talk freely, as we always have out here. He knows why I've come. He says, *I'm sorry, Ms. Kuo.* I tell him, *You don't need to say you're sorry.* He promises me he'll go back again. I tell him, *Keep your chin up.* At this, he lifts his head, as if the phrase is meant literally. I tell him, *I'll be here to see you graduate.* He nods. I tell him that the Boys & Girls Club just opened; wouldn't he like to apply for a job there? We can even play Ping-Pong. I joke, *Hey, I'm Asian, Ping-Pong is in my blood; you don't stand a chance.* He smiles because I no longer seem angry. Tomorrow he'll prove himself. He'll show me his word is good. He rises to escort me to my car.

In my imagined life, I do not leave the Delta; he does not drop out of school. The night Marcus might have been killed, Patrick has decided to stay inside, studying for a test. He is focused and alert, because he has a task. Nobody asks him to look for his sister. When his father hears rustling noises outside, he gets up from the couch and says to the man, *Get out of here, or I'll call the police.* Marcus leaves. Patrick hears the commotion but thinks nothing of it; he continues reading. Nothing happens on the porch; the porch is just a porch. A place to chat when the weather is warm.

I KNOW WHAT I AM doing: wishful thinking, crazy thinking. I know that maybe nothing would be different if I had stayed, that Patrick might have kept living his life and I mine. And I know it sounds as if I think I could have saved him, as if I think I'm so important in his life. It's not like that.

Or maybe it is, in the sense that the alternative, the rational thought, would be to say to myself, *You can't do that much, you're not that important, there are so many forces in a person's life, good and bad, who do you think you are?* That's what I said to make myself feel better after I left the Delta, and sometimes I still say it. But then what is a human for? A person must matter to another, it must mean something for two people to have passed time together, to have put work into each other and into becoming more fully themselves. So even if I am wrong, if my dreaming is wrong, the alternative, to not dream at all, seems wrong, too.

It's not that I, in particular, could have altered the course of Patrick's life or that Patrick, in particular, would have responded to me. Rather, I have to believe that two people can make a powerful impression on one another, especially in a certain kind of place, where so many have left, and in a certain time, when we are coming of age, not worn down or hardened. In these times and places we are fragile and ready.

HABITS BEING HARD TO BREAK, he'd skip again. Driving along, I might catch him in the act, wandering along Valley Drive, while I run errands during my lunch break.

Patrick recognizes my car. I pull over, guiltily aware that I would not stop for just any student. I lean toward the passenger door and open it. Patrick climbs in and fiddles with the music, waiting for a reprimand. My hands grip the steering wheel. We drive a bit. He rolls down the window. Looking out, his eyes linger on what he sees. A homeless man squatting in the heat; a kid on a bike. I sense his shame—he feels he disappointed me, and himself, too. With shame one must be gentle. I turn off the music and ask simple questions. *How are you? Where are you going?* In the quiet of the car, we make plans for tomorrow.

I taught myself to feel free

I taught myself to feel free and alive
to wake up thankful to be here
and to know everything is a blessing
from my food, my family, and visits.
When the old man moans in his room
and the white guys tell sad stories,
I insist I'm fine.
I have perfect health and happiness.
I instantly realize the peaceful insects
flying across the room noiseless
and the bright light bulb
that shine like the sun for me every day
inside the county jail downtown
Only to a newcomer is it all startling.
If you ask me I'm not here
Just in my own world.

PATRICK, *April 2010*

AUTHOR'S NOTE

I am indebted to the profound work of historians who investigate African American life in the rural South. This list is not exhaustive, but I hope it recognizes sources that influenced me and points curious readers to the right places. Leon Litwack's *Trouble in Mind: Black Southerners in the Age of Jim Crow* (Knopf, 1998) and Robin D. G. Kelley's *Hammer and Hoe: Alabama Communists During the Great Depression* (University of North Carolina Press, 1990) were among my first introductions to Southern history and formed a lasting impact. I found indispensable Steven Hahn's *A Nation Under Our Feet: Black Political Struggles in the Rural South* (Harvard University Press, 2003), which powerfully chronicles the organizing of black rural poor in the South and brings to light the vibrant black social movements in Phillips County, Arkansas. Jeannie Whayne's *Delta Empire* (Louisiana State University Press, 2011) and *A New Plantation South* (University of Virginia, 1996) were essential to understanding broader socioeconomic transformations in the Delta from the nineteenth century to the middle of the twentieth century, as were Nan Woodruff's *American Congo* (Harvard University Press, 2003) and James Cobb's *The Most Southern Place on Earth* (Oxford University Press, 1992). I thank Jeannie Whayne and Paddy Riley for their generosity in pointing me to incisive and helpful sources.

On Frederick Douglass's opposition to the Black Exodus and to Back-to-Africa movements, I found helpful Waldo Martin's *The Mind of Frederick Douglass* (University of North Carolina Press, 1986) and Nell Irvin Painter's *Exodusters: Black Migration to Kansas After Reconstruction* (Norton, 1976). On the Back-to-Africa Movement in Arkansas, I consulted the work of Steven Hahn, Adell Patton, Jr., and Kenneth Barnes, which suggests that the rural black poor formed the early and most devoted constituency of Back-to-Africa Movements. I'm grateful to the work of Donald Holley on migration to Arkansas in the early twentieth century, and to S. Charles Bolton, Willard Gatewood, and Carl Moneyhon on inequality in Arkansas. On the Great Migration, Stewart Tolnay and E. M. Beck's studies comparing the economic status of those who migrated and those who stayed were eye-opening. Isabel Wilkerson's *The Warmth of Other Suns* (Random House, 2010) and Nicholas Lemann's *The Promised Land* (Vintage, 2010) offered panoramic views of the Great Migration that helped me contextualize and contrast the experiences of those who left with those who stayed.

On the first black institution of higher education west of the Mississippi, Thomas Kennedy's *A History of Southland College* (University of Arkansas Press, 2009) illuminated a fascinating local history of Quakers who came to teach and live in Phillips County and more broadly of black education in Arkansas. Randy Finley's *From Slavery to Uncertain Freedom* (University of Arkansas Press, 1996) offered a moving portrait of the Delta immediately after emancipation. I am grateful for Finley's research on the role of the Student Nonviolent Coordinating Committee in Arkansas.

On the massacre in Elaine, Arkansas, and racial violence in the Delta, I turned to Grif Stockley's *Blood In Their Eyes: The Elaine Race Massacre of 1919* (University of Arkansas Press, 2001); Woodruff's *American Congo*; the research of Karlos Hill; J. W. Butts and Dorothy James, "The Underlying Causes of the Elaine Race Riot of 1919," *Arkansas Historical Quarterly*, 20 (Spring 1961); and Jeannie Whayne, "Low Villains and Wickedness in High Places: Race and Class in the Elaine Riots," *Arkansas Historical Quarterly*, 58 (Autumn 1999).

On Japanese internment in the Arkansas Delta, I am indebted to Calvin Smith, William Anderson, Russell Bearden, and Jason Morgan Ward, and the oral histories at Densho (densho.org). On the experiences of Asians in the Delta, I consulted James Loewen's *The Mississippi Chinese: Between Black and White* (Waveland Press, 1971) and Leslie Bow's *Partly Colored: Asian Americans and Racial Anomaly in the Segregated South* (New York University Press, 2010).

On the history of criminal justice in the Delta and more generally the South, I turned to David Oshinsky's *Worse Than Slavery* (Free Press, 1996), Michael Klarman's *From Jim Crow to Civil Rights* (Oxford University Press, 2004), and Hortense Powdermaker's *After Freedom: A Cultural Study in the Deep South* (Viking, 1939).

On incarceration and justice in urban areas, I turned to William Stuntz's The *Collapse of American Criminal Justice* (Belknap Press, 2011), Michelle Alexander's *The New Jim Crow* (The New Press, 2010), Randall Kennedy's *Race, Crime, and the Law* (Vintage, 1996), Khalil Gibran Muhammad's *The Condemnation of Blackness* (Harvard University Press, 2011), and Elizabeth Hinton's *From the War on Poverty to the War on Crime* (Harvard University Press, 2016). On moral luck and criminal justice, I turned to Nir Eisikovits's work, published in *Law and Social Justice* (MIT Press, 2005). I deeply appreciated Lisa Pruitt's work on the dire shortage of lawyers in rural Arkansas.

I am grateful for the work of the Arkansas Advocates for Children and Families. Its February 2013 report on school discipline found that black students receive in-school suspension almost three times as often as white students, out-of-school suspension more than five times as often as white students, and corporal punishment almost twice as often as white students. On the battle for desegregation and the Civil Rights Movement, Richard Kluger's *Simple Justice* (Knopf, 1976) and Derrick Bell's work were formative. Robert Carter's essay was published in *Shades of* Brown: *New Perspectives on School Desegregation*, edited by Derrick Bell (Teachers College Press, 1980). On education policy and law more broadly, I find James Ryan's work penetrating. Richard Hofstadter's *Age of Reform* (Vintage, 1959) helped me think through the rural-urban divide. To understand challenges facing present-day rural America more broadly, I relied on Patrick Carr and Maria Kefalas's *Hollowing Out the Middle: The Rural Brain Drain and What It Means for America* (Beacon, 1999). We urgently need more research on criminal justice and education in the rural South today.

Mary Beth Hamilton's *In Search of the Blues* (Basic Books, 2005) formed an enduring influence on my own thinking about the Delta, and more broadly I admire the work of Ted Gioia, John Jeremiah Sullivan, and Elijah Wald in helping me understand the culture, history, and music of the Delta.

I thank Aida Levy-Hussen for pointing me to illuminating sources for over a decade and for her own penetrating work,

How to Read African American Literature (New York University Press, 2016). Her work has pushed me to understand the place of slavery in the American imagination and brilliantly articulated the projects of writers in the post–Civil Rights era. On Richard Wright's development, I consulted Michel Fabre's *The Unfinished Quest of Richard Wright* (University of Illinois Press, 1973) and Lawrence Jackson's *The Indignant Generation* (Princeton University Press, 2010). Robert Stepto's *From Behind the Veil* (University of Illinois Press, 1979) explores the relationship between African American narrative and literacy.

The Arkansas History Commission, in particular Tim Schultz, has provided microfilm of Arkansas newspapers. On desegregation and De Soto, I turned to Helena newspapers. For advertisements of slavery, I looked at *Southern Shield*. For a portrait of black life in Arkansas, I looked at *The Miller Spectator*. Thanks to Kevin Schultz for generously sharing materials on James Baldwin.

I have changed names of most people in this book to protect their privacy. No person in this book is a composite. I thank the patience and generosity of people in the Delta who shared their experiences and answered my endless questions. Those who have stayed, locals and interlopers alike, I view with admiration and esteem.

In one of his letters, Patrick quotes his favorite lines from Mary Oliver's poem "Mysteries, Yes" (Beacon, 2009). Here is the poem in full:

> *Truly, we live with mysteries too marvelous*
> *to be understood.*

> *How grass can be nourishing in the*
> *mouths of the lambs.*

How rivers and stones are forever
  in allegiance with gravity
    while we ourselves dream of rising.
How two hands touch and the bonds
  will never be broken.
How people come, from delight or the
  scars of damage,
to the comfort of a poem.

Let me keep my distance, always, from those
  who think they have the answers.

Let me keep company always with those who say
  "Look!" and laugh in astonishment,
  and bow their heads.

ACKNOWLEDGMENTS

It has taken me a long time to finish this book and I have incurred many debts while writing it. I first thank Patrick for trusting me to write this story and sharing so much of himself with me. I've learned from his insights, stories, and faith, and I am grateful for all the years we have known each other. I hope readers will encounter his extraordinary qualities as I have. I am deeply grateful to Patrick for giving me permission to share his words and writings in this book, and I honor his generosity with contributions to the Boys and Girls Club of Phillips County and a fund for his advancement. I thank also Patrick's family for sharing their stories with me. And I thank my students at Stars for the sensitivity, intelligence, and humor they brought to class and to my life.

Aida Levy-Hussen, Tim and Liz Schuringa, and Kathy Huang encouraged me to write, and I owe them profound thanks. Aida Levy-Hussen has read basically every word I've written for over a decade now; probably the earliest version of this writing began in email correspondence with her. Her fierce intellect, passionate and independent mind, generous friendship, humane imagination, and penetrating scholarship have shaped this project and formed a lasting impact on me. I'm indebted to Aida in ways I cannot measure. I thank as well the irreplaceable Tim and Liz Schuringa, the sort of people whom everybody dreams of having as friends. Since I met them in Arkansas, their kindness, wry humor, gentle temperament, home-cooked meals, and searching conversations have sustained me. I always measure the warmth of my home with theirs in mind. Thanks to Tim for his discerning comments on my writing for all these years, and hugs for Max and Owen. And I thank deeply Kathy Huang, my *jie jie* and a force of nature. For as long as I've known her, Kathy's grit, fearlessness, humor, courage in confronting life, and desire to live with integrity have inspired and emboldened me; I can't imagine a world in which I don't look up to her.

Deepest thanks to the home team, Kristin Naragon Gainey, Monica Castillo, Jennifer Leath, Sae Takada, and Rachel Rutishauser. Kristin Gainey's support and love are unfaltering and heroic. It's not a surprise that everyone I know turns to her for guidance and compassion. Monica Castillo's irrepressible humor, loyalty, and gentle wisdom have given me delight and comfort over the years. I treasure her friendship. Jen's passion and joy are infectious, and I can't think of a time when her presence hasn't generated intense laughter. I thank Sae for her wise encouragement; she is the steadiest of friends, and I am grateful to know her. And I thank Rachel for her uplifting spirit, indefatigable and seemingly unconditional empathy (let's keep testing it!), and glorious cooking.

Dror Ladin provided critical support, reading early and late drafts, and I've depended on his insight for a decade. Conversations with Dror give me the kind of joy and pride that comes with knowing truly amazing people and being able to claim them as your friends; it's hard not to be in awe of his clear mind, pursuit of justice, and capacity to leaven any situation with wit. Thanks, Dror, and with love to the warm and thoughtful Jenny Bress. I thank Julia Chuang, who provided much light and relief as I tried to write and guidance on drafts at crucial stages. Discovering Julia was one of the happiest things to happen in the past few years of my life, and I'm constantly marveling at her mixture of soul and analytical virtuosity.

I thank Chris Lim and Sarah Raff, ideal friends. Chris is the perfect comrade; his integrity, hilarious sense of humor, passionate beliefs, and friendship have encouraged and urged me on. I love Sarah Raff's luminous mind and sly brilliance, and send a hug to Aphra. I also want to express my deep affection and admiration for James Sheehan and Margaret Lavinia Anderson. Jim and Peggy welcomed me into their home, a site of warmth, wit, generosity, genius, and good cheer.

I am grateful to the generous people I have met in Arkansas and Mississippi. Peggy Webster has been a dear friend, offering music, a huge heart, and kindness. I was devastated by the loss of Maude Cain Howe and Jimmy Webster and think fondly of Maude's open and active mind. Thanks to Doug Friedlander and Anna Skorupa, who are still in the Delta, and whose dedication fills me with admiration. I love Grace Hu's spirit, loyalty, and wry observations. Noam Osband's humor, spirit, and poetry club were uplifting. Cathy Cunningham's dedication, warmth, and boundless energy are inspiring. Monique and Brian Miller are rock stars: I'm grateful for their friendship and thoughtful conversations. Amy Charpentier shepherded me through teaching, and her compassion and warmth have always inspired admiration. I'm in awe of Maisie Wright and Todd Dixon, who arrived the year I left and are both now principals in the Delta. Thanks to Ben Steinberg and Alexandra Terninko for their kindness and generosity. Mike Martin and Edlyn Smith, my mentors at Teach for America, were exceptional and dedicated. Sanford and Amanda Johnson, in Mississippi, have always inspired me with their passion and energy. I'm in awe of John Ruskey's work at the Quapaw Canoe Company and his joy in expanding knowledge of the Mississippi River and commitment to environmental justice. Orlena Hill's love, faith, and sense of humor are fantastic. I thank Elijah Mondy for his generosity, help, and generally enlightened state of being. Thanks to Joseph Whitfield for his generosity in speaking with me and for his inspiring words. Thanks also to Jacob and Katie Austin, Holly Peters, Harris Golden, Amoz Eckerson, Martin Mudd, Tom Kaiser, Luke van de Walle, Orlena Hill, Dr. Joyce Cottoms, the First Presbyterian Church of Helena, John Bennetts, Ann and John King, Carissa Godwin, Suzanne Rowland Brothers, Sarah Campbell, Emily Cook, Carrianne Scheib, Lauren Rush, Liselotte Schluender, Zipporah Mondy, Ollie Neal, Steve Mancini, Jay Barth, Warwick Sabin, Richard Wormser, Catherine Bahn, Ida Gill, Michael Steinbeck, Krystal and Michael Cormack, John Hsu, Joshua Biber, and Ron Nurnberg. Thanks to the Boys and Girls Club of Phillips County and Jason Rollett for their support and work; the Phillips County Library; Joshua Youngblood at the University of Arkansas; and the Arkansas History Commission and Tim Schultz for providing microfilm on Helena. I thank Jeannie Whayne for sharing her lovely spirit and consummate knowledge about the history of the Arkansas Delta.

I am grateful to my agent, Sam Stoloff, at the Frances Goldin Literary Agency. Sam is the greatest. Ever since I met Sam, I've been sure I'm in safe hands and, over the years, my admiration for his virtues has only deepened. I thank Sam for his patience and vision, honesty and wise instincts, graciousness and conviction. He is a champion, mentor, and friend. I also thank the wonderful Ilena Silverman, whose warmth and insight I am grateful for. Thanks to everyone at Frances Goldin, in particular Matt McGowan.

At Random House I thank Hilary Redmon, my brilliant editor. Thanks, Hilary, for being all perfection: meticulous, thoughtful, incisive, conscientious, and uplifting. Hilary's empathy and vision radiate, and I felt her love on the pages everywhere. I wouldn't have finished without her encouragement. I am also deeply grateful to David Ebershoff for acquiring this book and believing in the project: David's penetrating insights, guidance on structure, and generosity were essential, and I am forever in his debt. I am grateful for Kathy Lord's copyediting, which reflected precision and care, Lucy Silag and Catherine Mikula for their insight and effervescence, Jess Bonet for her terrific guidance, Molly Turpin for her tireless support, and the stellar team at Random House, including Kelly Chian and Caitlin McKenna. I thank Robin Schiff for her jacket design and Alessandro Gottardo for his cover illustration. Andy Ward provided critical comments on my draft. I am grateful for the support and generosity of Susan Kamil, Tom Perry, and Gina Centrello.

I would like to express my thanks to Zennor Compton at Pan Macmillan for her support and Jon Butler for h is warm encouragement.

I wrote part of the book while working at Centro Legal de la Raza in Oakland, an immigrants' rights nonprofit, and I am grateful for the inspiration my colleagues offered daily: Esmeralda Izarra, Patricia Salazar, Lindsey Wheeler Lee, Laura Polstein, Luis Salas, Kyra Lilien (and Leo and Alex!), Nancy Hanna, Sarah Martin, Jennifer Miller, Bianca Sierra, Juan Vera, Paul Chavez, Carlos Almanza, Abby Figueroa, and Jesse Newmark, as well as the unstoppable duo of Elizabeth Cortez and Fernando Flores. I thank Esmeralda, my first friend in Oakland, for her soulful laughter, generosity, profound capacity to love, and all the pisco sours, and Jesse for being my idea of a real hero—fearless, uncompromising, rooted in community organizing, and deeply empathetic. Thanks, Jesse, for introducing me to Centro, offering clarity during my time as a confused law student, and for that epic evening in the Oakland dive bar. With love for Britton Schwartz, Jalen, and Sonora. I also thank Jody Lewen for her tremendous leadership at the Prison University Project (PUP), the staff at PUP, and the students at San Quentin Prison for the searching intelligence and preparation that they brought to the classroom.

In California, Eunice Cho's kindness and dedication to immigrants' rights were a constant inspiration, as anybody who knows her will attest. Shira Wakschlag's supernaturally good nature and wisdom delighted me. I treasure Ti Ngo's encouragement, humor, and insight. Chuck Witschorik and Adolfo Ponce have been inspiring, warm, and kind; to know them is a blessing. I am grateful for Merilyn Neher's warmth and illuminating conversations over the years. Rena Patel and James Andrews encouraged me to keep writing, and I think fondly of our hikes and runs. Omar Amir and Victoria Lee bring grace and light wherever they go. Devora Keller provided kind encouragement and understanding. Andrew Jones and I shared many terrific conversations over beer, saltfish and ackee, and I'm grateful for his characteristically gentle encouragement and impeccable taste. Paddy Riley read a chapter and offered perceptive, generous comments and a wealth of knowledge. Radhika Natarajan's effervescence is a joy. (May Muppets live forever.) Shah Ali's kindness and whimsy brightened my days. Evelyn Lew has been like a second mom to me, spoiling me with kindness, moon cakes, airport pickups, and excellent hugs.

Scott Lee has been like a brother to me, and our lifelong friendship has seen many belief-shaping conversations. Shonu Gandhi shared with me her (trademark) superhuman spirit as I wrote, injecting my life with her ebullience and addictive sense of humor. I dearly love Summer Silversmith's humor, conviction, Scrabble prowess, and integrity. Krish Subrahmanian encouraged this project from the start, trusting it would bear fruit, and his wisdom and friendship are a source of comfort. Avi and Lindsey Singh provided early support, and Avi's experience as a public defender and advice on criminal-justice issues helped tremendously. Emma MacKinnon read a draft and I've been elated to rekindle our old friendship. Hannah Simpson read early drafts and offered discerning and warm advice. Cyrus Habib has been an infectious source of joy for many years. Hannah Callaway is a delight to know: Her company is all ease, graciousness, and intelligence. Shobitha Bhat, soulful and generous, read early drafts and was extraordinarily kind. Victor and Jennifer Lin and Asher have been a jubilant source of love, music, and support. For many years now Karen Sim and Tom Rutishauser have opened up their home, sharing their excellent taste, delicious meals, and keen observations. Emily Stokes, brilliant, provided vital encouragement when I first started writing. Nirvana Tanoukhi offered essential and trenchant advice, and it's thrilling to know her.

Warm thanks to Chris Gainey, David Thacker, John Minardi, Sarah Beiderman, Amy Barsky, Jondou Chen, Peiting Li, Daniel Steinmetz-Jenkins, Thomas Chatterton Williams, Ryan Calder, Kathryn Eidmann, Manav Kumar, Albert Wang, Rahul Kanakia, Roy Chan, Jacob Mikanowski, Ryan Acton, Alvin Henry, Hannah Murphy, Andy Staudt, and Jake and Dorli Lamar, with gratitude to Dorli for her transcendent singing lessons and support. Deep thanks to Chris Gainey for his wonderful music and Alex Bushe for his beautiful work in film editing. Pouya Shahbazian and Chris McEwen have been encouraging, insightful, and supportive.

I am grateful to have had wonderful teachers and mentors. Susan Cole and Michael Gregory's Education Advocacy Clinic/ Trauma Policy Learning Initiative, advocating for children impacted by family violence and students with disabilities, helped sustain my soul in law school. Jane Bestor was an immense source of encouragement and wisdom. I am indebted to Darcy Frey, whose encouraging and perceptive comments early on gave me the confidence to keep writing. Claire Messud's brilliance and kindness deeply inspired me. I am grateful to Bret Johnston for his generosity and insight all these years and for being a champion of his students. Thanks to Randall Kennedy for his incisive questions and alert mind. Carol Steiker's passionate dedication to justice and steady encouragement of her students are extraordinary. I thank Judy Murciano for her indefatigable spirit and encouragement. I thank Monika Wadman, Oona Ceder, Cynthia Monteiro, Katherine Vaz, Gish Jen, Mr. Larson, Jorie Graham, Ms. Stieve, Mrs. Arwady, Mrs. Jilek, Scott Friesner, Mrs. Leong, Dr. Elzinga, Dr. Yang, Mr. and Mrs. Scheidt, Mr. Sinclair, Mr. Streeter, Ms. Addison, Mrs. Hach, Mrs. King, Mrs. Hunt, Rebecca Jansen, Brian Snell, Jim Menchinger, and other teachers in Portage and Kalamazoo.

Susan Butler Plum, director of the Skadden Fellowship, has been an inspirational source of support, a true advocate and champion of her fellows. Thanks to John Glassie for his thoughtful edits on the "Lives" column piece. Thanks to the *L.A. Review of Books*, in particular Evan Kindley, Laurie Winer, and Tom Lutz. I thank my dear friend and mentor Warren Ilchman at the Paul and Daisy Soros Fellowship for his insight, kindness, and steadfast encouragement.

I thank the Honorable Judge John T. Noonan and Mary Lee Noonan. Judge Noonan's integrity, erudition, conviction, and extraordinary writing offer a model for a jurisprudence that is humane and intelligent. Thanks to Mary Lee for her generosity, warmth, and support over the years.

My community at American University of Paris has been supportive as I entered the final stages of writing. I'm grateful for Stephen Sawyer's warmth and generosity, Miranda Spieler's loyalty and brilliance (and Althea's radiance), Elena Berg's inspiring dedication, Philip Golub's incisive passion, Susan Perry's generous mentorship, and Peter Hagel's always-considerate and uplifting spirit. With warm thanks to Michael Stoepel, Kerstin Carlson, Linda Martz, Elizabeth Kinne, and the inimitable Brenda Torney. I am grateful for a Mellon grant from AUP that allowed me to view microfilm on Helena's history and to the library staff for its support. I thank the wonderful students at AUP, who come from all corners of the world and have energized and inspired me.

This book is dedicated to my dad and mom, Ming-Shang Kuo and Hwa-Mei Lin Kuo, who have made so much in my life possible. I thank them for being the heart of everything and for all their generosity, humor, and support throughout my life. My older brother, Alex Kuo, has always been there for me, ever since I waddled off, spoke late as a child, or readied myself for a high school speech contest: Alex was there to find me, translate me, and, later, coach me. Thanks to my sister-in-law Maria Jimenez Buedo for her laughter and astute insights, and to dear Felix for his heart-stopping charm. I thank my grandma, Yee-Rong Yu, for her stories and Mandarin lessons. I thank my in-laws, Maw-Kuen Wu and Hui-chin Tang Wu, for their kindness and encouragement, and Debby Chang and Phil Wu for their exceptional generosity and open hearts, and Micah for his winning smile. Thanks to my excellent cousins, uncles, and aunts.

And last I thank Albert Wu, my best friend, collaborator, great love, and ideal reader. I didn't know they made people like Albert, and sometimes I still can't believe he exists. I am the ever-indebted beneficiary of his sunny, bright spirit, unbounded kindness, insanely versatile brain, and curiosity about basically everything. Thank you, Albert, for taking the high road without blinking, for lacking a petty bone in your body, and for your joy and compassion, feelings that seem as natural to you as air. You were by my side as I wrote; you didn't doubt when I did. Love you.

READING
with
PATRICK

———

Michelle Kuo

A READER'S GUIDE

QUESTIONS AND TOPICS FOR DISCUSSION

1. What challenges do rural areas such as the Arkansas and Mississippi Deltas face, and how are they different from urban areas? Why do you think we hear so little about rural education, employment, and crime in the news? Why do they get underresearched and underreported?

2. Can the classroom protect students from the deprivation outside of it? Can it further that deprivation? How do Michelle's experiences confirm or challenge your ideas about the transformative power of the classroom?

3. How is reading alone different from reading together? Consider experiences you've had being read to or instances where you've read to others.

4. What does poetry do that other texts can't? Consider the "I Am" poem in school and poetry in the county jail.

5. What changes do you see in Michelle as a teacher? How

would you compare her individual lessons with Patrick to her time as a formal teacher?

6. Patrick is a stranger when Michelle meets him, but over time she begins to feel an ethical responsibility for his life. Why? Does she owe him anything? Why does she think she does, and how does he respond?

7. Michelle and Patrick ask each other their favorite lines from literature. Why does this act of sharing open up conversation between them? What are some of your favorite lines from the book? (This can include lines from the poetry and books that they read together.)

8. Patrick does not blame his circumstances for his hard life. Michelle clearly does. What do you make of their disagreement? Would you have tried to convince him otherwise?

9. Among other histories, we witness passages on migration, rural organizing of Back-to-Africa movements, and violence in the Arkansas Delta. How do these historical scenes help us to make sense of the memoir's present-day circumstances and events?

10. This book is as much an Asian American story as it is an African American story. How does being Asian American help explain Michelle's choices, including the decision to go to the Delta and the decision to leave?

11. Can two people who have a radical power difference ever connect through a genuine feeling of equality? Michelle questions this idea, except for in one instance: when they read together. Why would literature, or any kind of art, open up that possibility of experiencing equality with one another? And why would she call that experience "fleeting"?

12. Michelle could have ended on the optimistic note of Part 3, where, after intensive daily work together, Patrick has become a writer of exquisite sentences and a sophisticated reader. But she doesn't. We are told that life after prison for Patrick—finding a job, feeling at home in the Delta—"was a new battle, excruciating, and, unlike incarceration, with no end date." Why do you think Michelle includes this information? Does it change the meaning of their seven months together if Patrick still struggles after?

MICHELLE KUO was born and raised in Kalamazoo, Michigan. Kuo's parents are immigrants from Taiwan. She taught English at an alternative school in the Arkansas Delta for two years. After teaching, she attended Harvard Law School as a Paul and Daisy Soros Fellow and worked legal aid at a nonprofit for Spanish-speaking immigrants in the Fruitvale district of Oakland, California, on a Skadden Fellowship, with a focus on tenants' and workers' rights. She has volunteered as a teacher at the Prison University Project, the only college-degree granting program in a California prison, and clerked for the Honorable John T. Noonan on the Ninth Circuit. Currently she teaches courses on race, law, and society at the American University of Paris, where she recently won the Board of Trustees Award for Distinguished Teaching.

michellekuo.net
Twitter: @kuokuomich

ABOUT THE TYPE

The text of this book was set in Janson, a typeface designed about 1690 by Nicholas Kis (1650–1702), a Hungarian living in Amsterdam, and for many years mistakenly attributed to the Dutch printer Anton Janson. In 1919, the matrices became the property of the Stempel Foundry in Frankfurt. It is an old-style book face of excellent clarity and sharpness. Janson serifs are concave and splayed; the contrast between thick and thin strokes is marked.